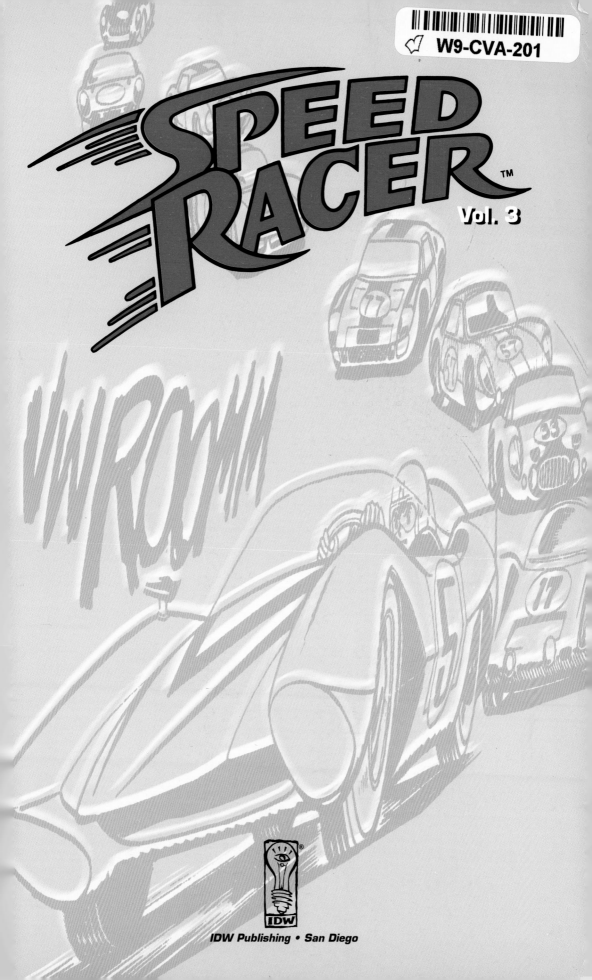

SPEED RACER™

Vol. 3

VWROOM

IDW Publishing • San Diego

W9-CVA-201

VROOM

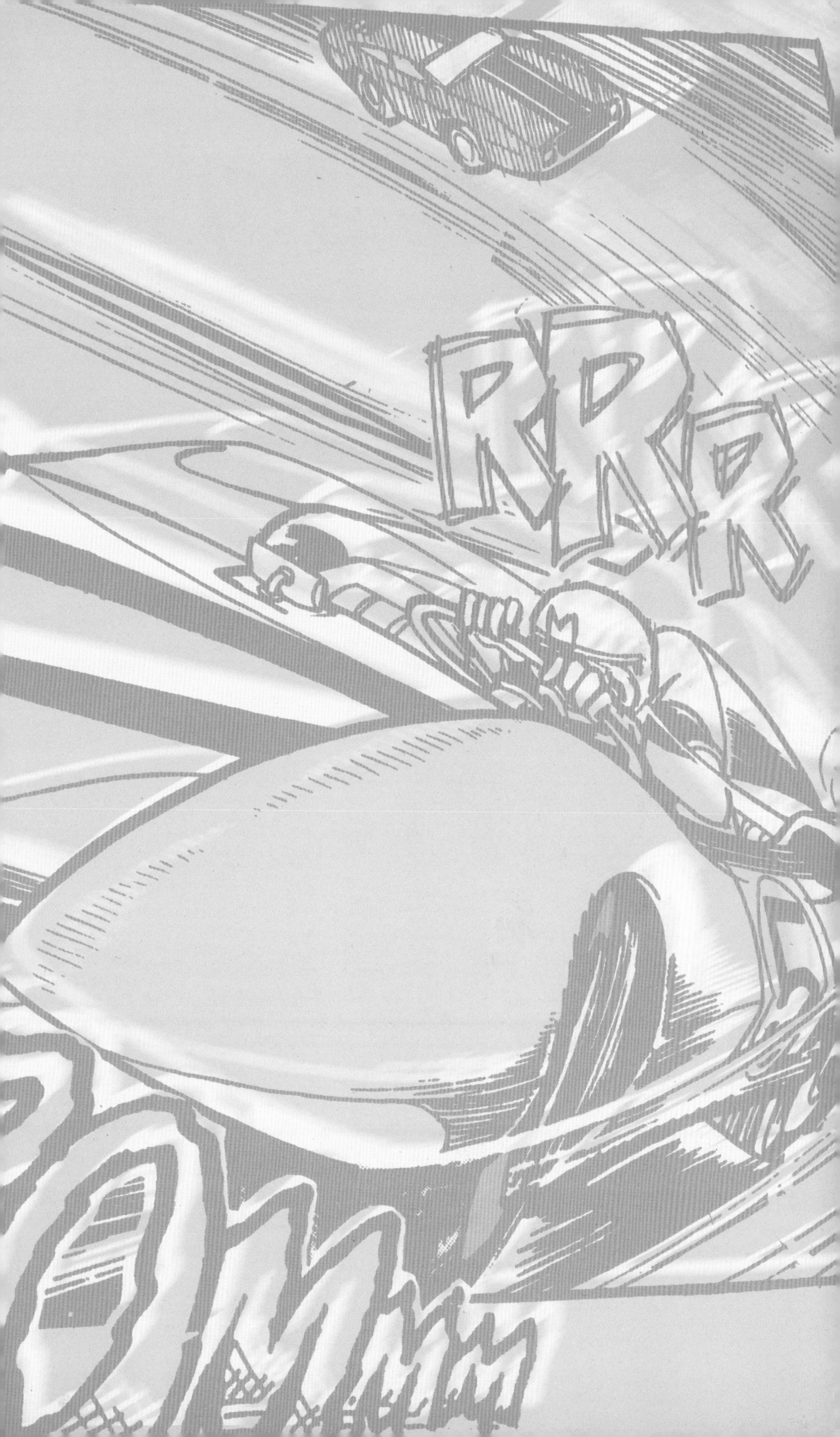
RRRR

IDW Publishing
Ted Adams, Preside
Robbie Robbins, EVP/Sr. Graphic Art
Chris Ryall, Publisher/Editor-in-Ch
Clifford Meth, EVP of Strategies/Editor
Alan Payne, VP of Sa
Marci Kahn, Executive Assista
Neil Uyetake, Art Direct
Tom Waltz, Edit
Andrew Steven Harris, Edi
Chris Mowry, Graphic Art
Amauri Osorio, Graphic Art
Dene Nee, Graphic Artist/Edi
Matthew Ruzicka, CPA, Control
Alonzo Simon, Shipping Manag
Kris Oprisko, Editor/Foreign Lic. Re

www.idwpublishing.com
www.speedracer.com

ISBN: 978-1-60010-176-3
11 10 09 08   1 2 3 4 5

This volume of collects Speed Racer, Vol. 1 #'s 14 to 19.

Speed Racer #14
page 6
Written by ***Lamar Waldron***
Pencilled by ***Joe Phillips***
Inked by ***John Dell III***
Lettered by ***Jim Massara***
Colored by ***John Vogel***

Speed Racer #15
page 32
Written by ***Lamar Waldron***
Pencilled by ***Joe Phillips***
Inked by ***John Dell III***
Lettered by ***Ken Holewczynski***
Colored by ***John Vogel***

Speed Racer #16
page 58
Written by ***Lamar Waldron***
Pencilled by ***Joe Phillips***
Inked by ***John Dell III***
Lettered by ***Ken Holewczynski***

Speed Racer #17
page 82
Written by ***Lamar Waldron***
Pencilled by ***Joe Phillips***
Inked by ***Brian Thomas***
Lettered by ***Ken Holewczynski***

Speed Racer #18
page 104
Written by ***Lamar Waldron***
Pencilled by ***Joe Phillips***
Inked by ***John Dell III***
Lettered by ***Ken Holewczynski***

Speed Racer #19
page 126
Written by ***Lamar Waldron***
Pencilled by ***Joe Phillips***
Inked by ***Dan McKinnon & David Mowry***
Lettered by ***Dan McKinnon***

Speed Racer Vol. 3 TPB

Cover by ***Ken Steacy***
Edited by ***Dene Nee***
Design and Remaster by ***Tom B. Long***

Speed Racer #14

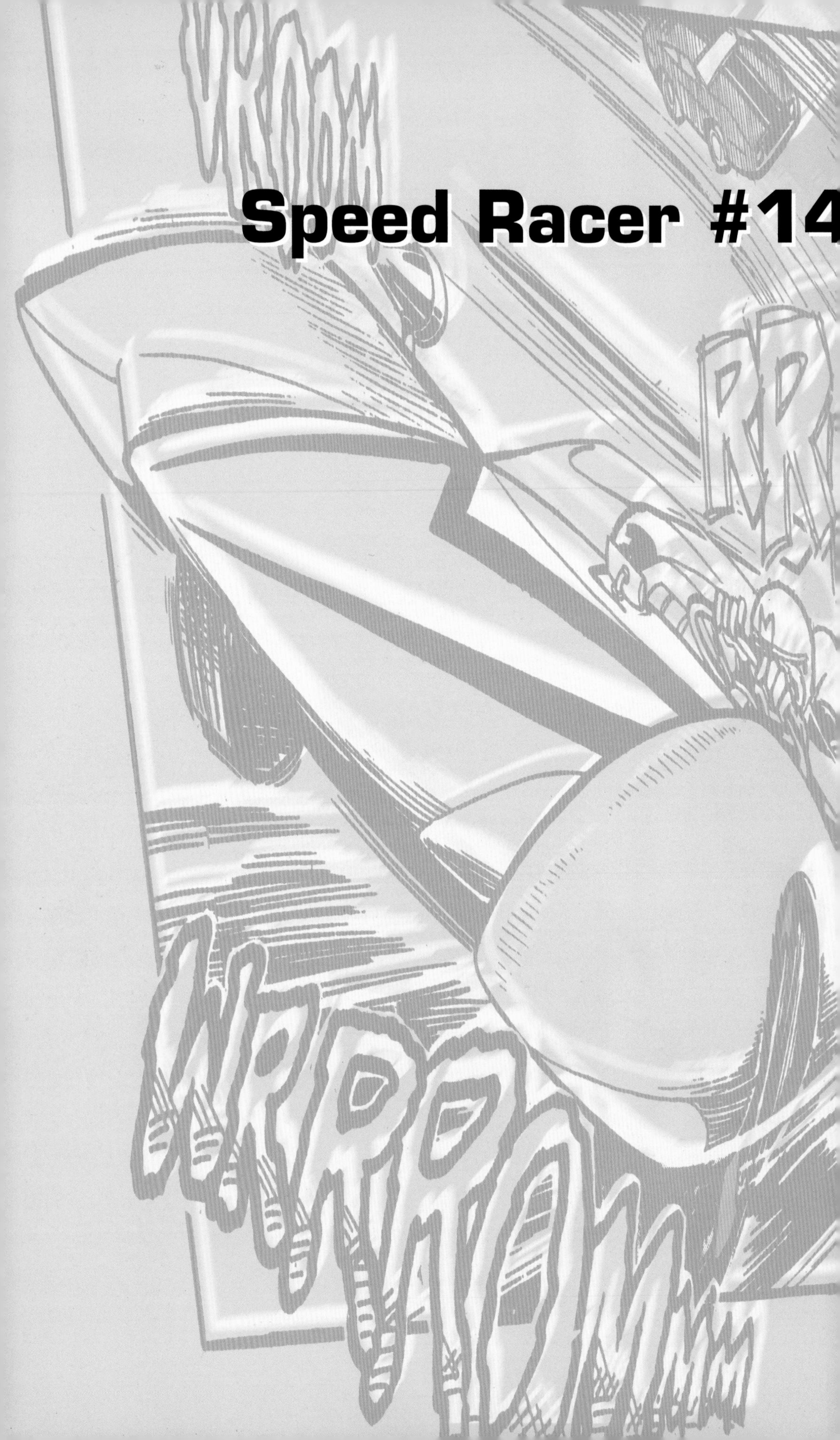

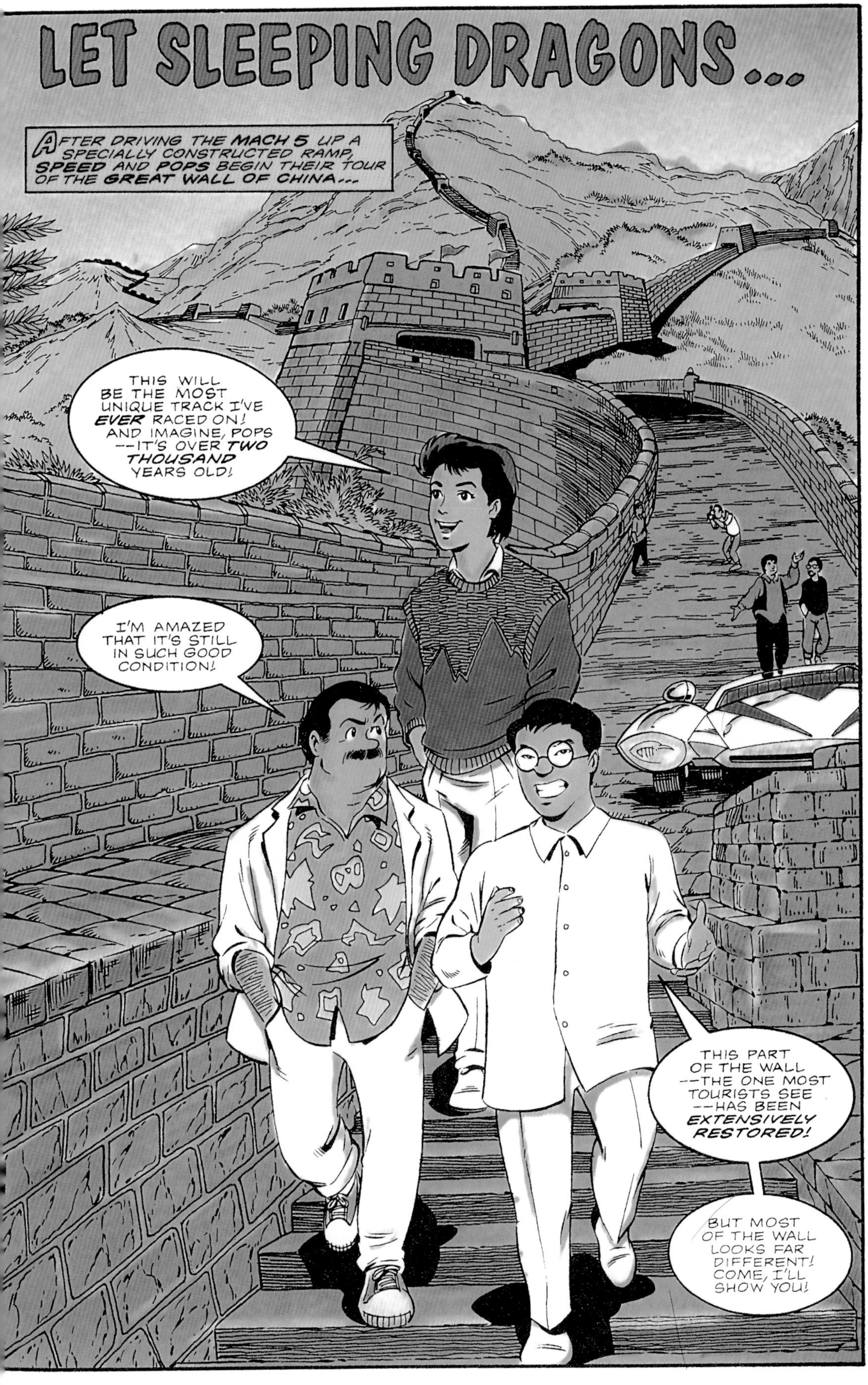

LET SLEEPING DRAGONS...
AFTER DRIVING THE MACH 5 UP A SPECIALLY CONSTRUCTED RAMP, SPEED AND POPS BEGIN THEIR TOUR OF THE GREAT WALL OF CHINA...
THIS WILL BE THE MOST UNIQUE TRACK I'VE EVER RACED ON! AND IMAGINE, POPS --IT'S OVER TWO THOUSAND YEARS OLD!
I'M AMAZED THAT IT'S STILL IN SUCH GOOD CONDITION!
THIS PART OF THE WALL --THE ONE MOST TOURISTS SEE --HAS BEEN EXTENSIVELY RESTORED!
BUT MOST OF THE WALL LOOKS FAR DIFFERENT! COME, I'LL SHOW YOU!

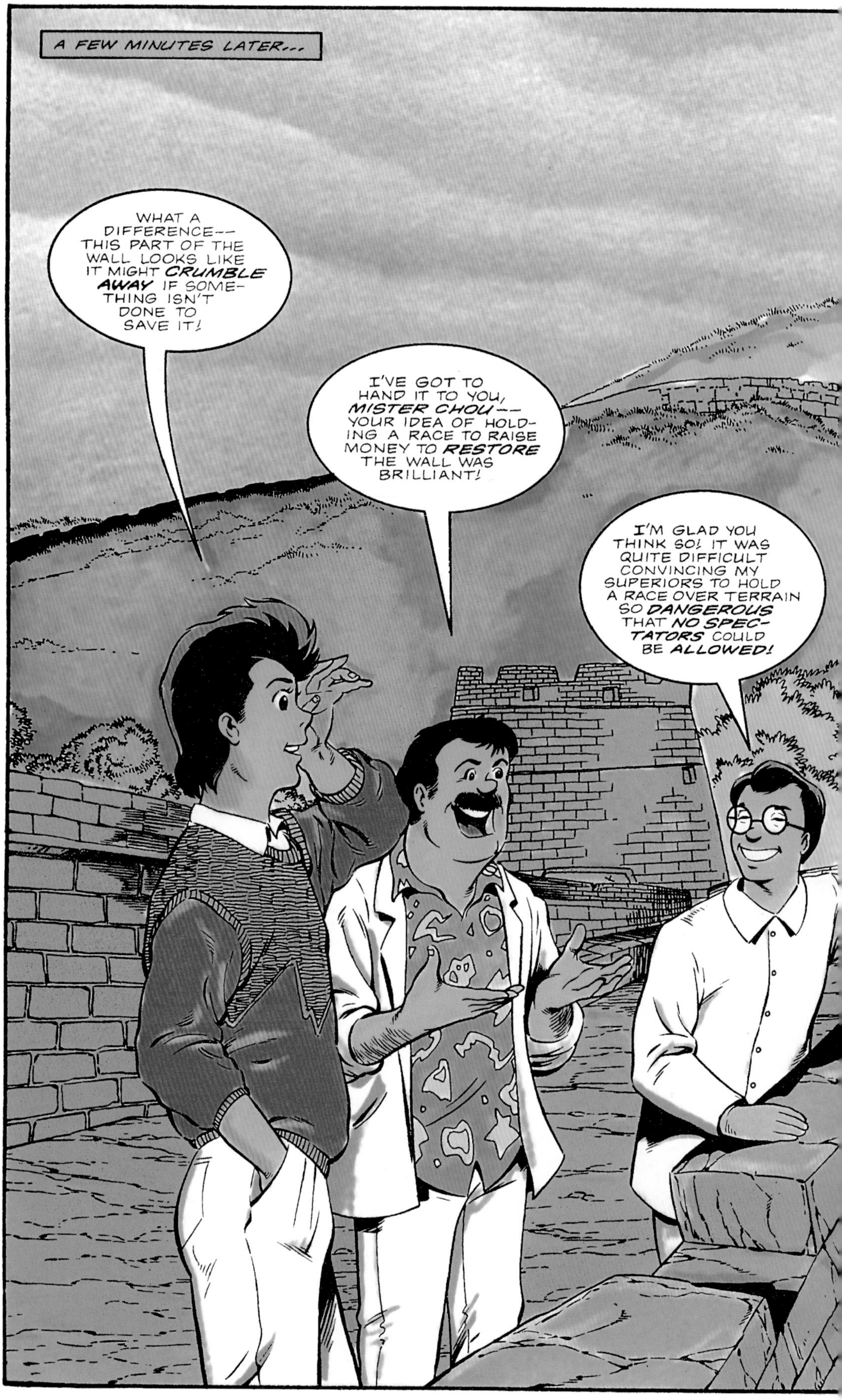
A FEW MINUTES LATER...
WHAT A DIFFERENCE-- THIS PART OF THE WALL LOOKS LIKE IT MIGHT CRUMBLE AWAY IF SOMETHING ISN'T DONE TO SAVE IT!
I'VE GOT TO HAND IT TO YOU, MISTER CHOU-- YOUR IDEA OF HOLDING A RACE TO RAISE MONEY TO RESTORE THE WALL WAS BRILLIANT!
I'M GLAD YOU THINK SO! IT WAS QUITE DIFFICULT CONVINCING MY SUPERIORS TO HOLD A RACE OVER TERRAIN SO DANGEROUS THAT NO SPECTATORS COULD BE ALLOWED!

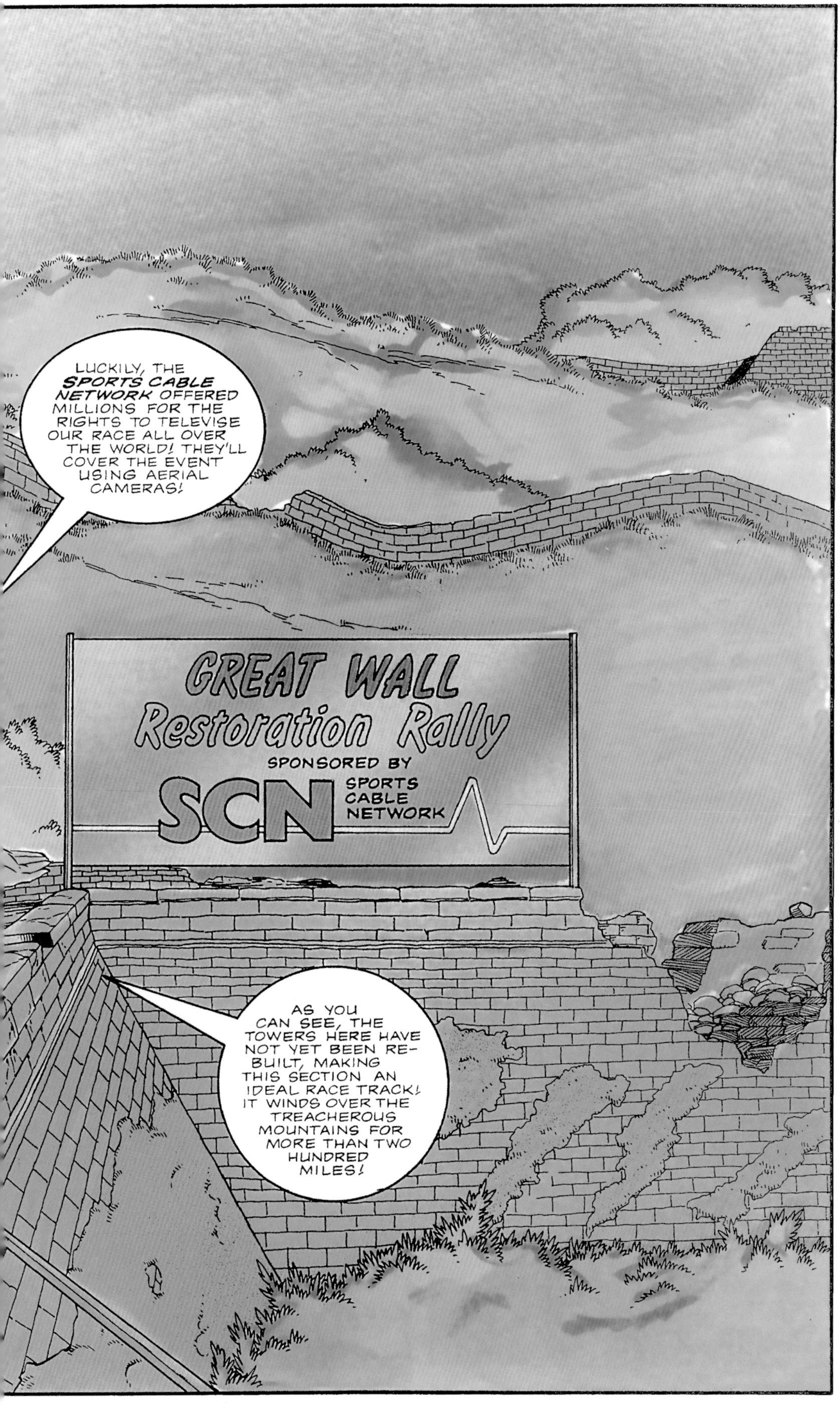
LUCKILY, THE SPORTS CABLE NETWORK OFFERED MILLIONS FOR THE RIGHTS TO TELEVISE OUR RACE ALL OVER THE WORLD! THEY'LL COVER THE EVENT USING AERIAL CAMERAS!
GREAT WALL Restoration Rally
SPONSORED BY
SCN SPORTS CABLE NETWORK
AS YOU CAN SEE, THE TOWERS HERE HAVE NOT YET BEEN RE-BUILT, MAKING THIS SECTION AN IDEAL RACE TRACK! IT WINDS OVER THE TREACHEROUS MOUNTAINS FOR MORE THAN TWO HUNDRED MILES!

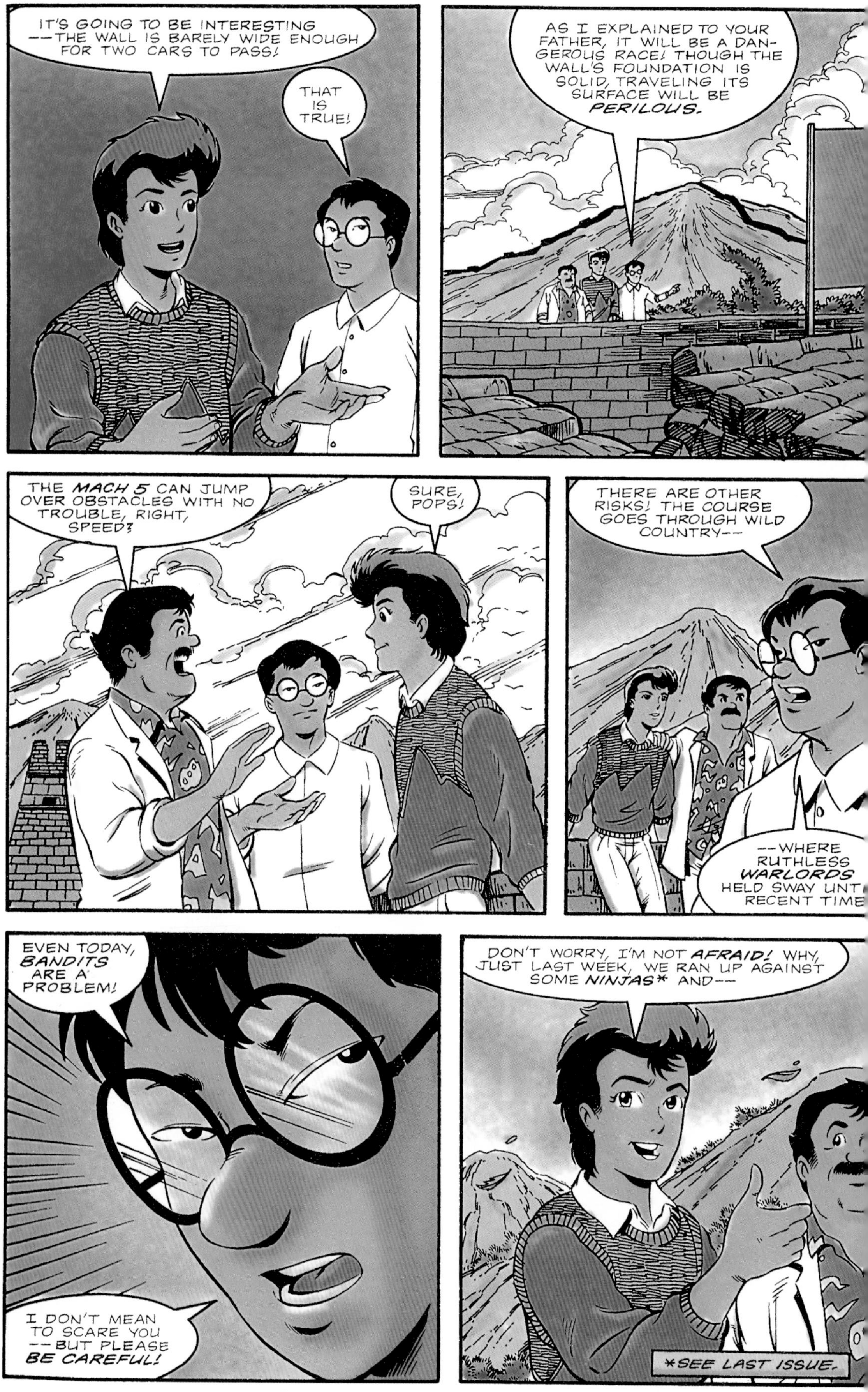
IT'S GOING TO BE INTERESTING --THE WALL IS BARELY WIDE ENOUGH FOR TWO CARS TO PASS!
THAT IS TRUE!
AS I EXPLAINED TO YOUR FATHER, IT WILL BE A DANGEROUS RACE! THOUGH THE WALL'S FOUNDATION IS SOLID, TRAVELING ITS SURFACE WILL BE PERILOUS.
THE MACH 5 CAN JUMP OVER OBSTACLES WITH NO TROUBLE, RIGHT, SPEED?
SURE, POPS!
THERE ARE OTHER RISKS! THE COURSE GOES THROUGH WILD COUNTRY--
--WHERE RUTHLESS WARLORDS HELD SWAY UNTI RECENT TIME
EVEN TODAY, BANDITS ARE A PROBLEM!
I DON'T MEAN TO SCARE YOU --BUT PLEASE BE CAREFUL!
DON'T WORRY, I'M NOT AFRAID! WHY, JUST LAST WEEK, WE RAN UP AGAINST SOME NINJAS* AND--
*SEE LAST ISSUE.

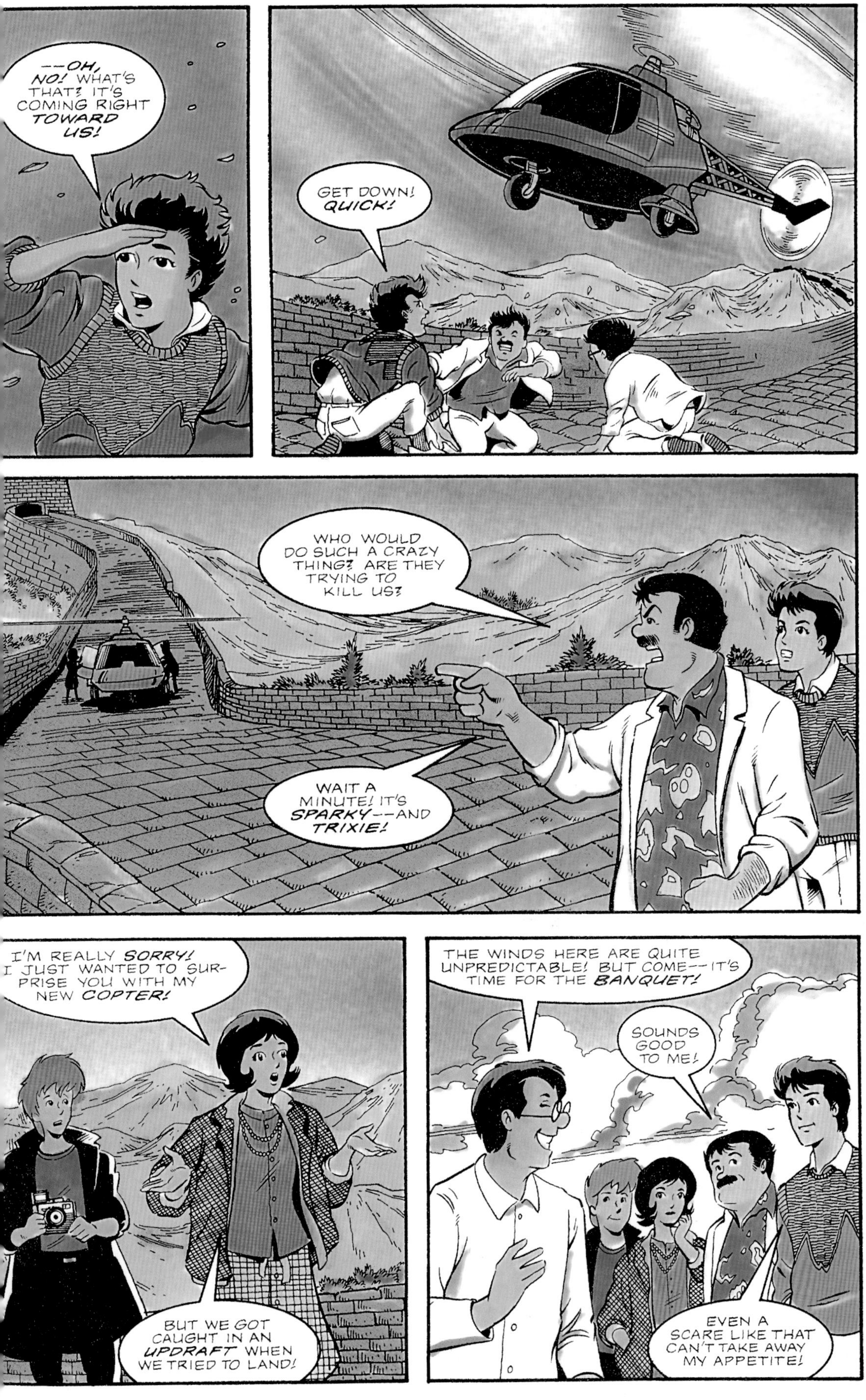
--OH, NO! WHAT'S THAT? IT'S COMING RIGHT TOWARD US!
GET DOWN! QUICK!
WHO WOULD DO SUCH A CRAZY THING? ARE THEY TRYING TO KILL US?
WAIT A MINUTE! IT'S SPARKY--AND TRIXIE!
I'M REALLY SORRY! I JUST WANTED TO SURPRISE YOU WITH MY NEW COPTER!
BUT WE GOT CAUGHT IN AN UPDRAFT WHEN WE TRIED TO LAND!
THE WINDS HERE ARE QUITE UNPREDICTABLE! BUT COME--IT'S TIME FOR THE BANQUET!
SOUNDS GOOD TO ME!
EVEN A SCARE LIKE THAT CAN'T TAKE AWAY MY APPETITE!

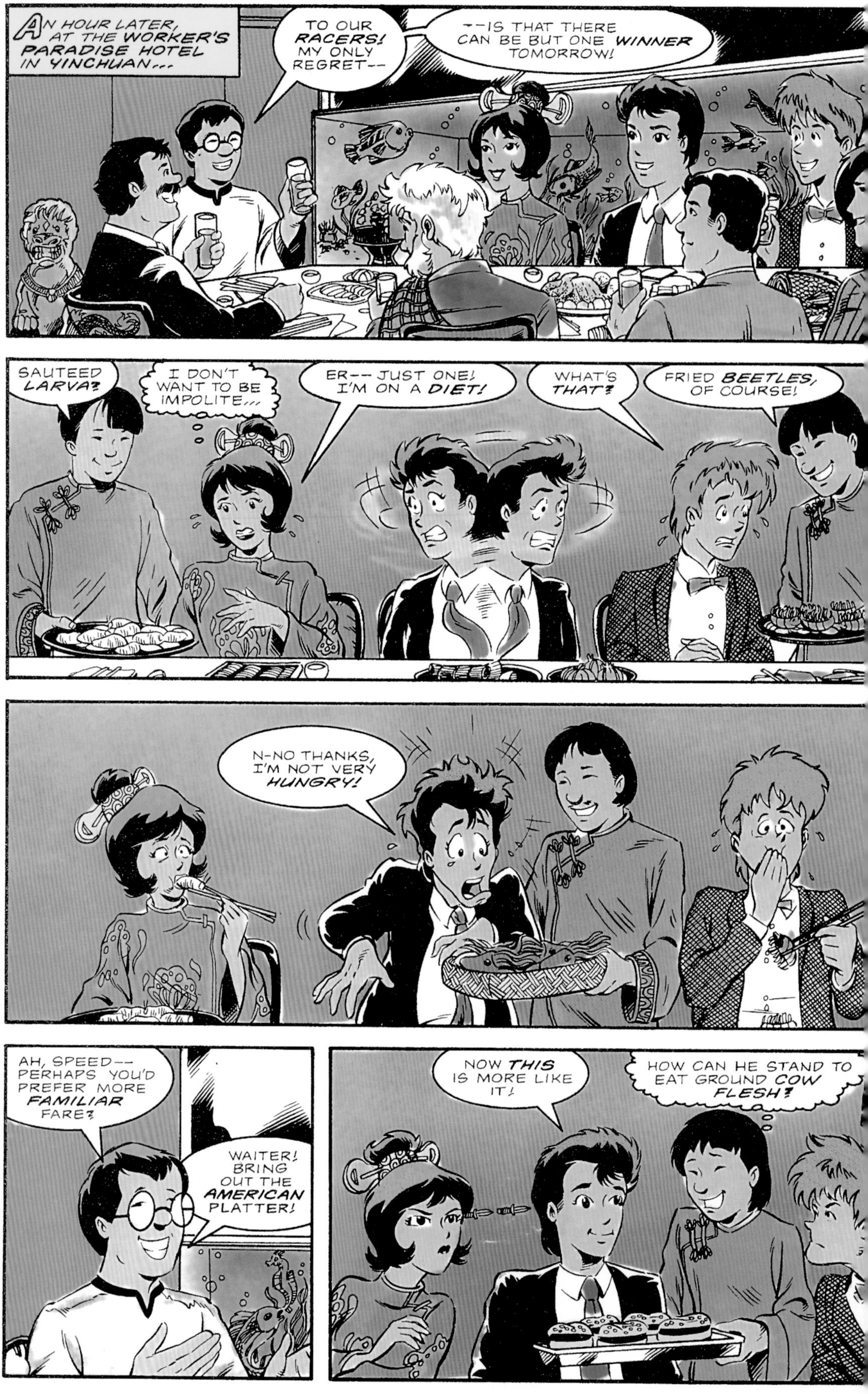
AN HOUR LATER, AT THE WORKER'S PARADISE HOTEL IN YINCHUAN...
TO OUR RACERS! MY ONLY REGRET--
--IS THAT THERE CAN BE BUT ONE WINNER TOMORROW!
SAUTEED LARVA?
I DON'T WANT TO BE IMPOLITE...
ER-- JUST ONE! I'M ON A DIET!
WHAT'S THAT?
FRIED BEETLES, OF COURSE!
N-NO THANKS, I'M NOT VERY HUNGRY!
AH, SPEED-- PERHAPS YOU'D PREFER MORE FAMILIAR FARE?
WAITER! BRING OUT THE AMERICAN PLATTER!
NOW THIS IS MORE LIKE IT!
HOW CAN HE STAND TO EAT GROUND COW FLESH?

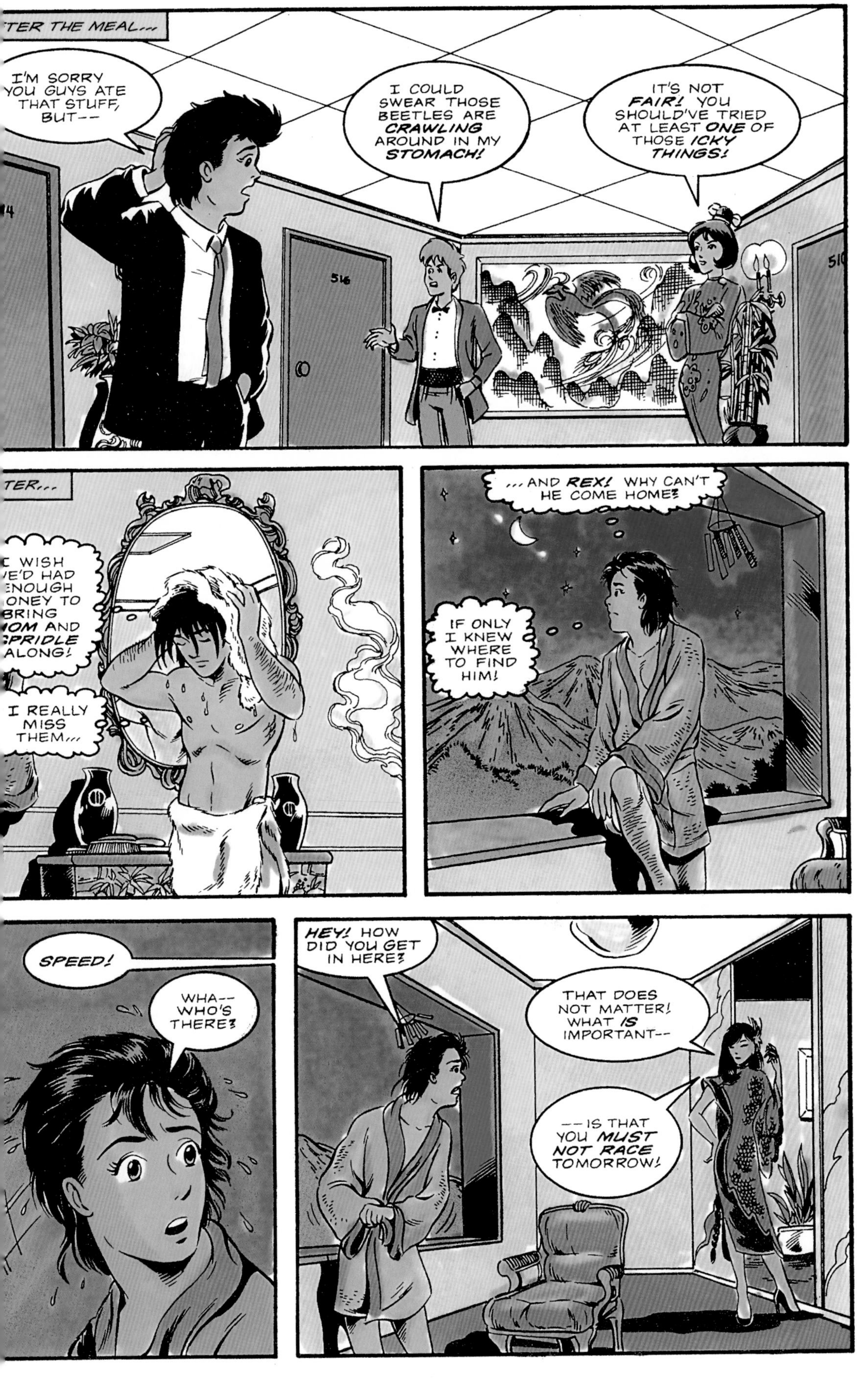
TER THE MEAL...
I'M SORRY YOU GUYS ATE THAT STUFF, BUT--
I COULD SWEAR THOSE BEETLES ARE CRAWLING AROUND IN MY STOMACH!
IT'S NOT FAIR! YOU SHOULD'VE TRIED AT LEAST ONE OF THOSE ICKY THINGS!
TER...
WISH 'E'D HAD ENOUGH ONEY TO BRING IOM AND PRIDLE ALONG!
I REALLY MISS THEM...
...AND REX! WHY CAN'T HE COME HOME?
IF ONLY I KNEW WHERE TO FIND HIM!
SPEED!
WHA-- WHO'S THERE?
HEY! HOW DID YOU GET IN HERE?
THAT DOES NOT MATTER! WHAT IS IMPORTANT--
--IS THAT YOU MUST NOT RACE TOMORROW!

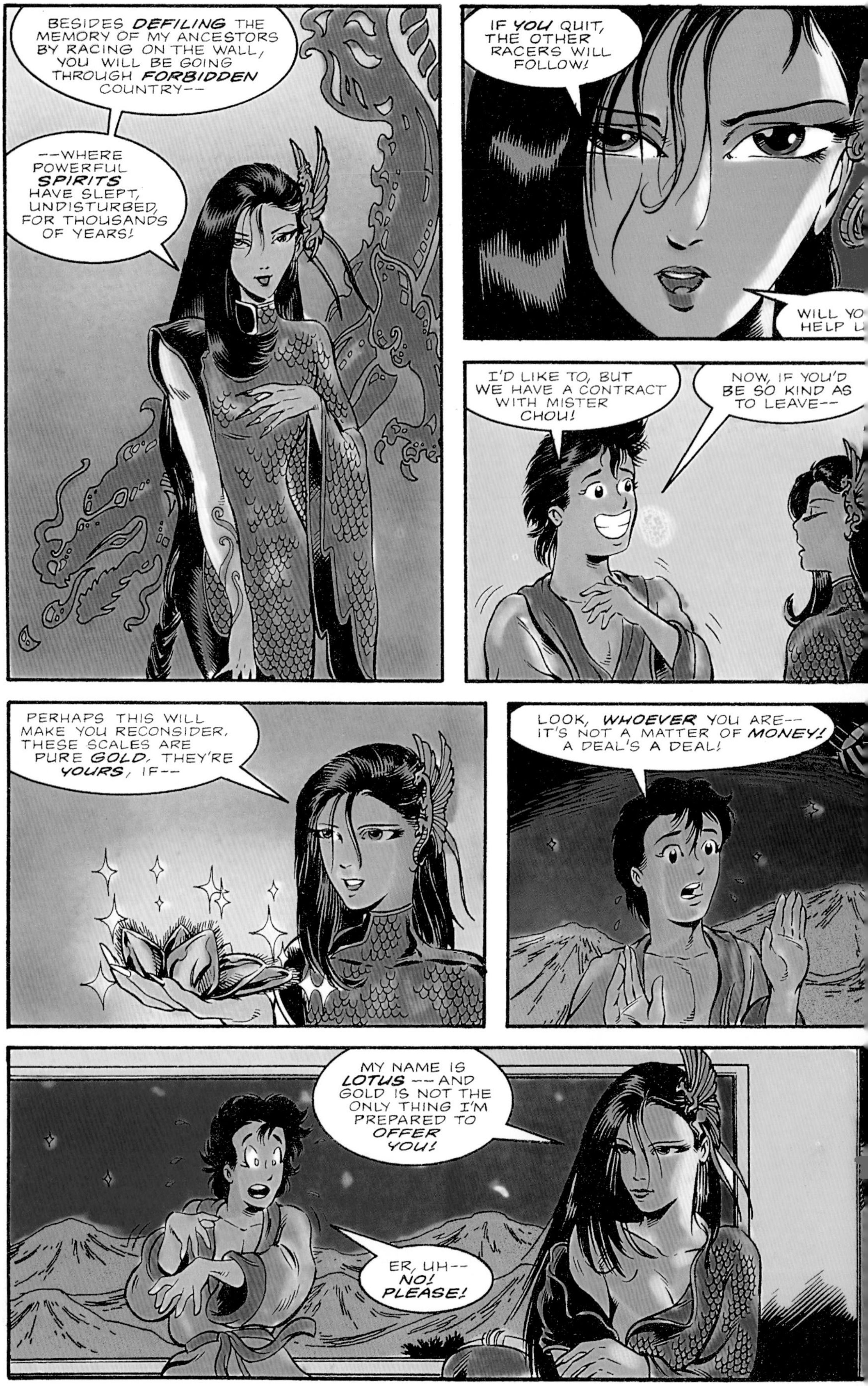
BESIDES DEFILING THE MEMORY OF MY ANCESTORS BY RACING ON THE WALL, YOU WILL BE GOING THROUGH FORBIDDEN COUNTRY--
--WHERE POWERFUL SPIRITS HAVE SLEPT, UNDISTURBED, FOR THOUSANDS OF YEARS!
IF YOU QUIT, THE OTHER RACERS WILL FOLLOW!
WILL YO HELP U
I'D LIKE TO, BUT WE HAVE A CONTRACT WITH MISTER CHOU!
NOW, IF YOU'D BE SO KIND AS TO LEAVE--
PERHAPS THIS WILL MAKE YOU RECONSIDER. THESE SCALES ARE PURE GOLD. THEY'RE YOURS, IF--
LOOK, WHOEVER YOU ARE-- IT'S NOT A MATTER OF MONEY! A DEAL'S A DEAL!
MY NAME IS LOTUS --AND GOLD IS NOT THE ONLY THING I'M PREPARED TO OFFER YOU!
ER, UH-- NO! PLEASE!

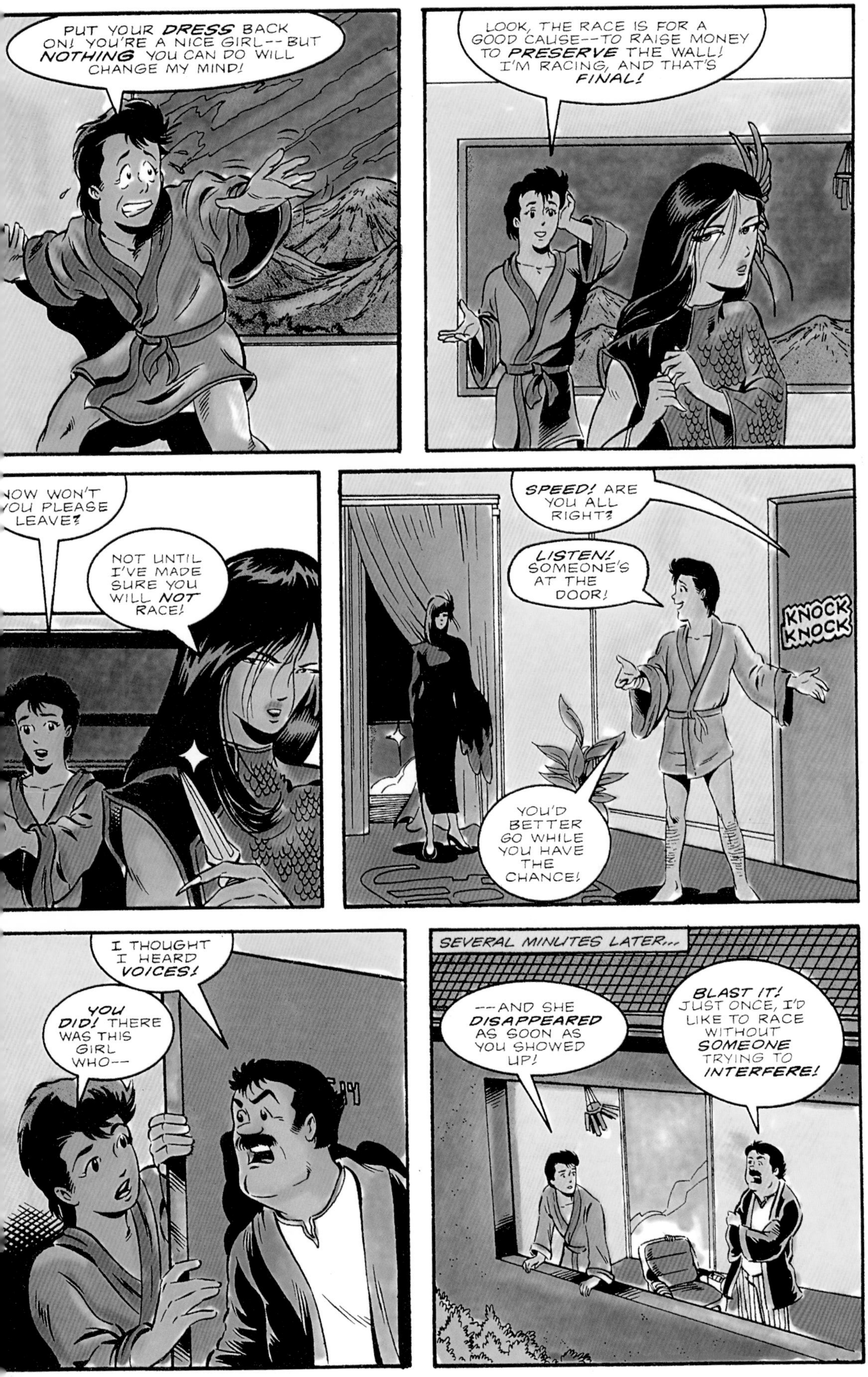
PUT YOUR DRESS BACK ON! YOU'RE A NICE GIRL--BUT NOTHING YOU CAN DO WILL CHANGE MY MIND!
LOOK, THE RACE IS FOR A GOOD CAUSE--TO RAISE MONEY TO PRESERVE THE WALL! I'M RACING, AND THAT'S FINAL!
NOW WON'T YOU PLEASE LEAVE?
NOT UNTIL I'VE MADE SURE YOU WILL NOT RACE!
SPEED! ARE YOU ALL RIGHT?
KNOCK KNOCK
LISTEN! SOMEONE'S AT THE DOOR!
YOU'D BETTER GO WHILE YOU HAVE THE CHANCE!
I THOUGHT I HEARD VOICES!
YOU DID! THERE WAS THIS GIRL WHO--
SEVERAL MINUTES LATER...
--AND SHE DISAPPEARED AS SOON AS YOU SHOWED UP!
BLAST IT! JUST ONCE, I'D LIKE TO RACE WITHOUT SOMEONE TRYING TO INTERFERE!

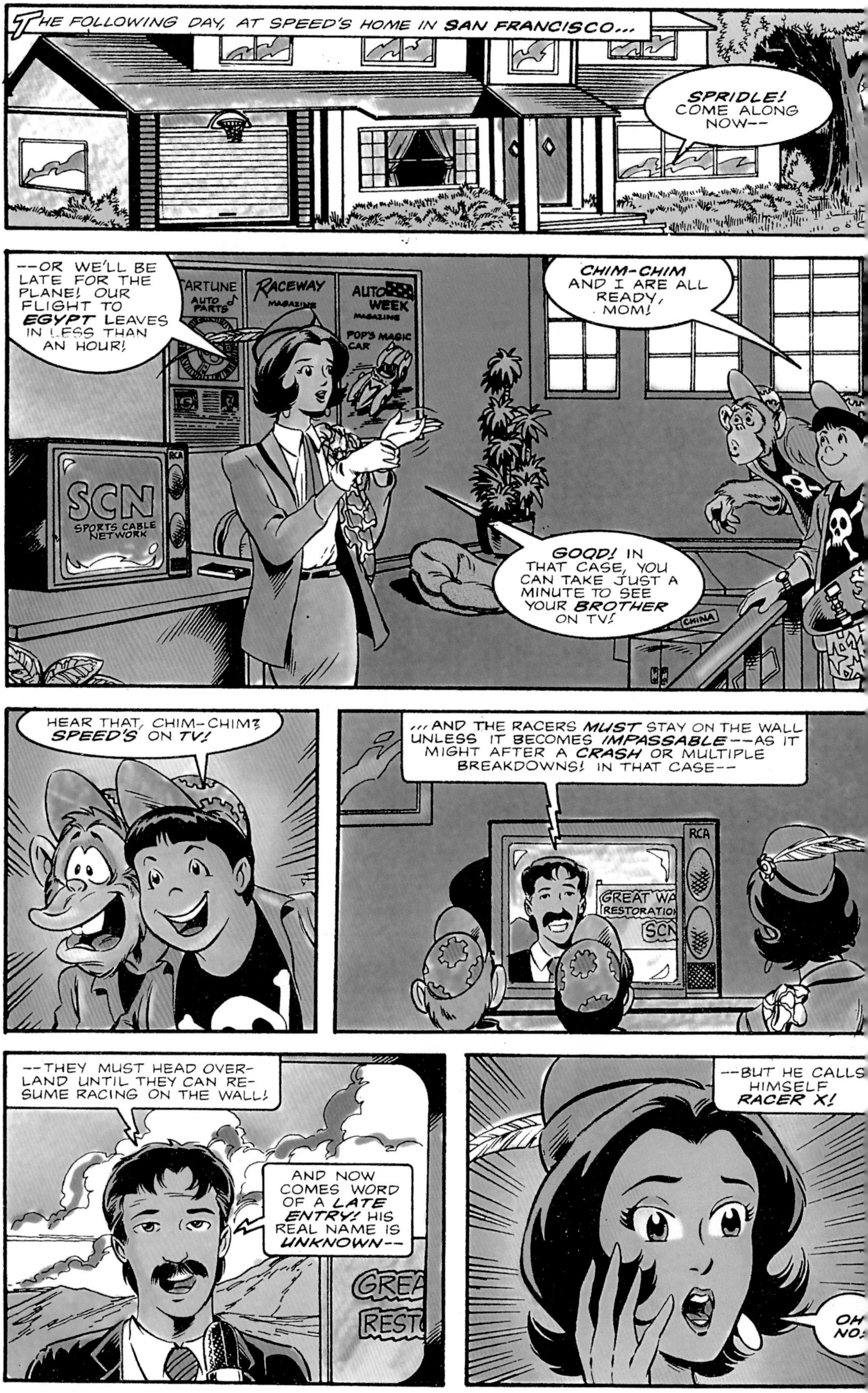
THE FOLLOWING DAY, AT SPEED'S HOME IN SAN FRANCISCO...
SPRIDLE! COME ALONG NOW--
--OR WE'LL BE LATE FOR THE PLANE! OUR FLIGHT TO EGYPT LEAVES IN LESS THAN AN HOUR!
CHIM-CHIM AND I ARE ALL READY, MOM!
GOOD! IN THAT CASE, YOU CAN TAKE JUST A MINUTE TO SEE YOUR BROTHER ON TV!
HEAR THAT, CHIM-CHIM? SPEED'S ON TV!
...AND THE RACERS MUST STAY ON THE WALL UNLESS IT BECOMES IMPASSABLE--AS IT MIGHT AFTER A CRASH OR MULTIPLE BREAKDOWNS! IN THAT CASE--
--THEY MUST HEAD OVER-LAND UNTIL THEY CAN RE-SUME RACING ON THE WALL!
AND NOW COMES WORD OF A LATE ENTRY! HIS REAL NAME IS UNKNOWN--
--BUT HE CALLS HIMSELF RACER X!
OH NO!

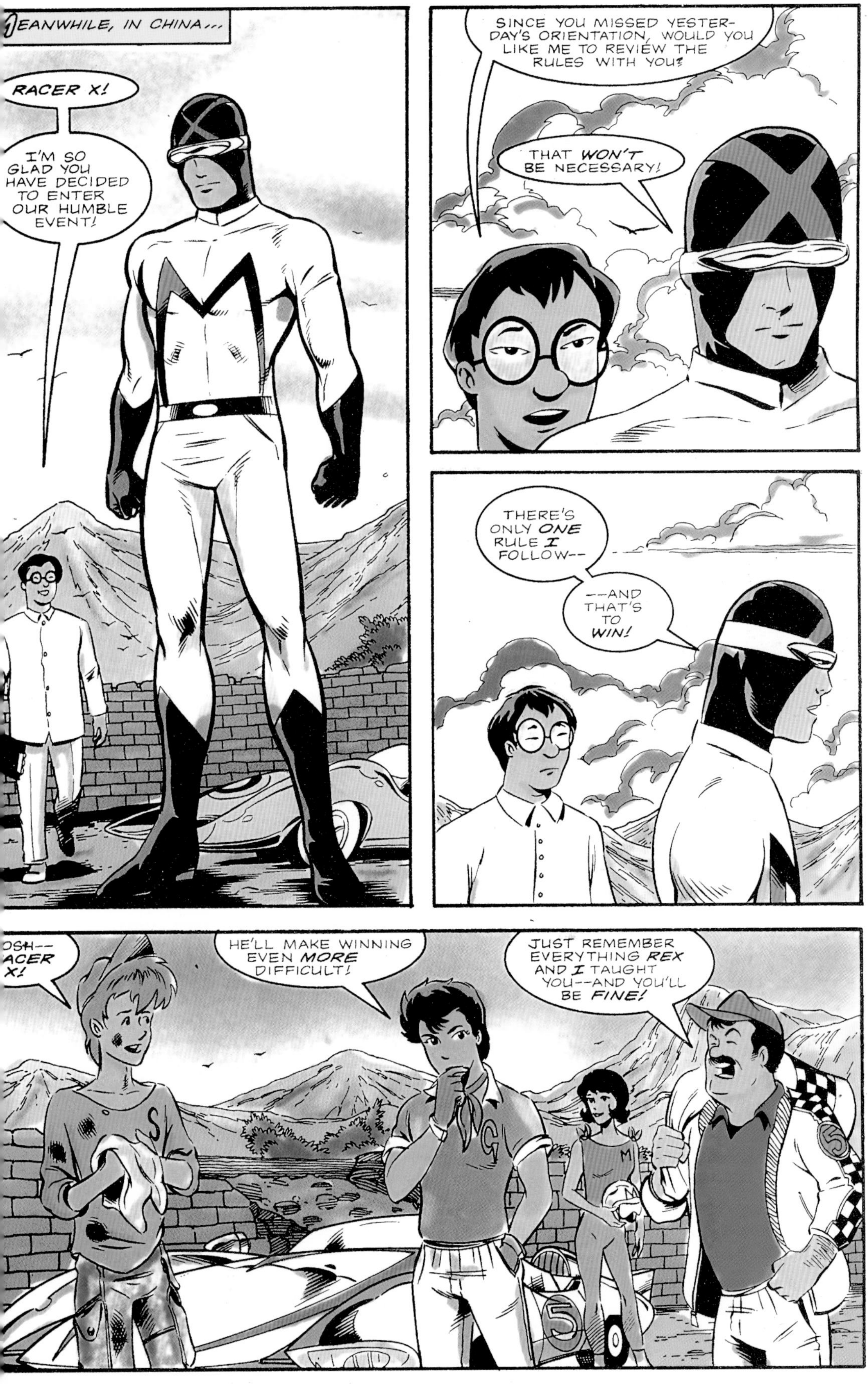
MEANWHILE, IN CHINA...
RACER X!
I'M SO GLAD YOU HAVE DECIDED TO ENTER OUR HUMBLE EVENT!
SINCE YOU MISSED YESTERDAY'S ORIENTATION, WOULD YOU LIKE ME TO REVIEW THE RULES WITH YOU?
THAT WON'T BE NECESSARY!
THERE'S ONLY ONE RULE I FOLLOW--
--AND THAT'S TO WIN!
OSH--
ACER X!
HE'LL MAKE WINNING EVEN MORE DIFFICULT!
JUST REMEMBER EVERYTHING REX AND I TAUGHT YOU--AND YOU'LL BE FINE!

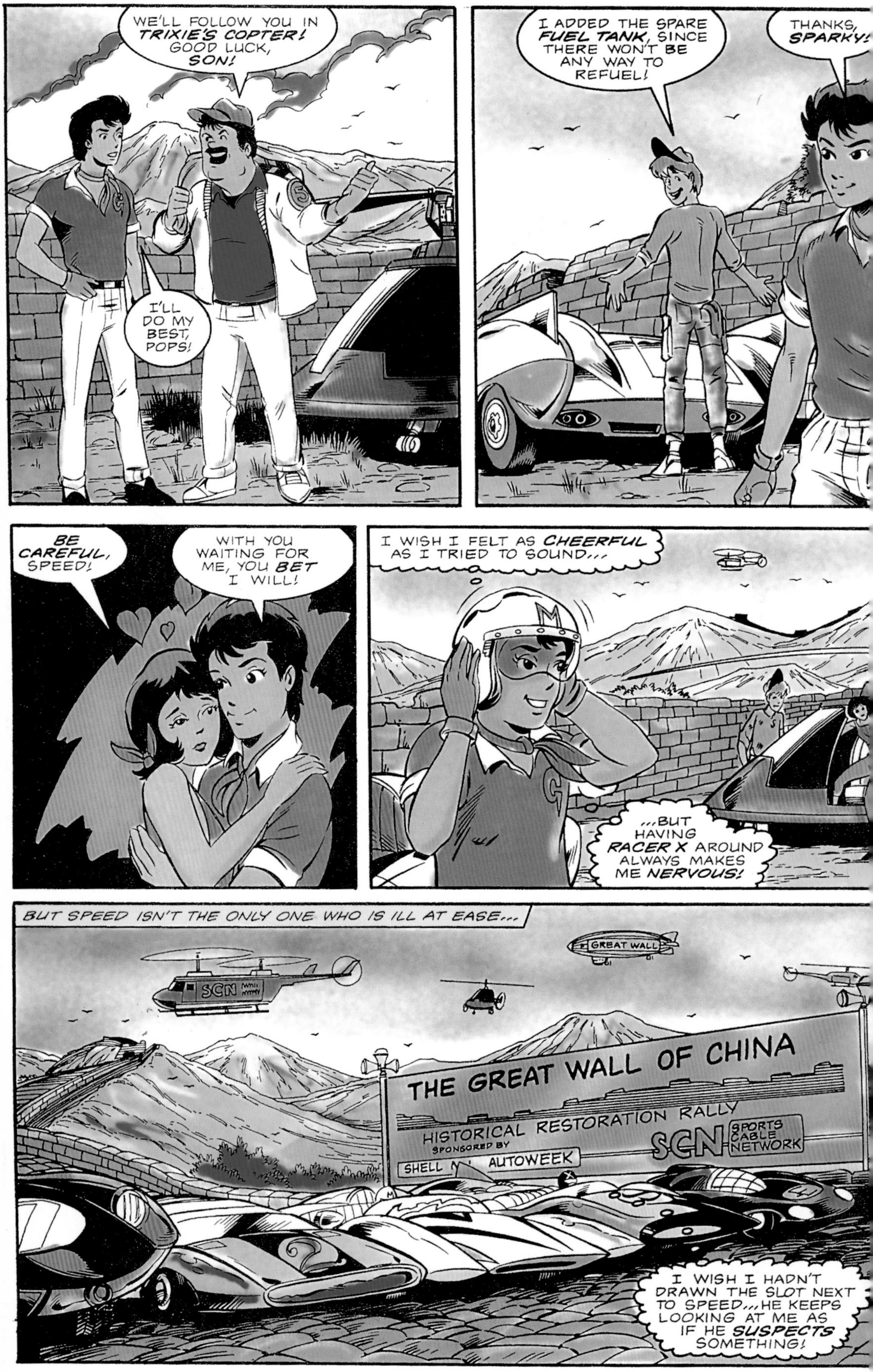
WE'LL FOLLOW YOU IN TRIXIE'S COPTER! GOOD LUCK, SON!
I'LL DO MY BEST, POPS!
I ADDED THE SPARE FUEL TANK, SINCE THERE WON'T BE ANY WAY TO REFUEL!
THANKS, SPARKY!
BE CAREFUL, SPEED!
WITH YOU WAITING FOR ME, YOU BET I WILL!
I WISH I FELT AS CHEERFUL AS I TRIED TO SOUND...
...BUT HAVING RACER X AROUND ALWAYS MAKES ME NERVOUS!
BUT SPEED ISN'T THE ONLY ONE WHO IS ILL AT EASE...
SCN
GREAT WALL
THE GREAT WALL OF CHINA
HISTORICAL RESTORATION RALLY
SPONSORED BY
SHELL
AUTOWEEK
SCN SPORTS CABLE NETWORK
I WISH I HADN'T DRAWN THE SLOT NEXT TO SPEED... HE KEEPS LOOKING AT ME AS IF HE SUSPECTS SOMETHING!

I'M NOT SURE IF IT'S HIS VOICE OR THE WAY HE LOOKS... BUT SOMETHING ABOUT RACER X SEEMS AWFULLY FAMILIAR!
I HOPE SPEED NEVER REALIZES I'M ACTUALLY HIS BROTHER, REX ...IT WOULD PUT HIM IN TOO MUCH DANGER!
DENLY, THE SOUND OF THE TING GUN FILLS THE AIR, THE CARS ROAR TO LIFE!
OH, NO... I WAS BUSY THINKING ABOUT RACER X AND LET THOSE CARS GET A JUMP ON ME!
BBBROOM! BROOM!
THE WALL'S TOO NARROW TO GO BETWEEN THEM... SO I'LL HAVE TO RISK PASSING ON THE OUTSIDE!

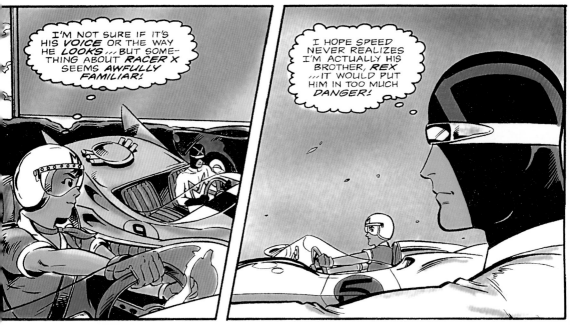

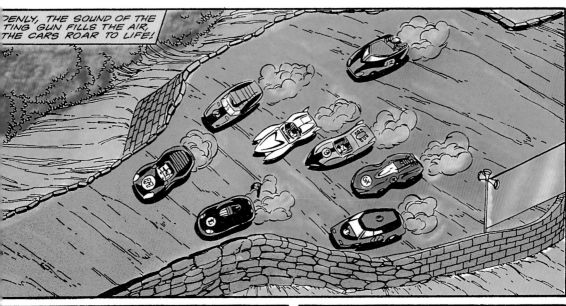

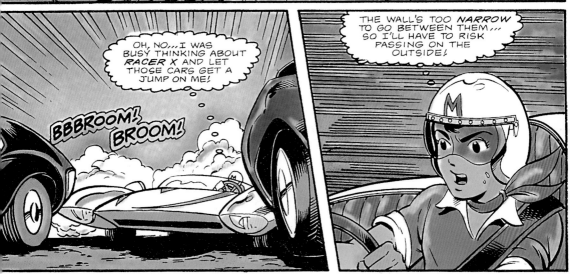

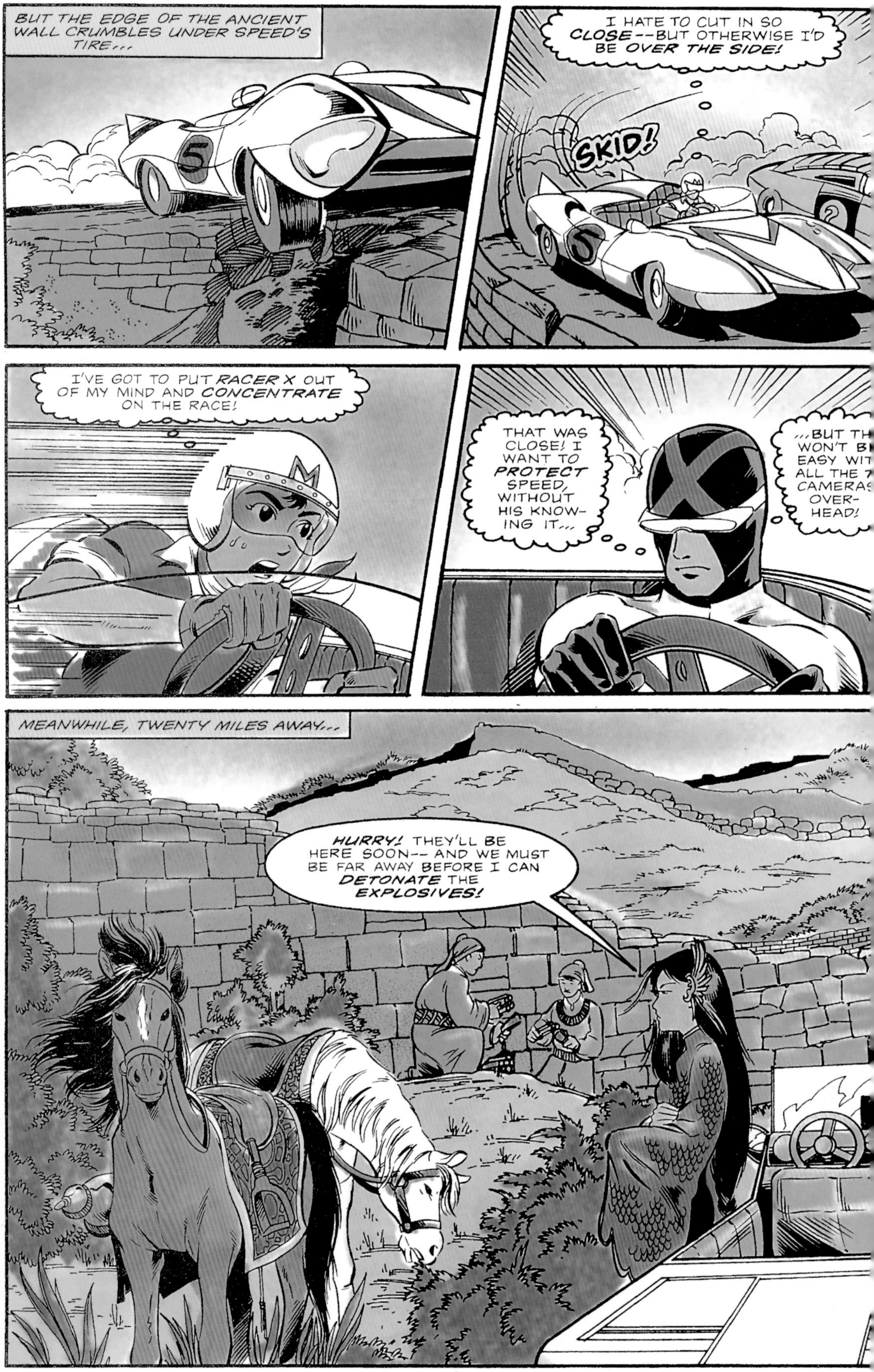

BUT THE EDGE OF THE ANCIENT WALL CRUMBLES UNDER SPEED'S TIRE...
I HATE TO CUT IN SO CLOSE--BUT OTHERWISE I'D BE OVER THE SIDE!
SKID!
I'VE GOT TO PUT RACER X OUT OF MY MIND AND CONCENTRATE ON THE RACE!
THAT WAS CLOSE! I WANT TO PROTECT SPEED, WITHOUT HIS KNOWING IT...
...BUT TH WON'T B EASY WIT ALL THE CAMERAS OVER-HEAD!
MEANWHILE, TWENTY MILES AWAY...
HURRY! THEY'LL BE HERE SOON-- AND WE MUST BE FAR AWAY BEFORE I CAN DETONATE THE EXPLOSIVES!

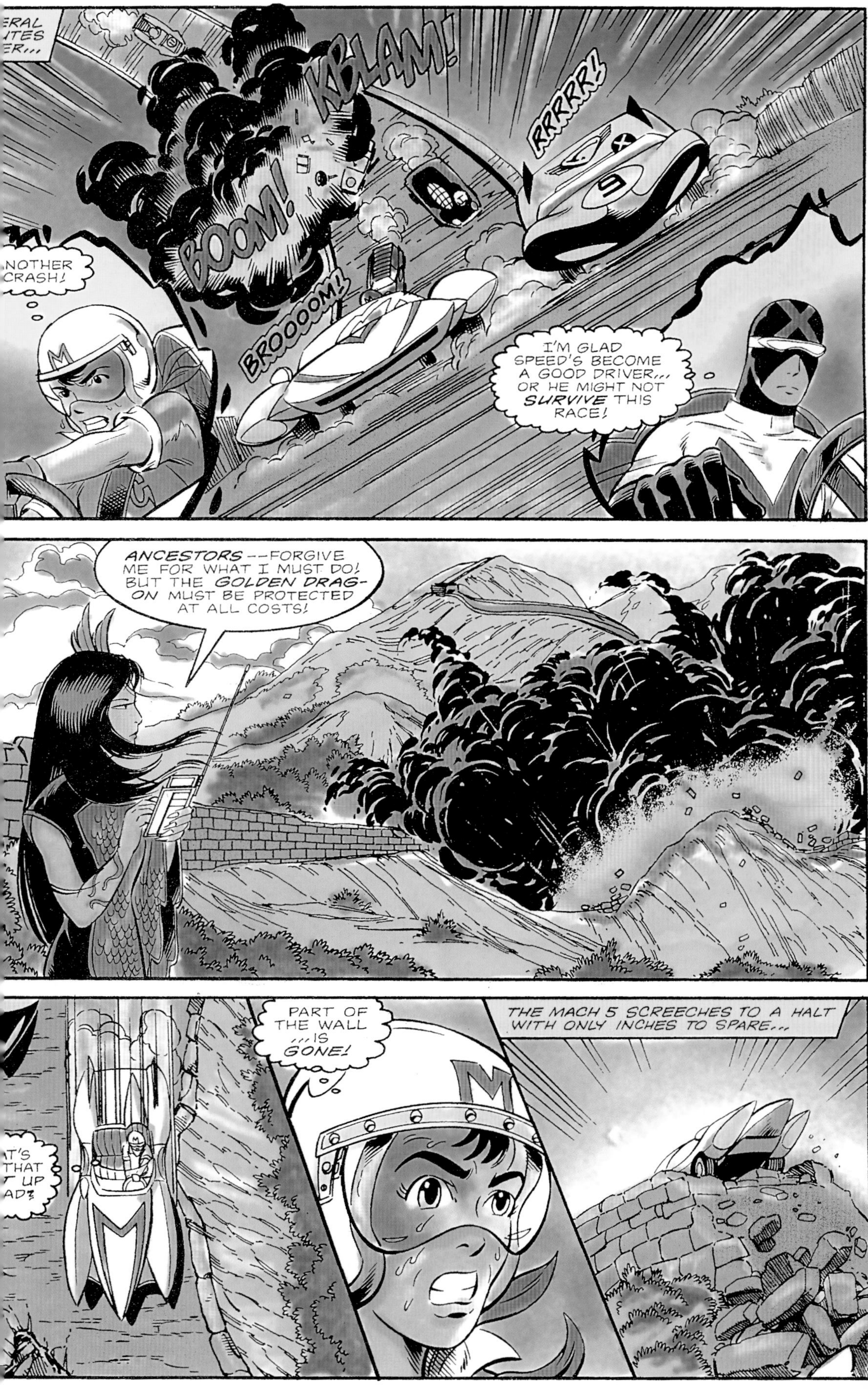
ERAL
UTES
ER...
KBLAM!
BOOM!
RRRRR!
NOTHER
CRASH!
BROOOOM!
I'M GLAD SPEED'S BECOME A GOOD DRIVER... OR HE MIGHT NOT SURVIVE THIS RACE!
ANCESTORS--FORGIVE ME FOR WHAT I MUST DO! BUT THE GOLDEN DRAGON MUST BE PROTECTED AT ALL COSTS!
T'S
THAT
T UP
AD?
PART OF THE WALL ...IS GONE!
THE MACH 5 SCREECHES TO A HALT WITH ONLY INCHES TO SPARE...

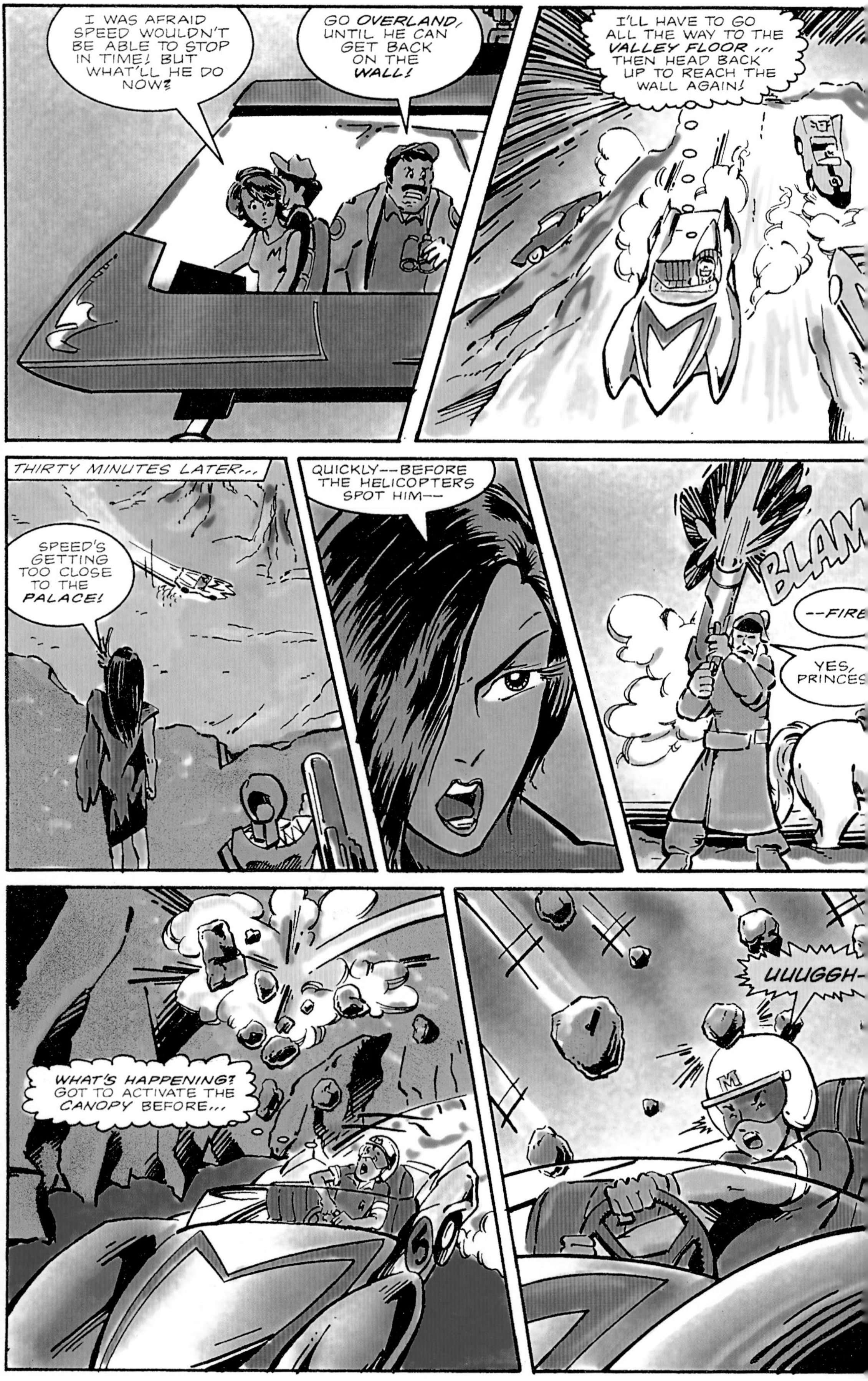

I WAS AFRAID SPEED WOULDN'T BE ABLE TO STOP IN TIME! BUT WHAT'LL HE DO NOW?
GO OVERLAND, UNTIL HE CAN GET BACK ON THE WALL!
I'LL HAVE TO GO ALL THE WAY TO THE VALLEY FLOOR ... THEN HEAD BACK UP TO REACH THE WALL AGAIN!
THIRTY MINUTES LATER...
SPEED'S GETTING TOO CLOSE TO THE PALACE!
QUICKLY--BEFORE THE HELICOPTERS SPOT HIM--
--FIRE
YES, PRINCES
BLAM
WHAT'S HAPPENING? GOT TO ACTIVATE THE CANOPY BEFORE...
UUUGGH-

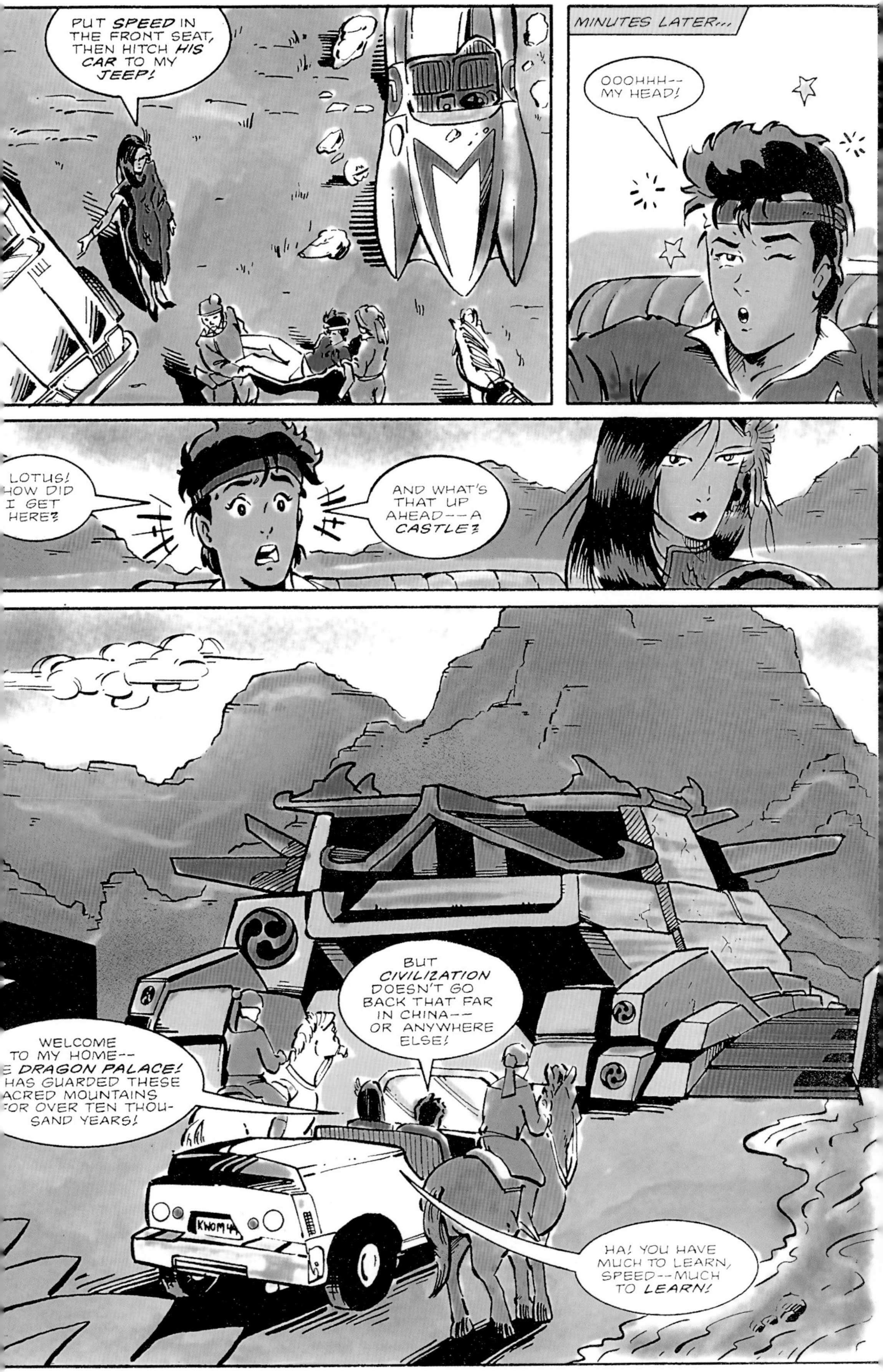
PUT SPEED IN THE FRONT SEAT, THEN HITCH HIS CAR TO MY JEEP!
MINUTES LATER...
OOOHHH-- MY HEAD!
LOTUS! HOW DID I GET HERE?
AND WHAT'S THAT UP AHEAD--A CASTLE?
WELCOME TO MY HOME-- E DRAGON PALACE! HAS GUARDED THESE ACRED MOUNTAINS FOR OVER TEN THOU- SAND YEARS!
BUT CIVILIZATION DOESN'T GO BACK THAT FAR IN CHINA-- OR ANYWHERE ELSE!
HA! YOU HAVE MUCH TO LEARN, SPEED--MUCH TO LEARN!

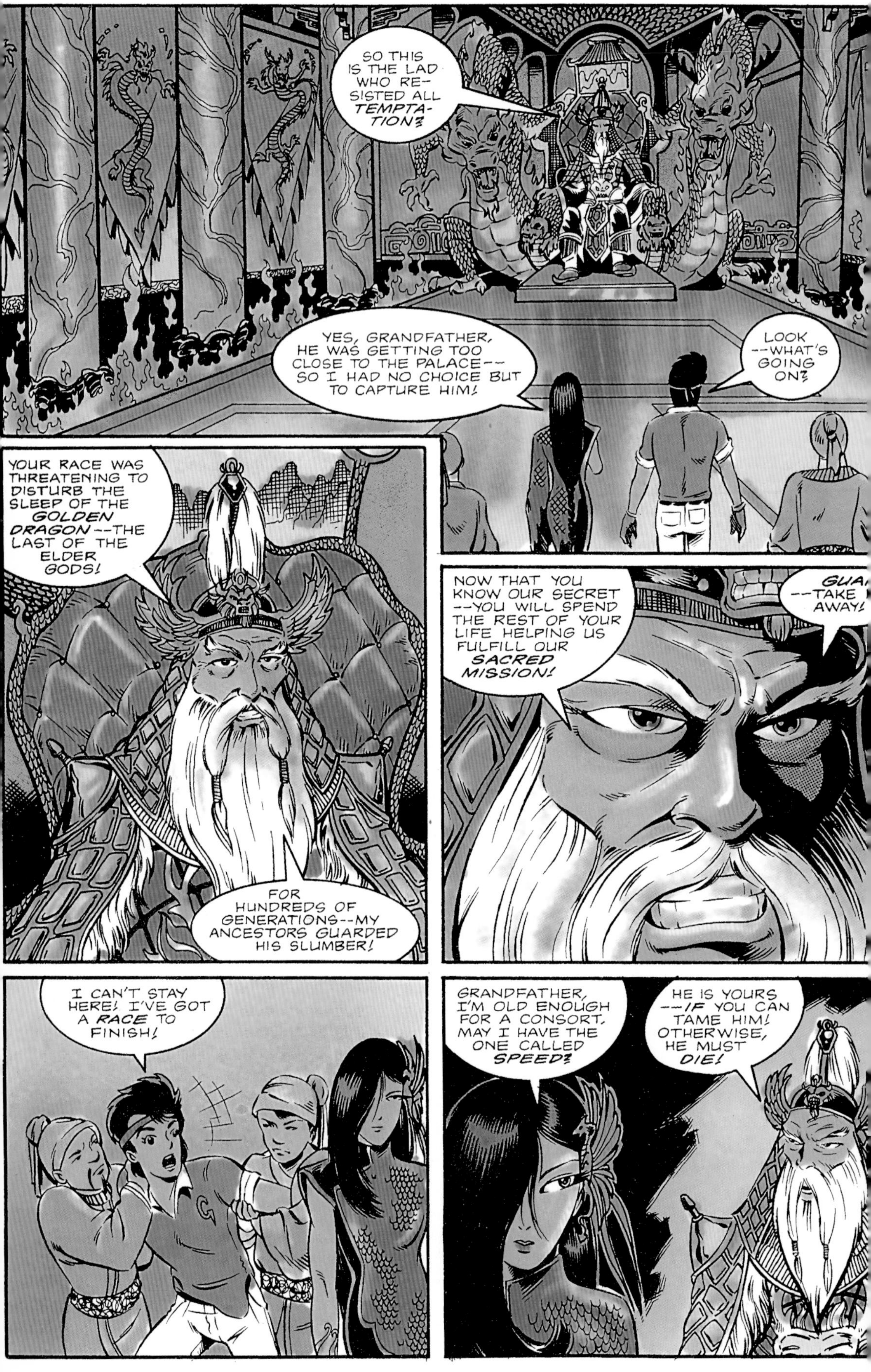
SO THIS IS THE LAD WHO RESISTED ALL TEMPTATION?
YES, GRANDFATHER, HE WAS GETTING TOO CLOSE TO THE PALACE-- SO I HAD NO CHOICE BUT TO CAPTURE HIM!
LOOK --WHAT'S GOING ON?
YOUR RACE WAS THREATENING TO DISTURB THE SLEEP OF THE GOLDEN DRAGON--THE LAST OF THE ELDER GODS!
FOR HUNDREDS OF GENERATIONS--MY ANCESTORS GUARDED HIS SLUMBER!
NOW THAT YOU KNOW OUR SECRET --YOU WILL SPEND THE REST OF YOUR LIFE HELPING US FULFILL OUR SACRED MISSION!
--TAKE AWAY!
I CAN'T STAY HERE! I'VE GOT A RACE TO FINISH!
GRANDFATHER, I'M OLD ENOUGH FOR A CONSORT. MAY I HAVE THE ONE CALLED SPEED?
HE IS YOURS --IF YOU CAN TAME HIM! OTHERWISE, HE MUST DIE!

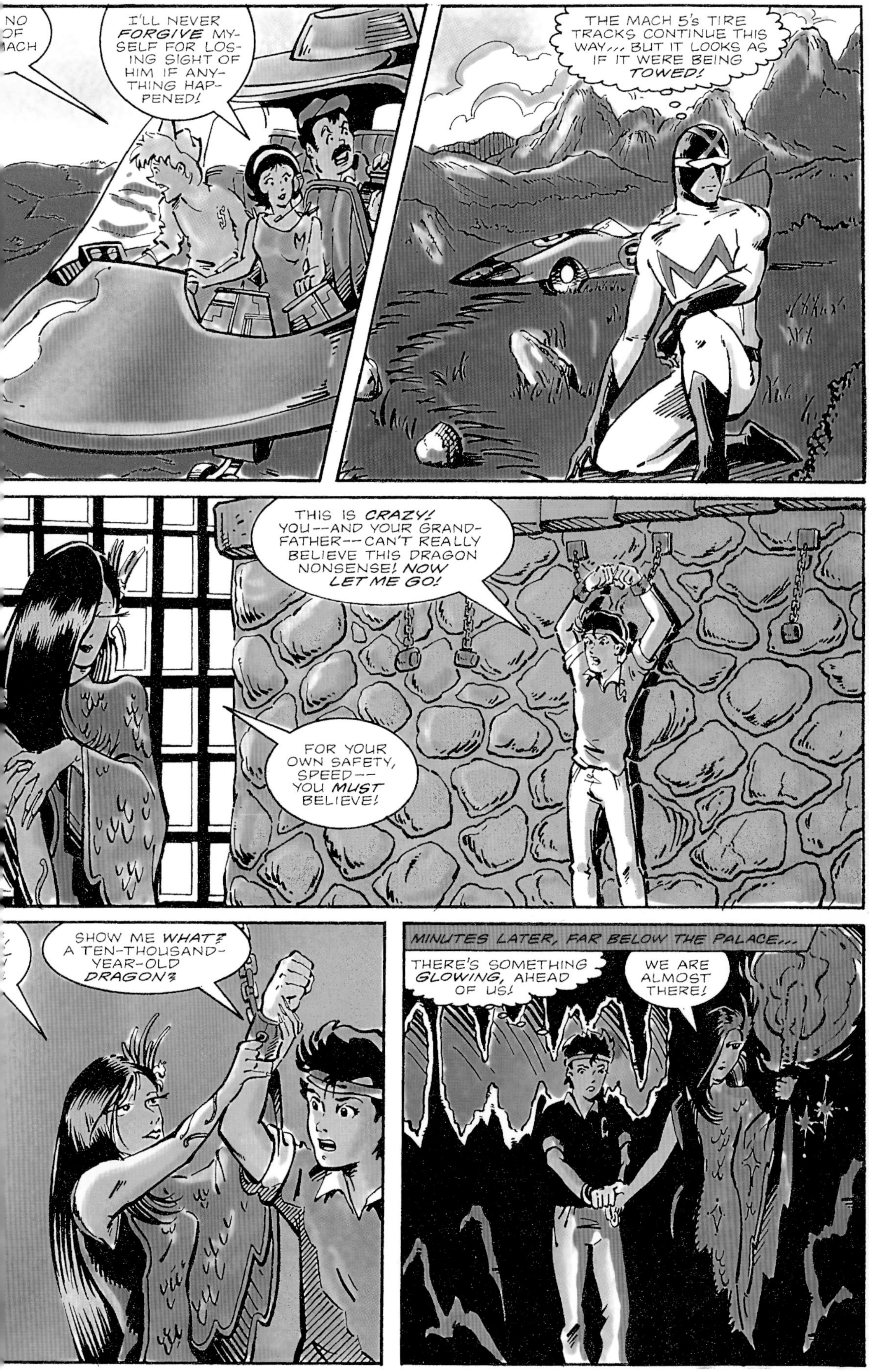
I'LL NEVER FORGIVE MYSELF FOR LOSING SIGHT OF HIM IF ANYTHING HAPPENED!
THE MACH 5's TIRE TRACKS CONTINUE THIS WAY... BUT IT LOOKS AS IF IT WERE BEING TOWED!
THIS IS CRAZY! YOU--AND YOUR GRANDFATHER--CAN'T REALLY BELIEVE THIS DRAGON NONSENSE! NOW LET ME GO!
FOR YOUR OWN SAFETY, SPEED-- YOU MUST BELIEVE!
SHOW ME WHAT? A TEN-THOUSAND-YEAR-OLD DRAGON?
MINUTES LATER, FAR BELOW THE PALACE...
THERE'S SOMETHING GLOWING, AHEAD OF US!
WE ARE ALMOST THERE!

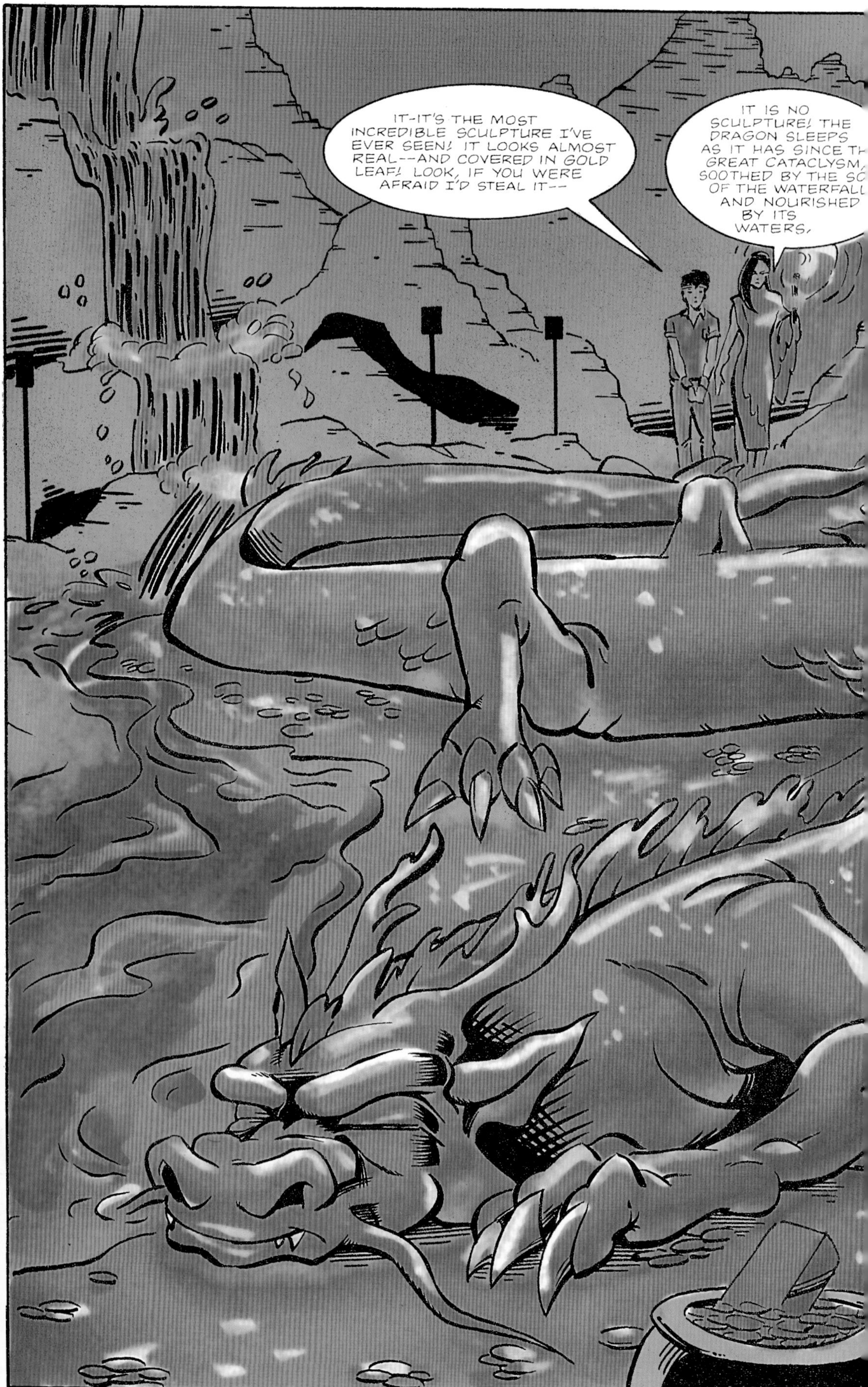
IT-IT'S THE MOST INCREDIBLE SCULPTURE I'VE EVER SEEN! IT LOOKS ALMOST REAL--AND COVERED IN GOLD LEAF! LOOK, IF YOU WERE AFRAID I'D STEAL IT--
IT IS NO SCULPTURE! THE DRAGON SLEEPS AS IT HAS SINCE TH GREAT CATACLYSM, SOOTHED BY THE SO OF THE WATERFALL AND NOURISHED BY ITS WATERS.

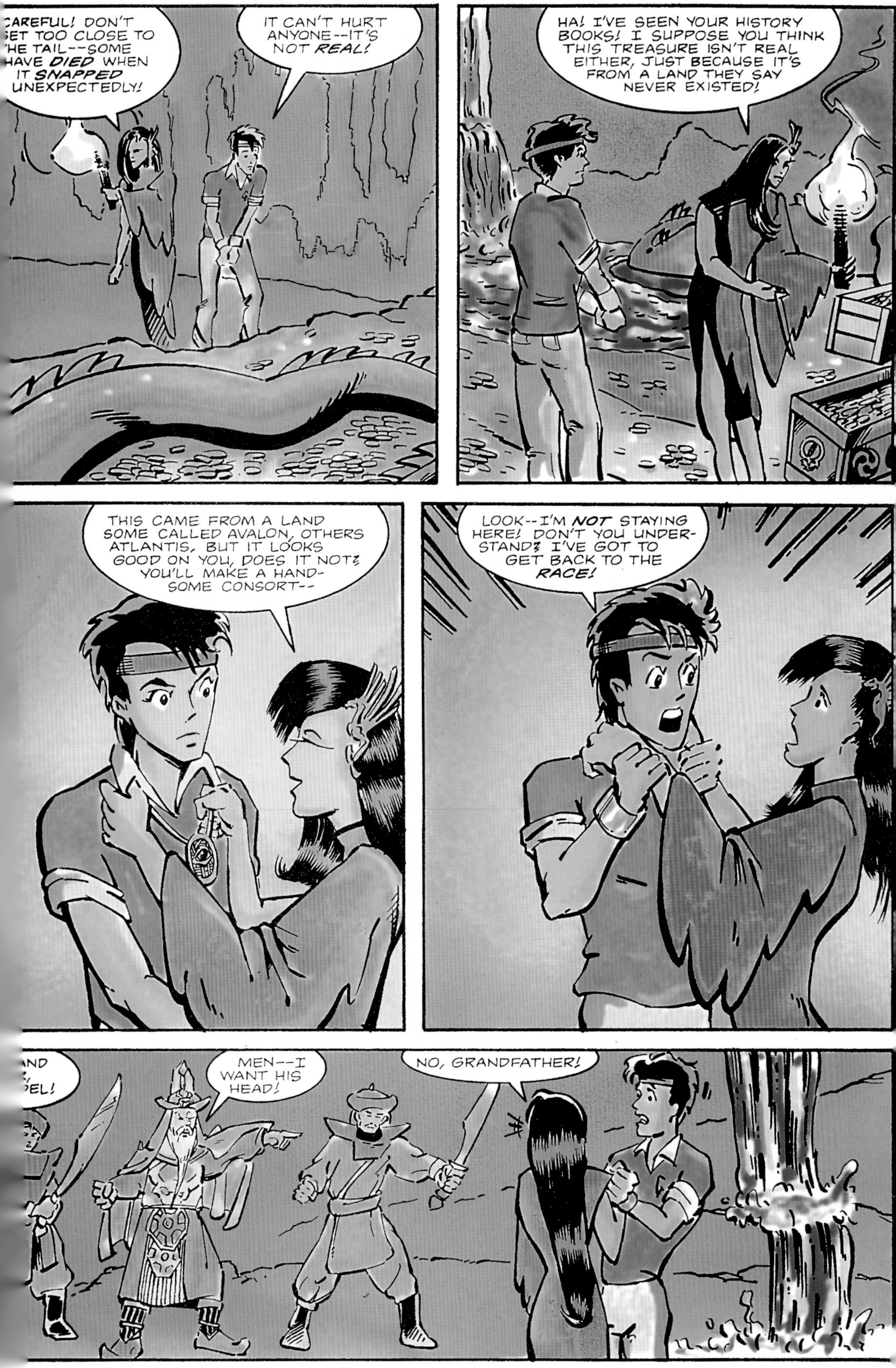

CAREFUL! DON'T GET TOO CLOSE TO THE TAIL--SOME HAVE DIED WHEN IT SNAPPED UNEXPECTEDLY!
IT CAN'T HURT ANYONE--IT'S NOT REAL!
HA! I'VE SEEN YOUR HISTORY BOOKS! I SUPPOSE YOU THINK THIS TREASURE ISN'T REAL EITHER, JUST BECAUSE IT'S FROM A LAND THEY SAY NEVER EXISTED!
THIS CAME FROM A LAND SOME CALLED AVALON, OTHERS ATLANTIS, BUT IT LOOKS GOOD ON YOU, DOES IT NOT? YOU'LL MAKE A HANDSOME CONSORT--
LOOK--I'M NOT STAYING HERE! DON'T YOU UNDERSTAND? I'VE GOT TO GET BACK TO THE RACE!
MEN--I WANT HIS HEAD!
NO, GRANDFATHER!

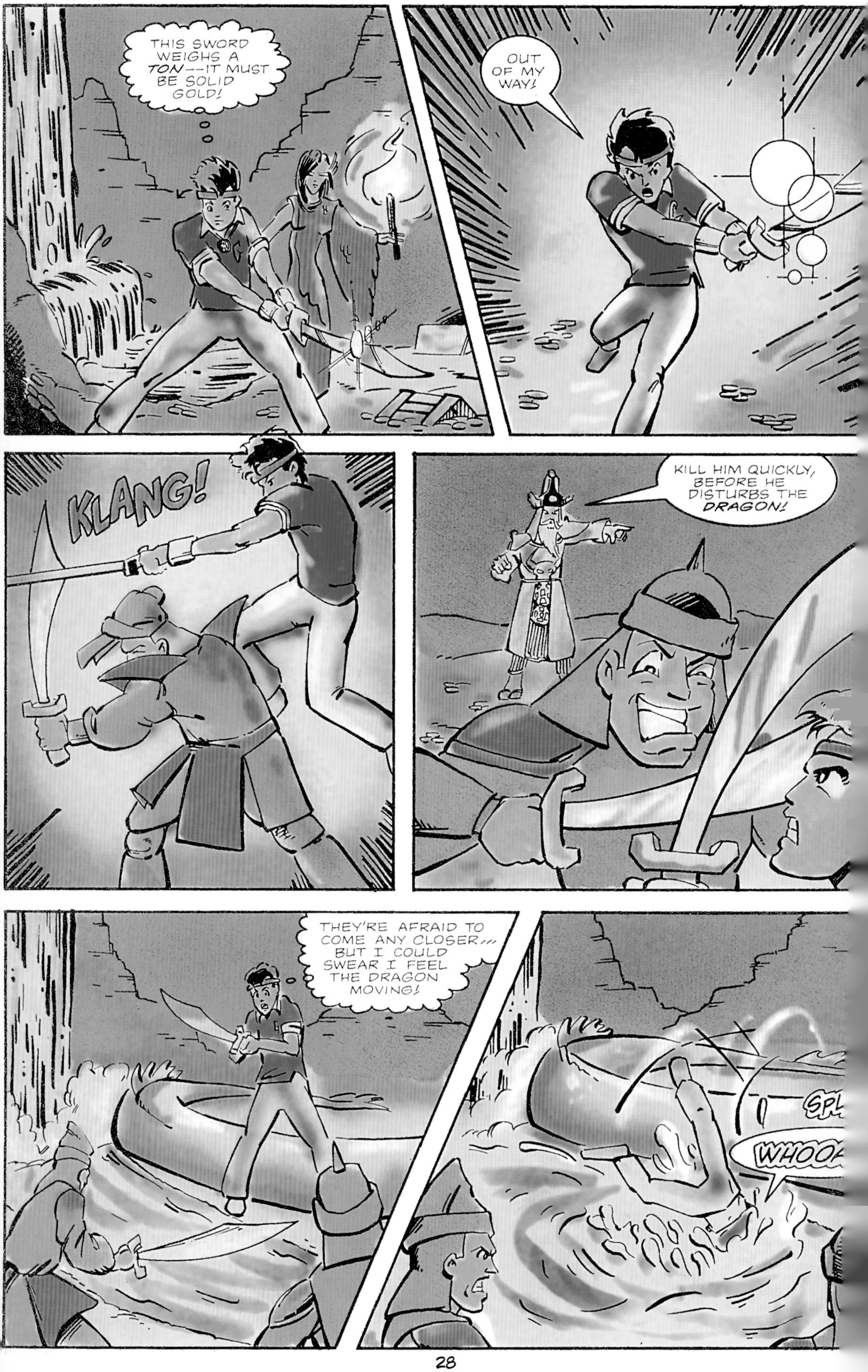

THIS SWORD WEIGHS A *TON*--IT MUST BE SOLID GOLD!
OUT OF MY WAY!
KLANG!
KILL HIM QUICKLY, BEFORE HE DISTURBS THE *DRAGON!*
THEY'RE AFRAID TO COME ANY CLOSER... BUT I COULD SWEAR I FEEL THE DRAGON MOVING!

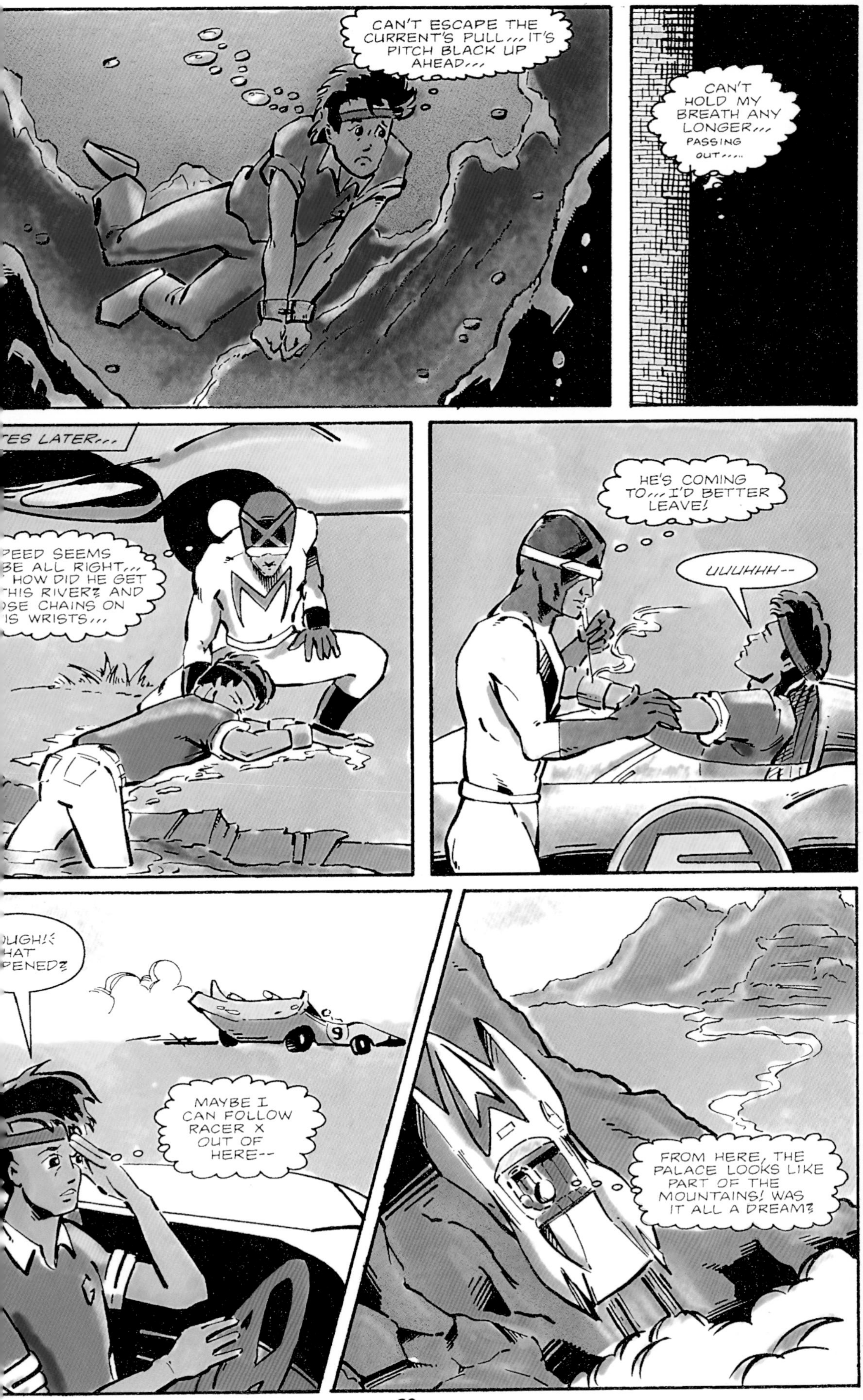
CAN'T ESCAPE THE CURRENT'S PULL... IT'S PITCH BLACK UP AHEAD...
CAN'T HOLD MY BREATH ANY LONGER... PASSING OUT.....
TES LATER...
PEED SEEMS BE ALL RIGHT... HOW DID HE GET HIS RIVER? AND OSE CHAINS ON IS WRISTS...
HE'S COMING TO... I'D BETTER LEAVE!
UUUHHH--
UGH! HAT PENED?
MAYBE I CAN FOLLOW RACER X OUT OF HERE--
FROM HERE, THE PALACE LOOKS LIKE PART OF THE MOUNTAINS! WAS IT ALL A DREAM?

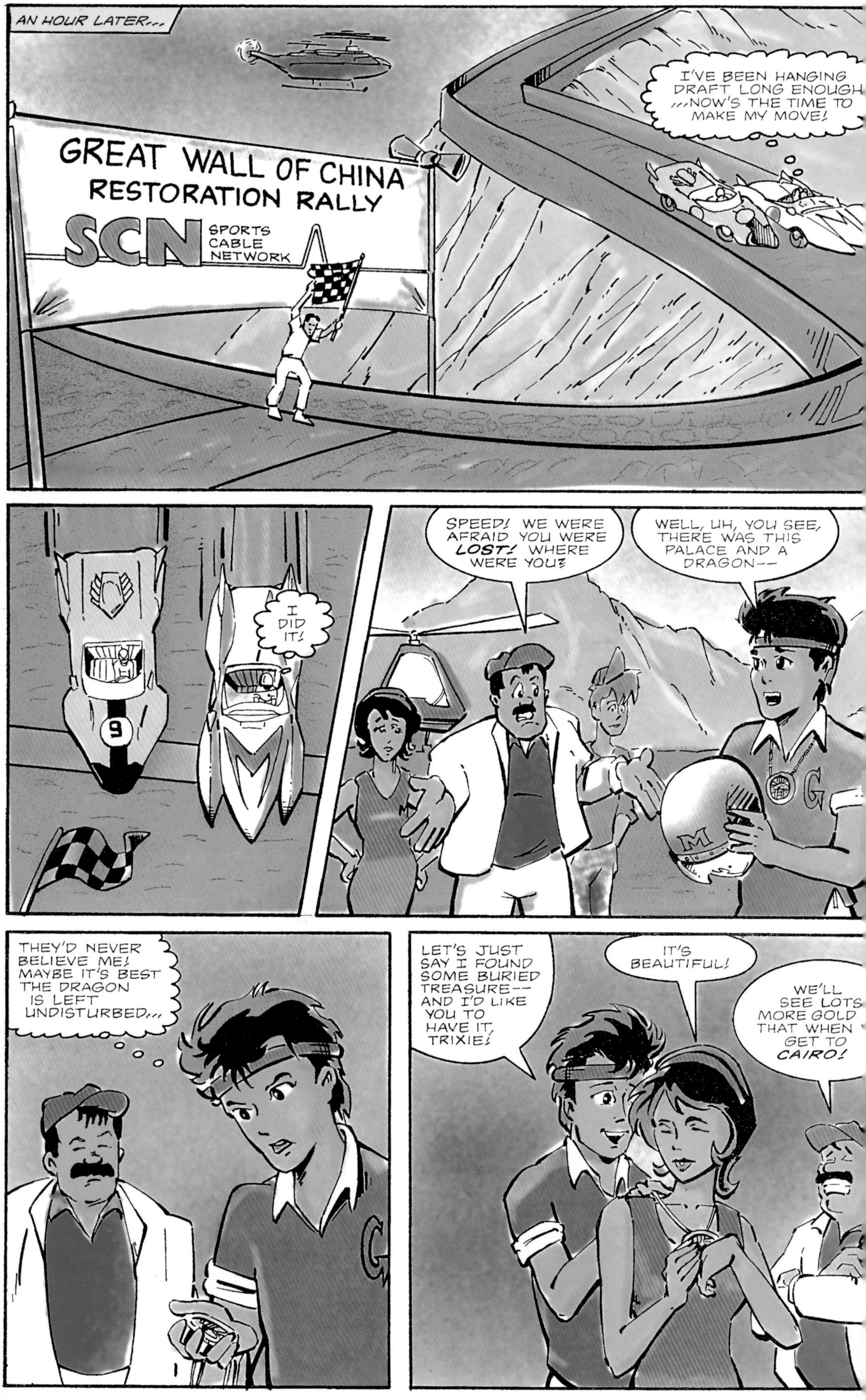
AN HOUR LATER...
GREAT WALL OF CHINA RESTORATION RALLY
SCN SPORTS CABLE NETWORK
I'VE BEEN HANGING DRAFT LONG ENOUGH ...NOW'S THE TIME TO MAKE MY MOVE!
I DID IT!
SPEED! WE WERE AFRAID YOU WERE LOST! WHERE WERE YOU?
WELL, UH, YOU SEE, THERE WAS THIS PALACE AND A DRAGON--
THEY'D NEVER BELIEVE ME! MAYBE IT'S BEST THE DRAGON IS LEFT UNDISTURBED...
LET'S JUST SAY I FOUND SOME BURIED TREASURE-- AND I'D LIKE YOU TO HAVE IT, TRIXIE!
IT'S BEAUTIFUL!
WE'LL SEE LOTS MORE GOLD THAT WHEN GET TO CAIRO!

Speed Racer #15

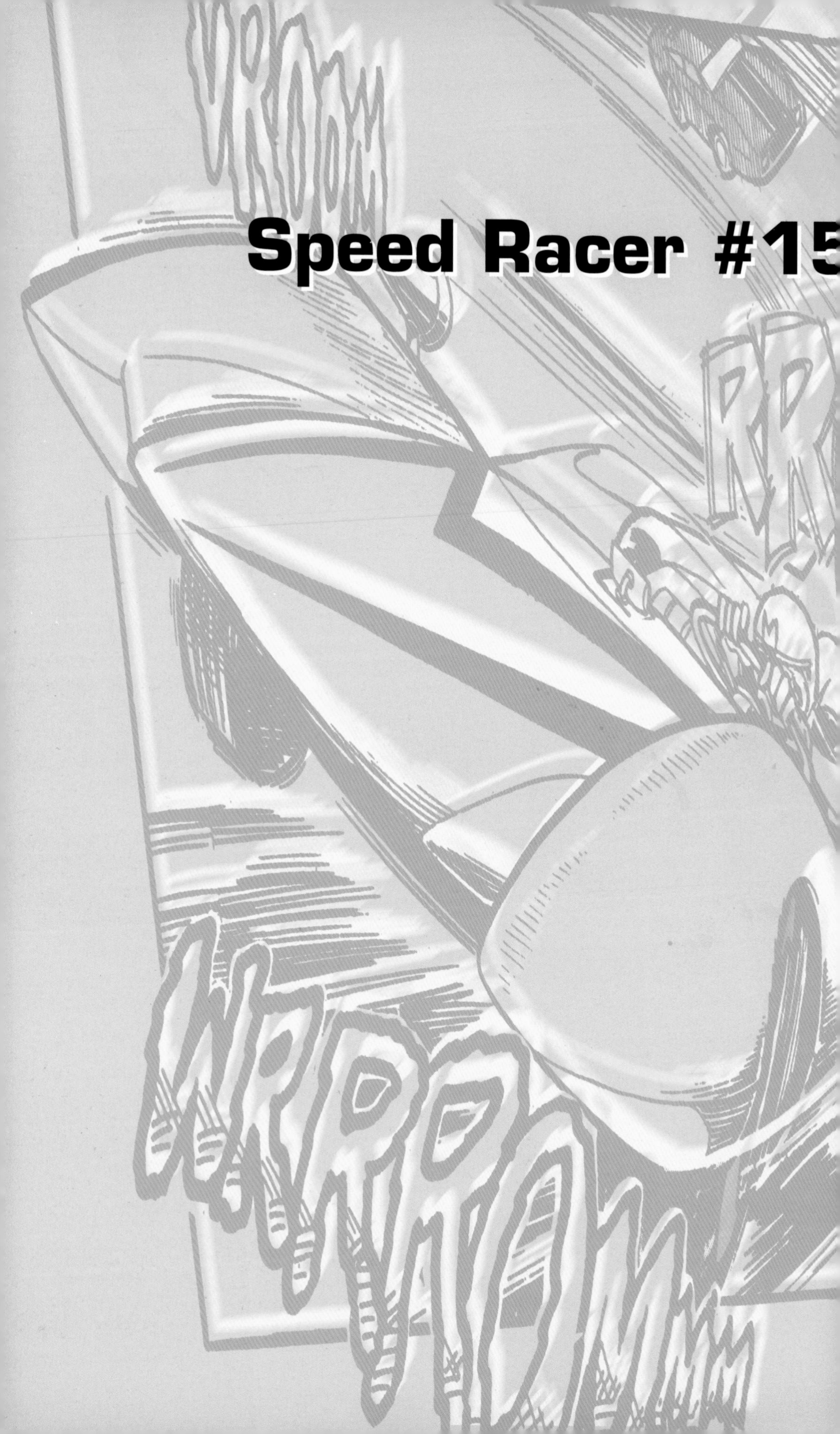

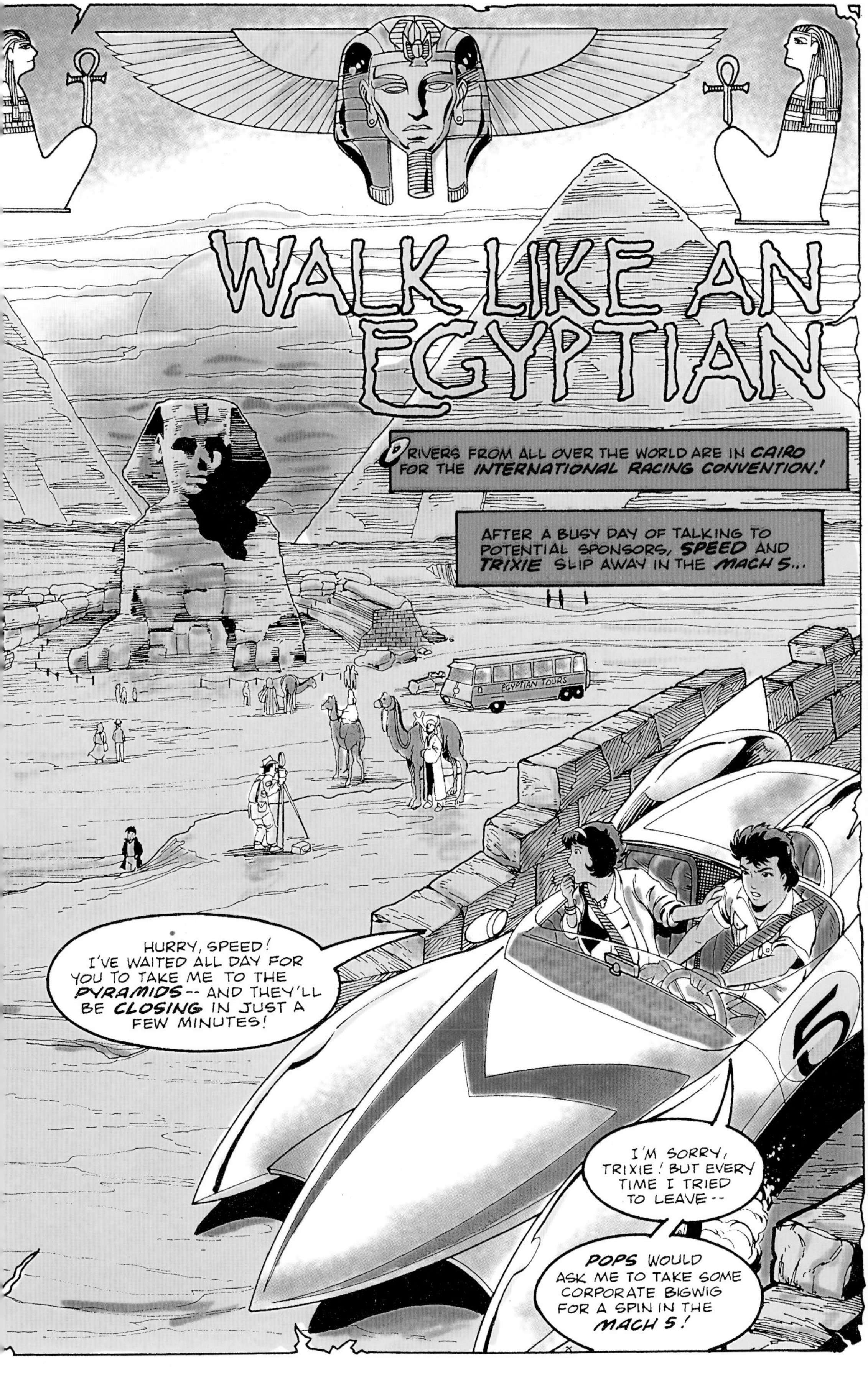
WALK LIKE AN EGYPTIAN
DRIVERS FROM ALL OVER THE WORLD ARE IN CAIRO FOR THE INTERNATIONAL RACING CONVENTION!
AFTER A BUSY DAY OF TALKING TO POTENTIAL SPONSORS, SPEED AND TRIXIE SLIP AWAY IN THE MACH 5...
EGYPTIAN TOURS
HURRY, SPEED! I'VE WAITED ALL DAY FOR YOU TO TAKE ME TO THE PYRAMIDS-- AND THEY'LL BE CLOSING IN JUST A FEW MINUTES!
I'M SORRY, TRIXIE! BUT EVERY TIME I TRIED TO LEAVE--
POPS WOULD ASK ME TO TAKE SOME CORPORATE BIGWIG FOR A SPIN IN THE MACH 5!

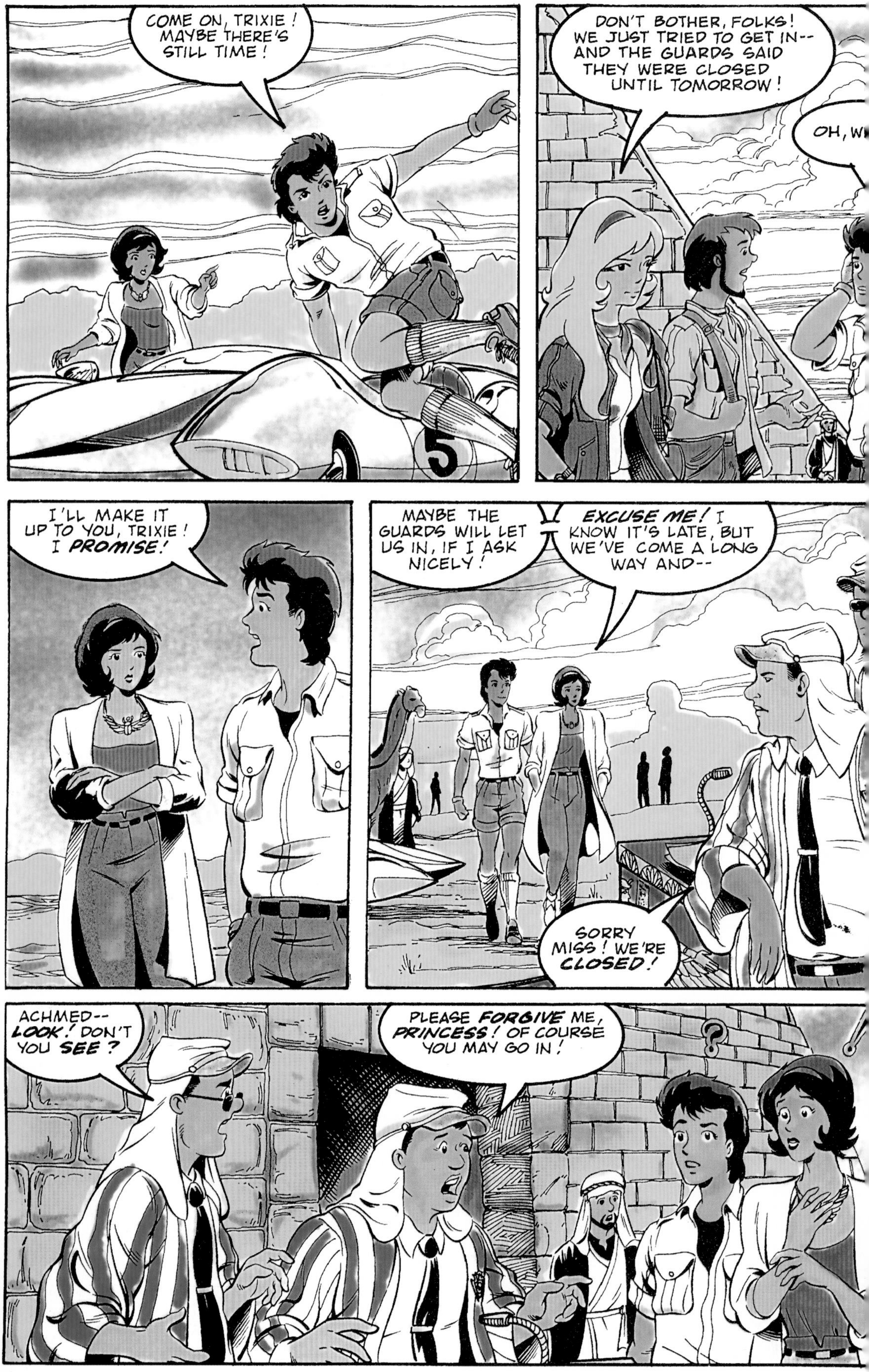
COME ON, TRIXIE! MAYBE THERE'S STILL TIME!
DON'T BOTHER, FOLKS! WE JUST TRIED TO GET IN-- AND THE GUARDS SAID THEY WERE CLOSED UNTIL TOMORROW!
I'LL MAKE IT UP TO YOU, TRIXIE! I PROMISE!
MAYBE THE GUARDS WILL LET US IN, IF I ASK NICELY!
EXCUSE ME! I KNOW IT'S LATE, BUT WE'VE COME A LONG WAY AND--
SORRY MISS! WE'RE CLOSED!
ACHMED-- LOOK! DON'T YOU SEE?
PLEASE FORGIVE ME, PRINCESS! OF COURSE YOU MAY GO IN!
?

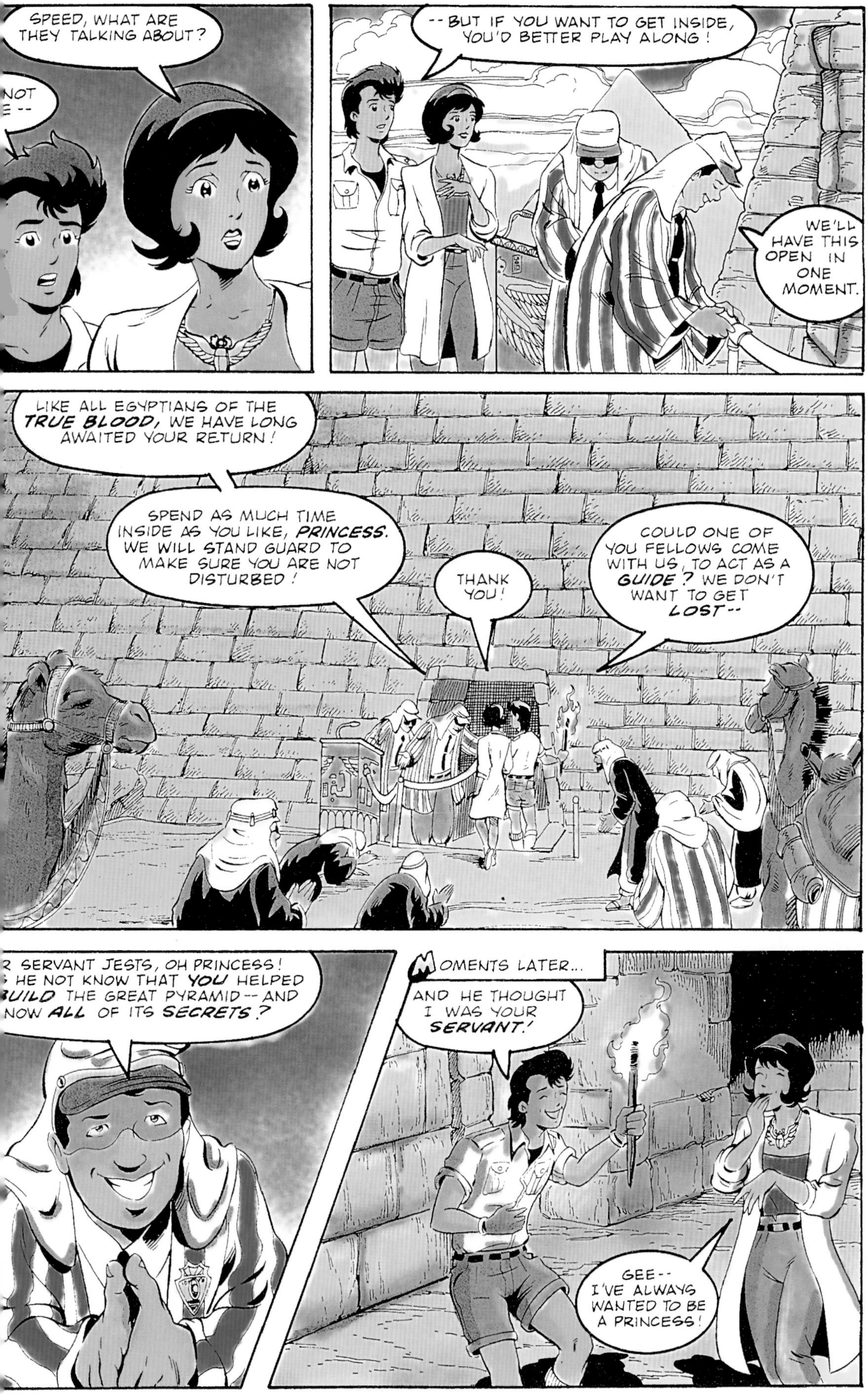

SPEED, WHAT ARE THEY TALKING ABOUT?
NOT E --
-- BUT IF YOU WANT TO GET INSIDE, YOU'D BETTER PLAY ALONG!
WE'LL HAVE THIS OPEN IN ONE MOMENT.
LIKE ALL EGYPTIANS OF THE TRUE BLOOD, WE HAVE LONG AWAITED YOUR RETURN!
SPEND AS MUCH TIME INSIDE AS YOU LIKE, PRINCESS. WE WILL STAND GUARD TO MAKE SURE YOU ARE NOT DISTURBED!
THANK YOU!
COULD ONE OF YOU FELLOWS COME WITH US, TO ACT AS A GUIDE? WE DON'T WANT TO GET LOST--
R SERVANT JESTS, OH PRINCESS! HE NOT KNOW THAT YOU HELPED BUILD THE GREAT PYRAMID -- AND NOW ALL OF ITS SECRETS?
MOMENTS LATER...
AND HE THOUGHT I WAS YOUR SERVANT!
GEE -- I'VE ALWAYS WANTED TO BE A PRINCESS!

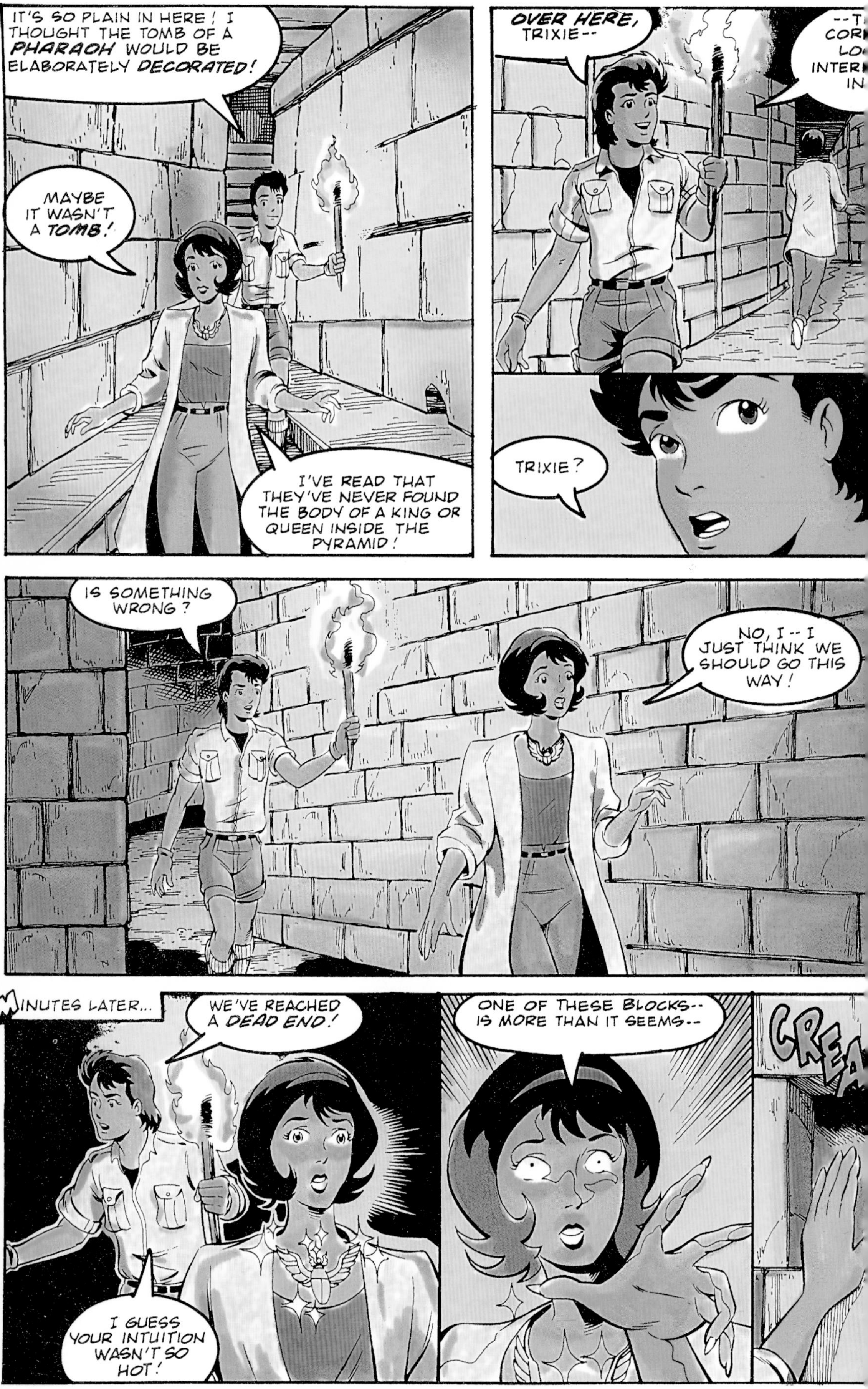
IT'S SO PLAIN IN HERE! I THOUGHT THE TOMB OF A PHARAOH WOULD BE ELABORATELY DECORATED!
MAYBE IT WASN'T A TOMB!
I'VE READ THAT THEY'VE NEVER FOUND THE BODY OF A KING OR QUEEN INSIDE THE PYRAMID!
OVER HERE, TRIXIE--
TRIXIE?
IS SOMETHING WRONG?
NO, I -- I JUST THINK WE SHOULD GO THIS WAY!
MINUTES LATER...
WE'VE REACHED A DEAD END!
I GUESS YOUR INTUITION WASN'T SO HOT!
ONE OF THESE BLOCKS-- IS MORE THAN IT SEEMS--

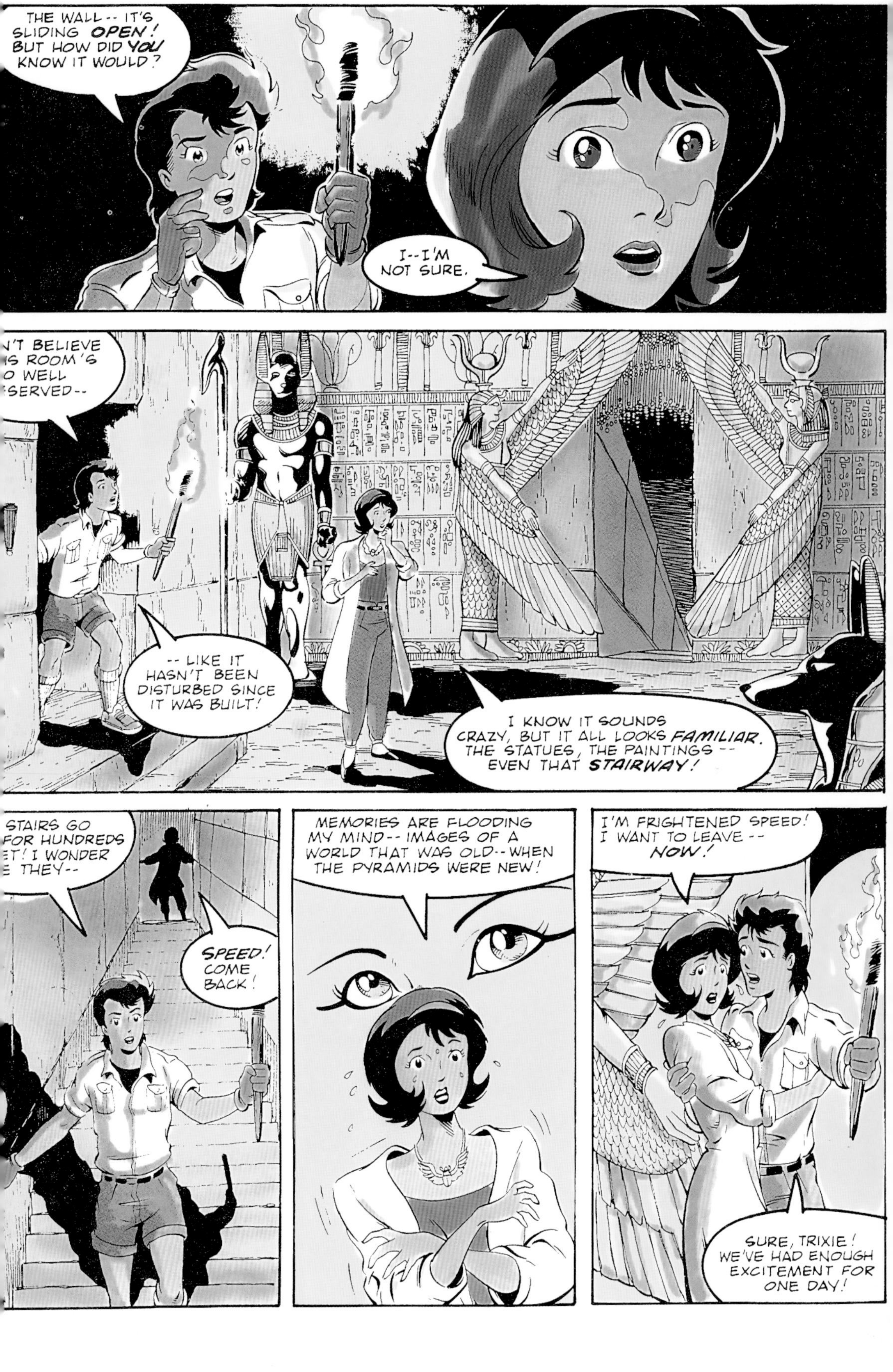
THE WALL -- IT'S SLIDING OPEN! BUT HOW DID YOU KNOW IT WOULD?
I--I'M NOT SURE.
N'T BELIEVE IS ROOM'S O WELL SERVED--
-- LIKE IT HASN'T BEEN DISTURBED SINCE IT WAS BUILT!
I KNOW IT SOUNDS CRAZY, BUT IT ALL LOOKS FAMILIAR. THE STATUES, THE PAINTINGS -- EVEN THAT STAIRWAY!
STAIRS GO FOR HUNDREDS ET! I WONDER E THEY--
SPEED! COME BACK!
MEMORIES ARE FLOODING MY MIND-- IMAGES OF A WORLD THAT WAS OLD-- WHEN THE PYRAMIDS WERE NEW!
I'M FRIGHTENED SPEED! I WANT TO LEAVE -- NOW!
SURE, TRIXIE! WE'VE HAD ENOUGH EXCITEMENT FOR ONE DAY!

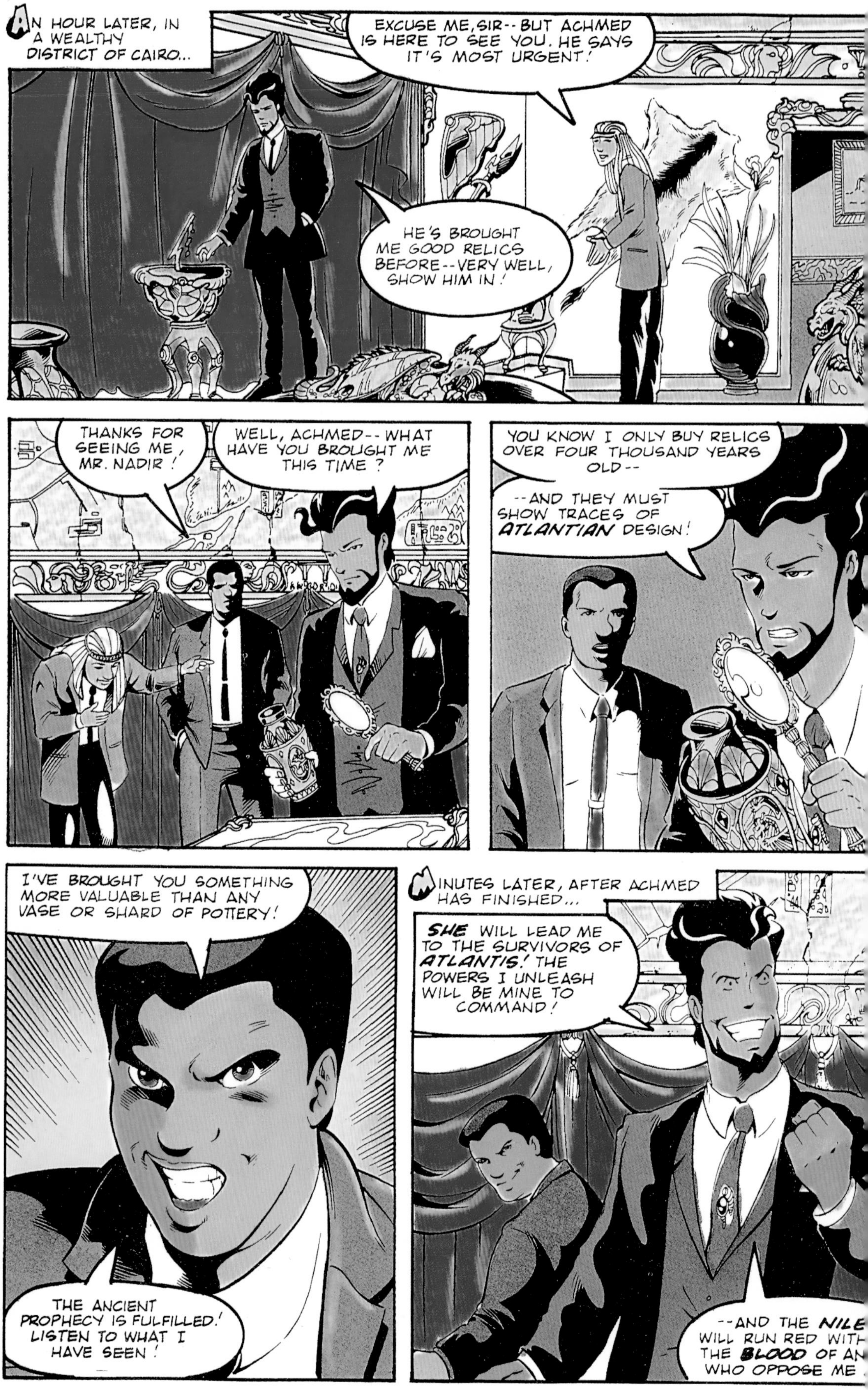
AN HOUR LATER, IN A WEALTHY DISTRICT OF CAIRO...
EXCUSE ME, SIR-- BUT ACHMED IS HERE TO SEE YOU. HE SAYS IT'S MOST URGENT!
HE'S BROUGHT ME GOOD RELICS BEFORE--VERY WELL, SHOW HIM IN!
THANKS FOR SEEING ME, MR. NADIR!
WELL, ACHMED-- WHAT HAVE YOU BROUGHT ME THIS TIME?
YOU KNOW I ONLY BUY RELICS OVER FOUR THOUSAND YEARS OLD--
--AND THEY MUST SHOW TRACES OF ATLANTIAN DESIGN!
I'VE BROUGHT YOU SOMETHING MORE VALUABLE THAN ANY VASE OR SHARD OF POTTERY!
THE ANCIENT PROPHECY IS FULFILLED! LISTEN TO WHAT I HAVE SEEN!
MINUTES LATER, AFTER ACHMED HAS FINISHED...
SHE WILL LEAD ME TO THE SURVIVORS OF ATLANTIS! THE POWERS I UNLEASH WILL BE MINE TO COMMAND!
--AND THE NILE WILL RUN RED WITH THE BLOOD OF AN WHO OPPOSE ME

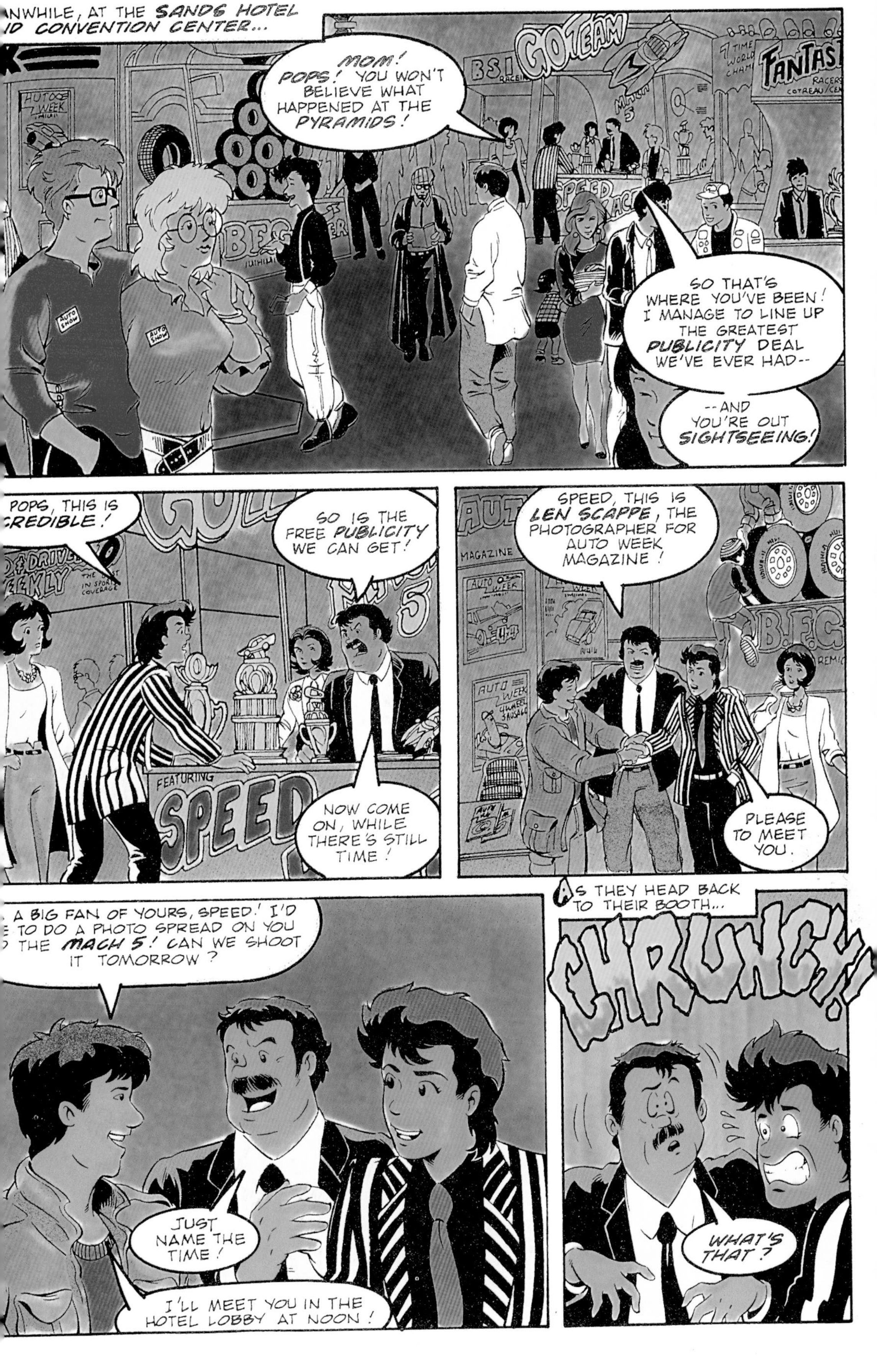

NWHILE, AT THE SANDS HOTEL
ID CONVENTION CENTER...
MOM! POPS! YOU WON'T BELIEVE WHAT HAPPENED AT THE PYRAMIDS!
SO THAT'S WHERE YOU'VE BEEN! I MANAGE TO LINE UP THE GREATEST PUBLICITY DEAL WE'VE EVER HAD--
--AND YOU'RE OUT SIGHTSEEING!
POPS, THIS IS CREDIBLE!
SO IS THE FREE PUBLICITY WE CAN GET!
NOW COME ON, WHILE THERE'S STILL TIME!
SPEED, THIS IS LEN SCAPPE, THE PHOTOGRAPHER FOR AUTO WEEK MAGAZINE!
PLEASE TO MEET YOU.
A BIG FAN OF YOURS, SPEED! I'D TO DO A PHOTO SPREAD ON YOU THE MACH 5! CAN WE SHOOT IT TOMORROW?
JUST NAME THE TIME!
I'LL MEET YOU IN THE HOTEL LOBBY AT NOON!
AS THEY HEAD BACK TO THEIR BOOTH...
CHRUNCH!!
WHAT'S THAT?

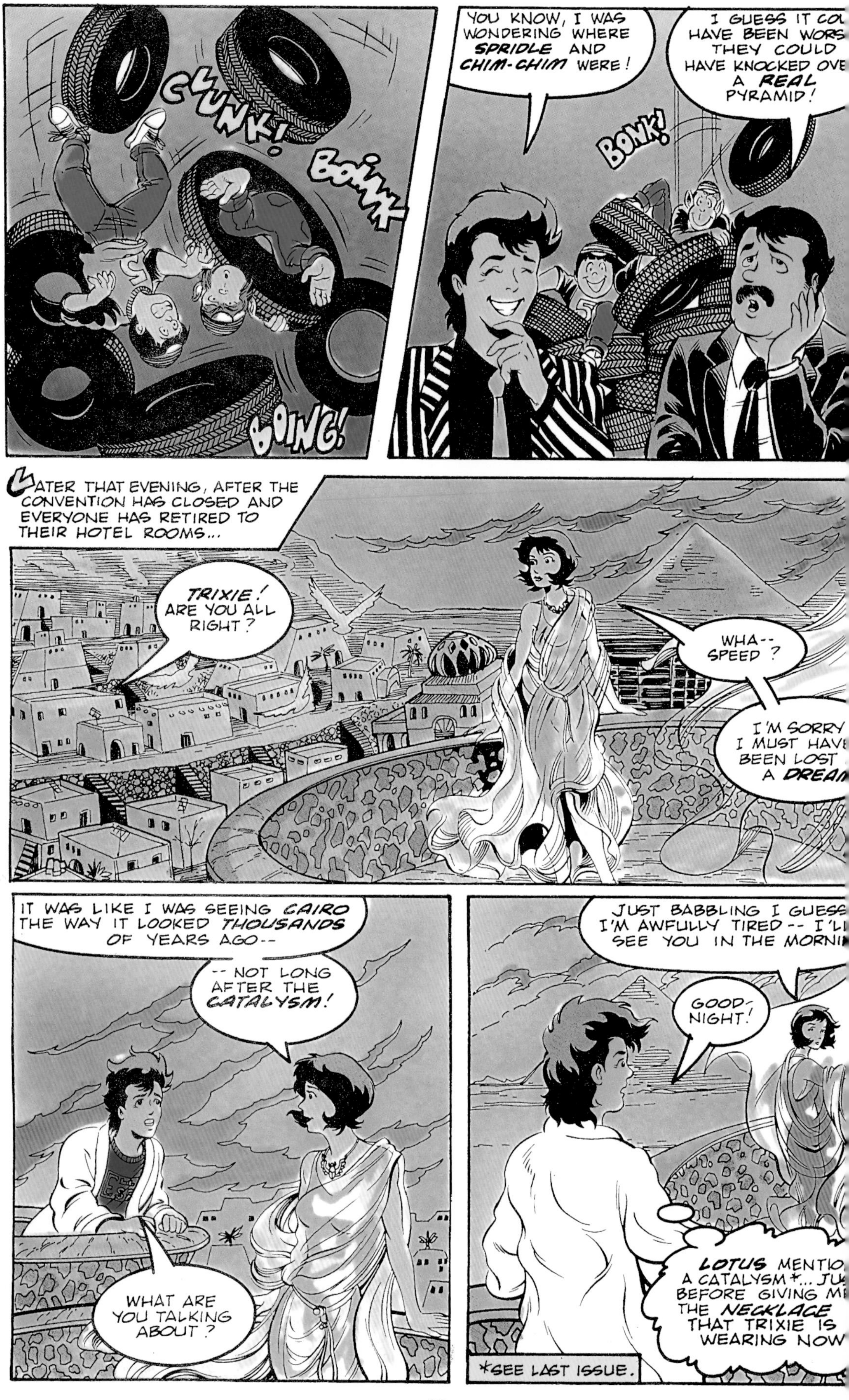
CLUNK!
BOINK
BOING!
YOU KNOW, I WAS WONDERING WHERE SPRIDLE AND CHIM-CHIM WERE!
I GUESS IT COU HAVE BEEN WORS THEY COULD HAVE KNOCKED OVE A REAL PYRAMID!
BONK!
LATER THAT EVENING, AFTER THE CONVENTION HAS CLOSED AND EVERYONE HAS RETIRED TO THEIR HOTEL ROOMS...
TRIXIE! ARE YOU ALL RIGHT?
WHA-- SPEED?
I'M SORRY I MUST HAVE BEEN LOST A DREAM
IT WAS LIKE I WAS SEEING CAIRO THE WAY IT LOOKED THOUSANDS OF YEARS AGO--
-- NOT LONG AFTER THE CATALYSM!
WHAT ARE YOU TALKING ABOUT?
JUST BABBLING I GUESS I'M AWFULLY TIRED -- I'LL SEE YOU IN THE MORNI
GOOD-NIGHT!
LOTUS MENTIO A CATALYSM*... JU BEFORE GIVING M THE NECKLACE THAT TRIXIE IS WEARING NOW
*SEE LAST ISSUE.

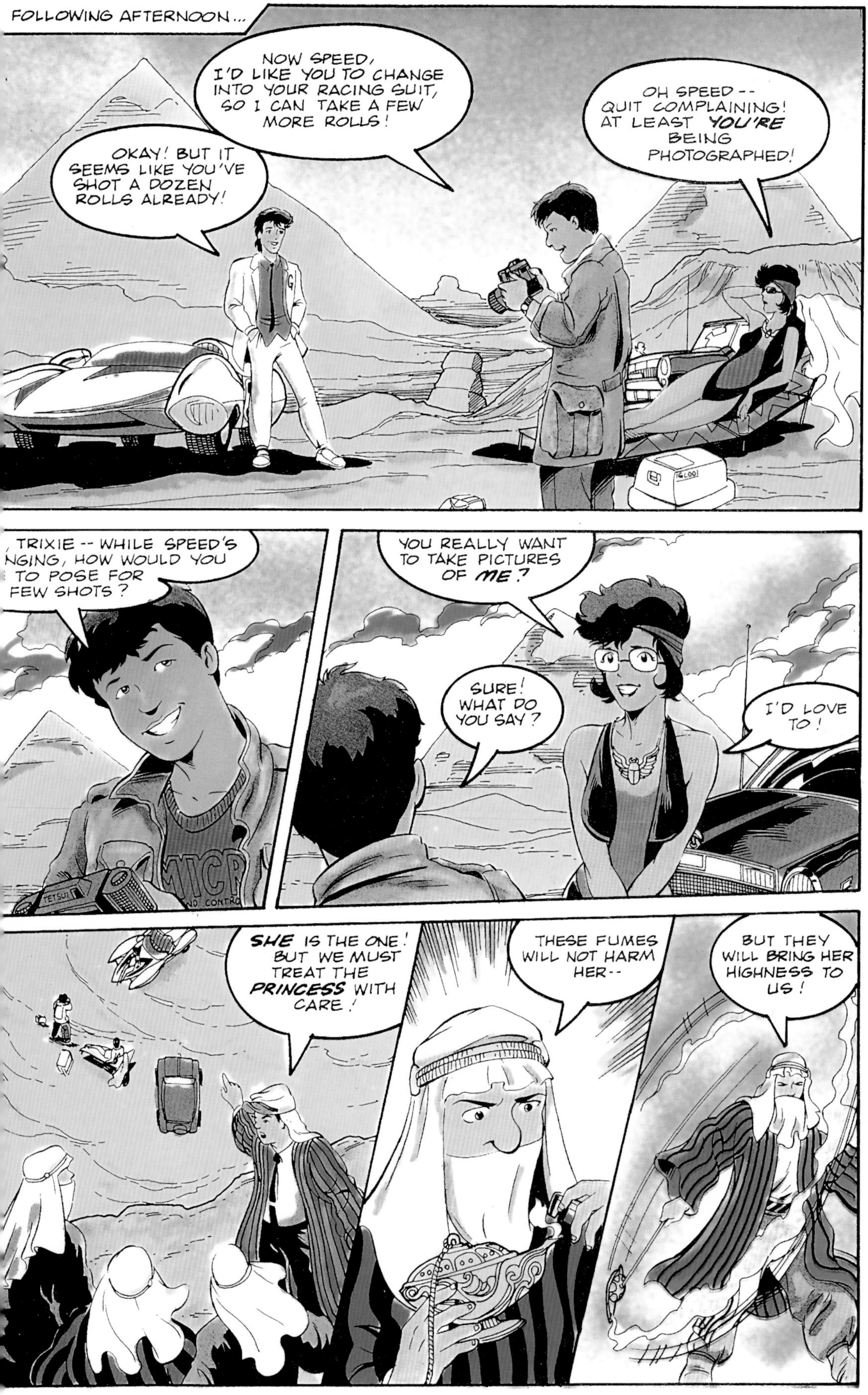

FOLLOWING AFTERNOON...
NOW SPEED, I'D LIKE YOU TO CHANGE INTO YOUR RACING SUIT, SO I CAN TAKE A FEW MORE ROLLS!
OKAY! BUT IT SEEMS LIKE YOU'VE SHOT A DOZEN ROLLS ALREADY!
OH SPEED -- QUIT COMPLAINING! AT LEAST YOU'RE BEING PHOTOGRAPHED!
TRIXIE -- WHILE SPEED'S NGING, HOW WOULD YOU TO POSE FOR FEW SHOTS?
YOU REALLY WANT TO TAKE PICTURES OF ME?
SURE! WHAT DO YOU SAY?
I'D LOVE TO!
SHE IS THE ONE! BUT WE MUST TREAT THE PRINCESS WITH CARE!
THESE FUMES WILL NOT HARM HER--
BUT THEY WILL BRING HER HIGHNESS TO US!

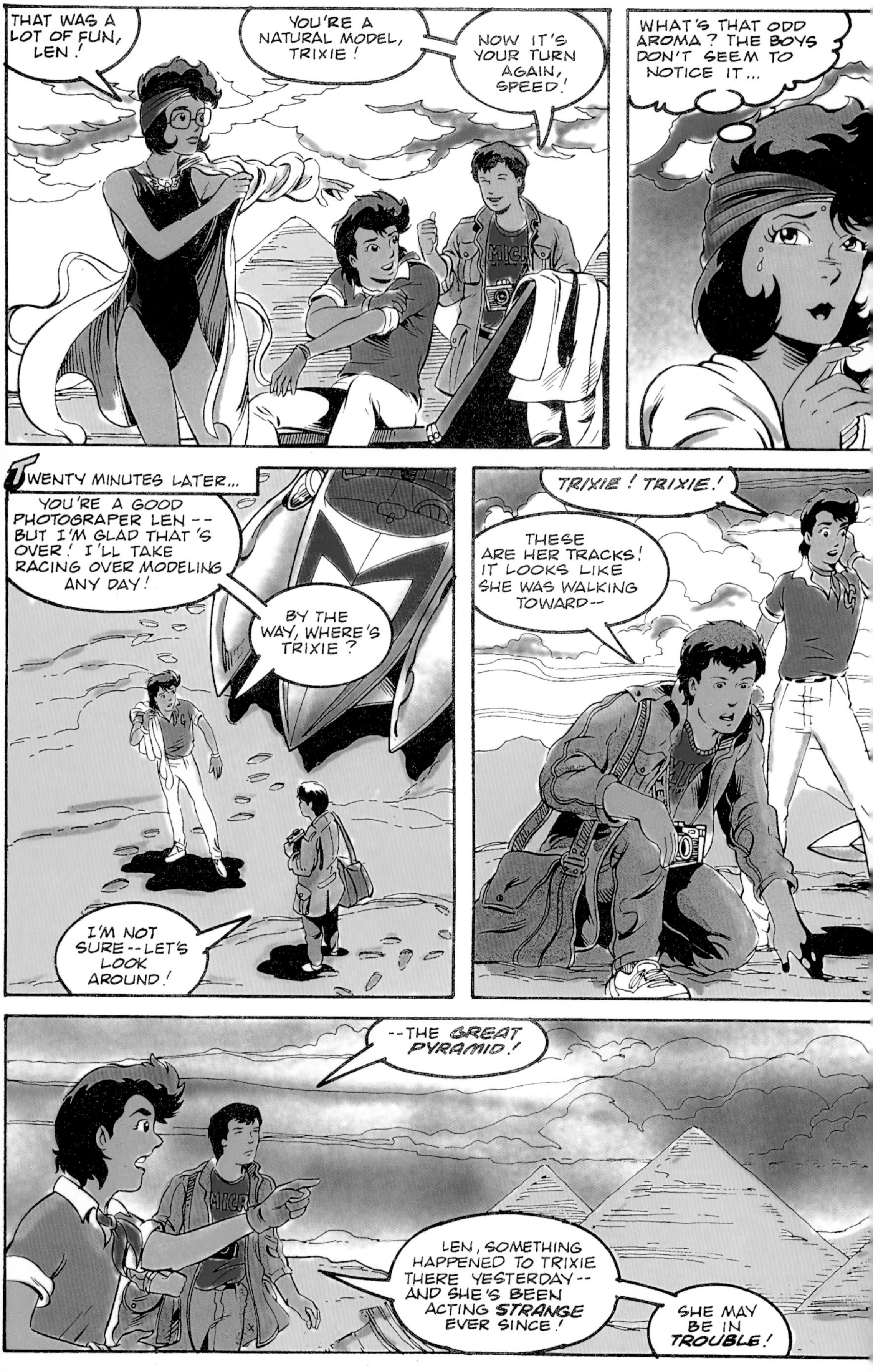
THAT WAS A LOT OF FUN, LEN!
YOU'RE A NATURAL MODEL, TRIXIE!
NOW IT'S YOUR TURN AGAIN, SPEED!
WHAT'S THAT ODD AROMA? THE BOYS DON'T SEEM TO NOTICE IT...
TWENTY MINUTES LATER...
YOU'RE A GOOD PHOTOGRAPER LEN -- BUT I'M GLAD THAT'S OVER! I'LL TAKE RACING OVER MODELING ANY DAY!
BY THE WAY, WHERE'S TRIXIE?
I'M NOT SURE -- LET'S LOOK AROUND!
TRIXIE! TRIXIE!
THESE ARE HER TRACKS! IT LOOKS LIKE SHE WAS WALKING TOWARD--
--THE GREAT PYRAMID!
LEN, SOMETHING HAPPENED TO TRIXIE THERE YESTERDAY -- AND SHE'S BEEN ACTING STRANGE EVER SINCE!
SHE MAY BE IN TROUBLE!

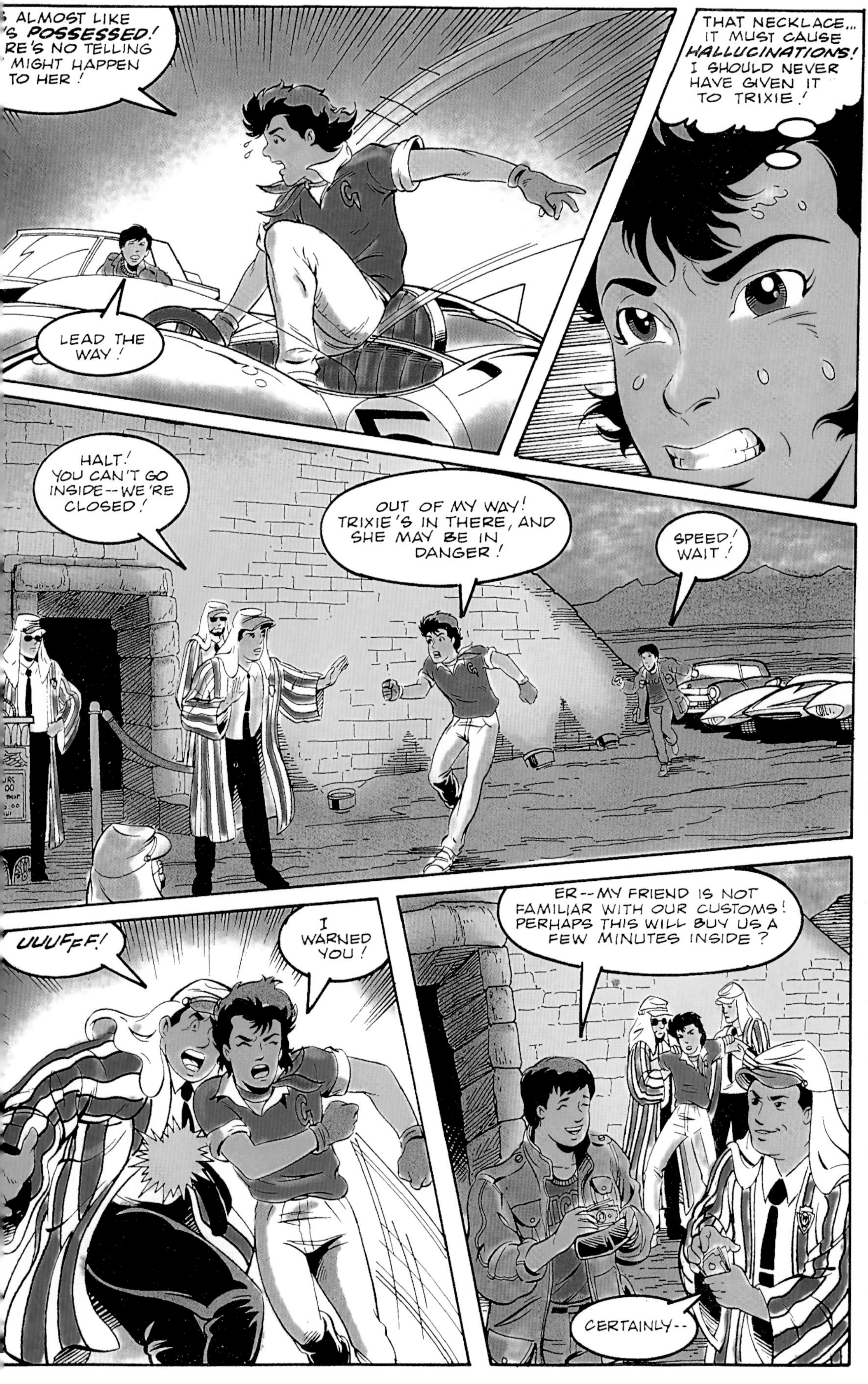

'S ALMOST LIKE 'S POSSESSED! RE'S NO TELLING MIGHT HAPPEN TO HER!
LEAD THE WAY!
THAT NECKLACE... IT MUST CAUSE HALLUCINATIONS! I SHOULD NEVER HAVE GIVEN IT TO TRIXIE!
HALT! YOU CAN'T GO INSIDE--WE'RE CLOSED!
OUT OF MY WAY! TRIXIE'S IN THERE, AND SHE MAY BE IN DANGER!
SPEED! WAIT!
UUUFFF!
I WARNED YOU!
ER--MY FRIEND IS NOT FAMILIAR WITH OUR CUSTOMS! PERHAPS THIS WILL BUY US A FEW MINUTES INSIDE?
CERTAINLY--

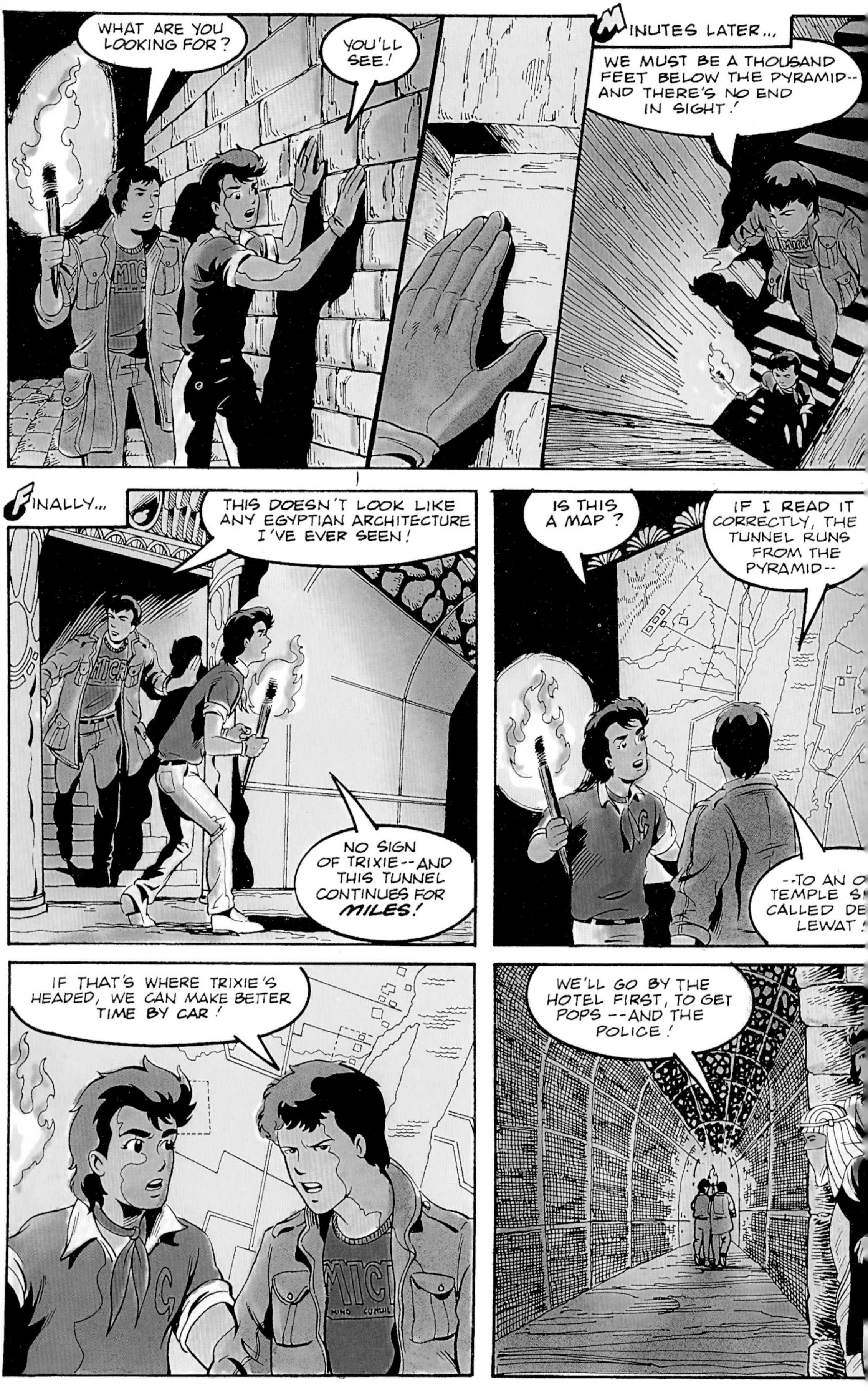
WHAT ARE YOU LOOKING FOR?
YOU'LL SEE!
MINUTES LATER...
WE MUST BE A THOUSAND FEET BELOW THE PYRAMID--AND THERE'S NO END IN SIGHT!
FINALLY...
THIS DOESN'T LOOK LIKE ANY EGYPTIAN ARCHITECTURE I'VE EVER SEEN!
NO SIGN OF TRIXIE--AND THIS TUNNEL CONTINUES FOR MILES!
IS THIS A MAP?
IF I READ IT CORRECTLY, THE TUNNEL RUNS FROM THE PYRAMID--
IF THAT'S WHERE TRIXIE'S HEADED, WE CAN MAKE BETTER TIME BY CAR!
WE'LL GO BY THE HOTEL FIRST, TO GET POPS --AND THE POLICE!

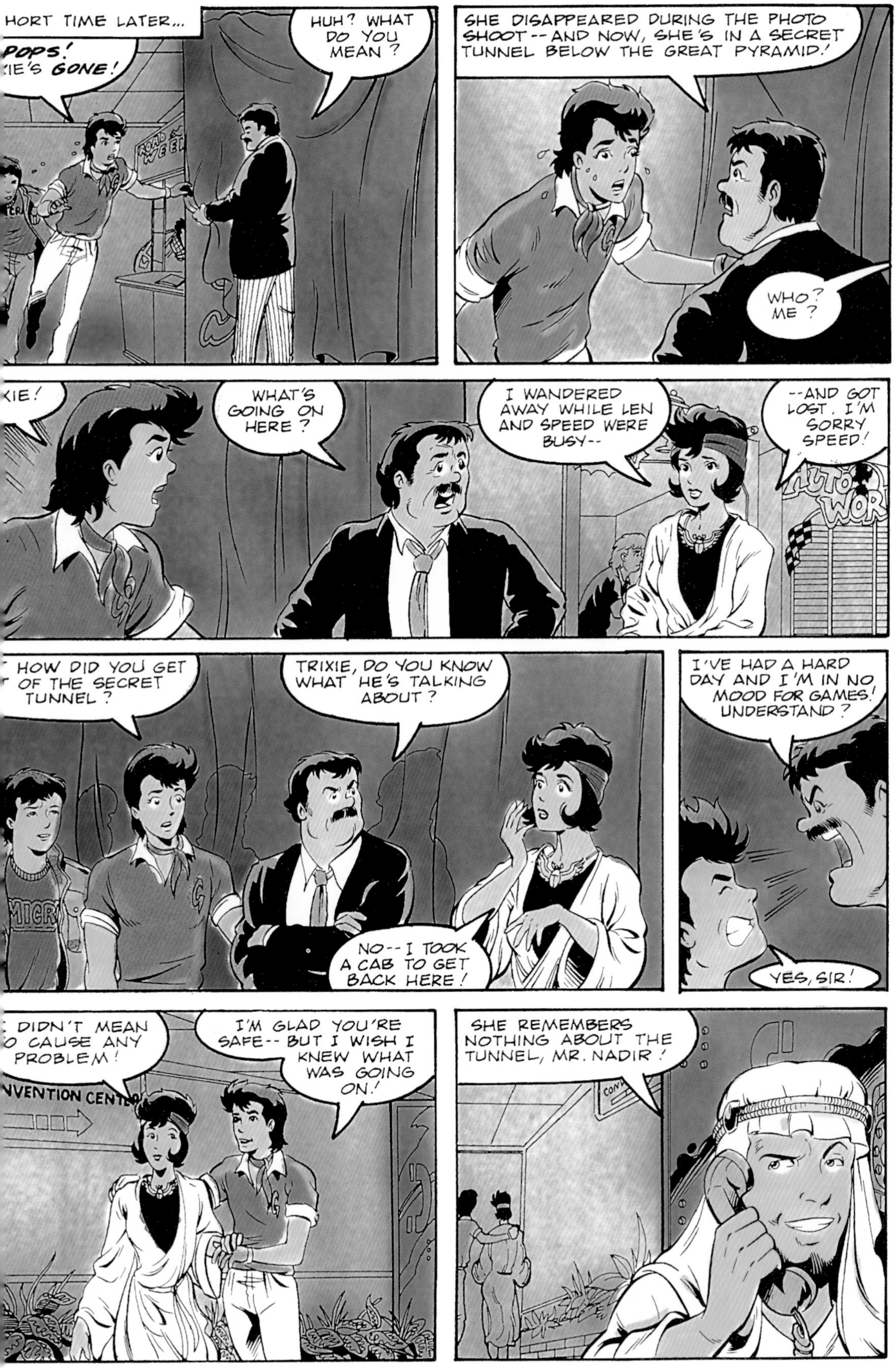

HORT TIME LATER...
POPS! IE'S GONE!
HUH? WHAT DO YOU MEAN?
SHE DISAPPEARED DURING THE PHOTO SHOOT -- AND NOW, SHE'S IN A SECRET TUNNEL BELOW THE GREAT PYRAMID!
WHO? ME?
IE!
WHAT'S GOING ON HERE?
I WANDERED AWAY WHILE LEN AND SPEED WERE BUSY--
--AND GOT LOST. I'M SORRY SPEED!
HOW DID YOU GET OF THE SECRET TUNNEL?
TRIXIE, DO YOU KNOW WHAT HE'S TALKING ABOUT?
NO-- I TOOK A CAB TO GET BACK HERE!
I'VE HAD A HARD DAY AND I'M IN NO MOOD FOR GAMES! UNDERSTAND?
YES, SIR!
DIDN'T MEAN O CAUSE ANY PROBLEM!
I'M GLAD YOU'RE SAFE-- BUT I WISH I KNEW WHAT WAS GOING ON!
NVENTION CENT
SHE REMEMBERS NOTHING ABOUT THE TUNNEL, MR. NADIR!

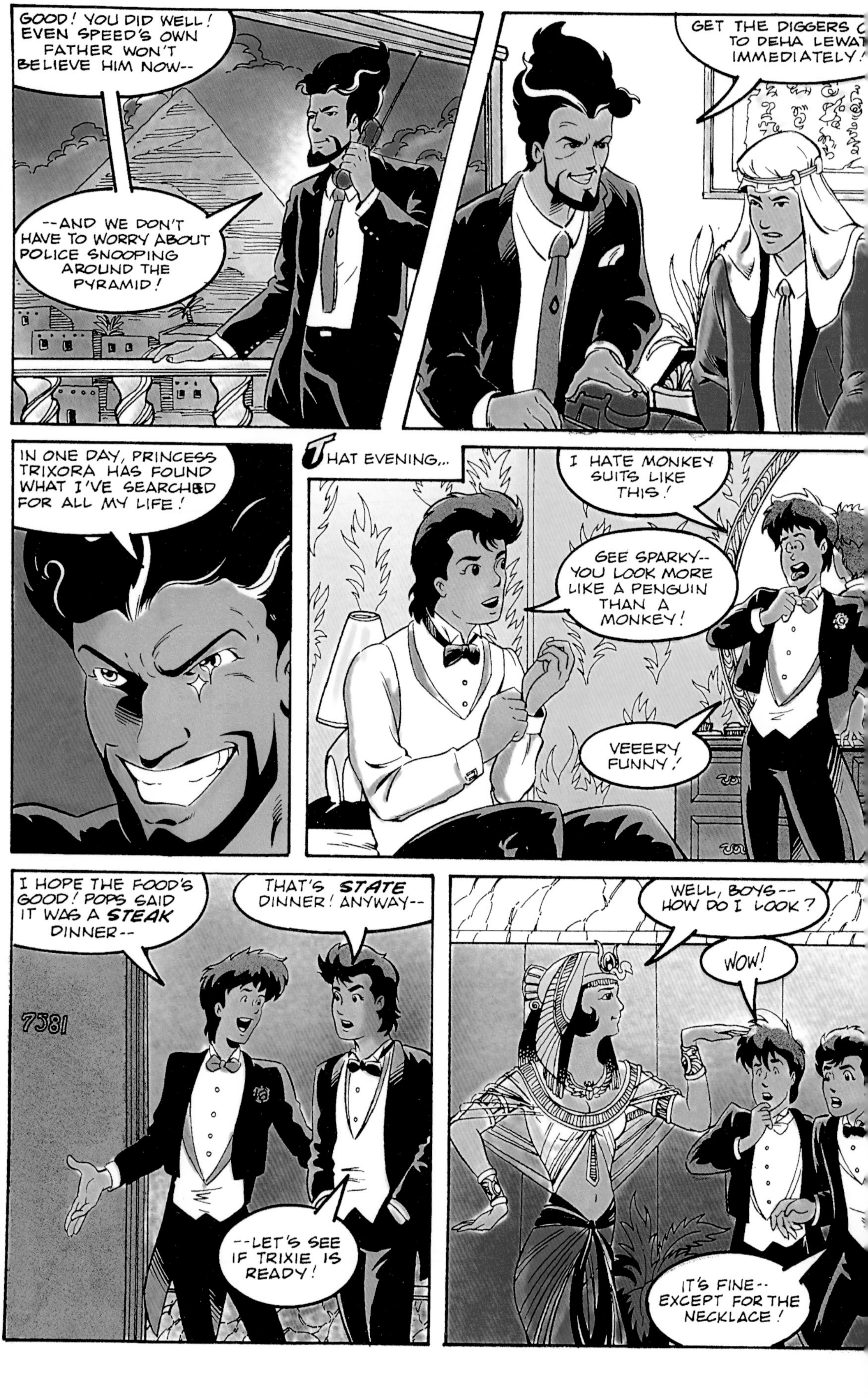
GOOD! YOU DID WELL! EVEN SPEED'S OWN FATHER WON'T BELIEVE HIM NOW--
--AND WE DON'T HAVE TO WORRY ABOUT POLICE SNOOPING AROUND THE PYRAMID!
GET THE DIGGERS TO DEHA LEWA IMMEDIATELY!
IN ONE DAY, PRINCESS TRIXORA HAS FOUND WHAT I'VE SEARCHED FOR ALL MY LIFE!
THAT EVENING...
I HATE MONKEY SUITS LIKE THIS!
GEE SPARKY-- YOU LOOK MORE LIKE A PENGUIN THAN A MONKEY!
VEEERY FUNNY!
I HOPE THE FOOD'S GOOD! POPS SAID IT WAS A STEAK DINNER--
THAT'S STATE DINNER! ANYWAY--
--LET'S SEE IF TRIXIE IS READY!
7381
WELL, BOYS-- HOW DO I LOOK?
WOW!
IT'S FINE-- EXCEPT FOR THE NECKLACE!

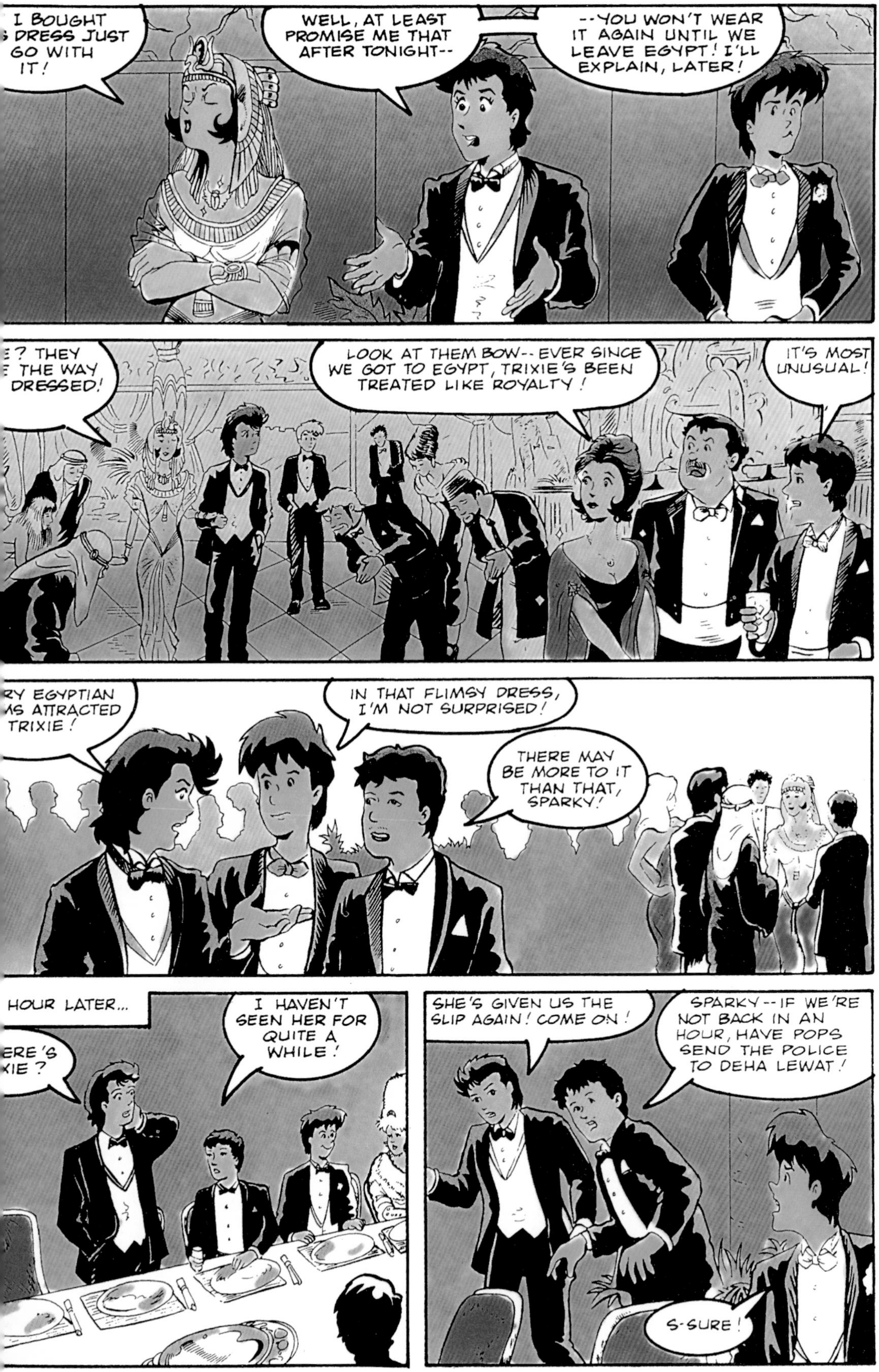

I BOUGHT
; DRESS JUST
GO WITH
IT!
WELL, AT LEAST PROMISE ME THAT AFTER TONIGHT--
--YOU WON'T WEAR IT AGAIN UNTIL WE LEAVE EGYPT! I'LL EXPLAIN, LATER!
? THEY
THE WAY
DRESSED!
LOOK AT THEM BOW-- EVER SINCE WE GOT TO EGYPT, TRIXIE'S BEEN TREATED LIKE ROYALTY!
IT'S MOST UNUSUAL!
RY EGYPTIAN
AS ATTRACTED
TRIXIE!
IN THAT FLIMSY DRESS, I'M NOT SURPRISED!
THERE MAY BE MORE TO IT THAN THAT, SPARKY!
HOUR LATER...
ERE'S
IE?
I HAVEN'T SEEN HER FOR QUITE A WHILE!
SHE'S GIVEN US THE SLIP AGAIN! COME ON!
SPARKY--IF WE'RE NOT BACK IN AN HOUR, HAVE POPS SEND THE POLICE TO DEHA LEWAT!
S-SURE!

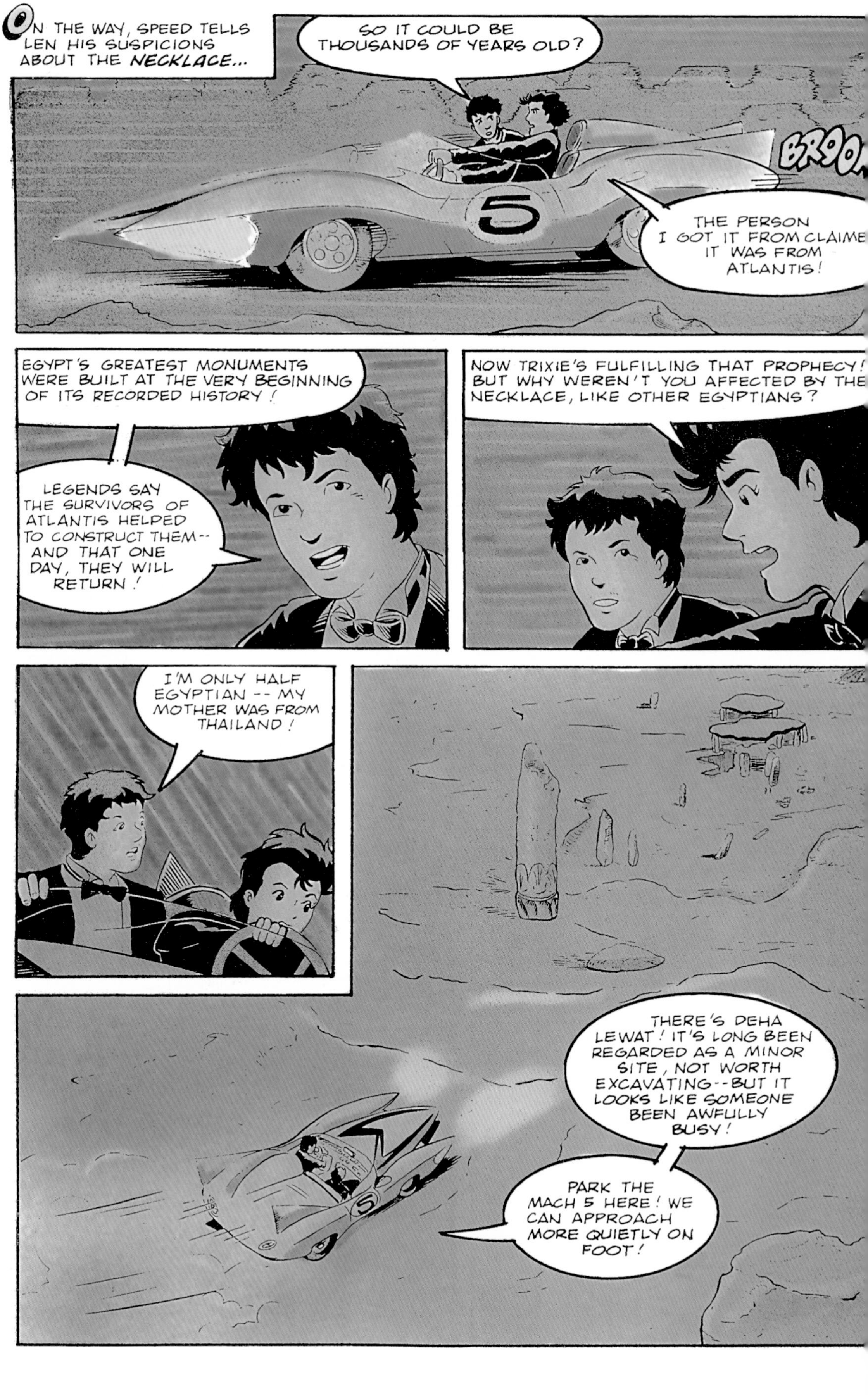

ON THE WAY, SPEED TELLS LEN HIS SUSPICIONS ABOUT THE NECKLACE...
SO IT COULD BE THOUSANDS OF YEARS OLD?
BROOM
THE PERSON I GOT IT FROM CLAIME IT WAS FROM ATLANTIS!
EGYPT'S GREATEST MONUMENTS WERE BUILT AT THE VERY BEGINNING OF ITS RECORDED HISTORY!
LEGENDS SAY THE SURVIVORS OF ATLANTIS HELPED TO CONSTRUCT THEM-- AND THAT ONE DAY, THEY WILL RETURN!
NOW TRIXIE'S FULFILLING THAT PROPHECY! BUT WHY WEREN'T YOU AFFECTED BY THE NECKLACE, LIKE OTHER EGYPTIANS?
I'M ONLY HALF EGYPTIAN -- MY MOTHER WAS FROM THAILAND!
THERE'S DEHA LEWAT! IT'S LONG BEEN REGARDED AS A MINOR SITE, NOT WORTH EXCAVATING--BUT IT LOOKS LIKE SOMEONE BEEN AWFULLY BUSY!
PARK THE MACH 5 HERE! WE CAN APPROACH MORE QUIETLY ON FOOT!

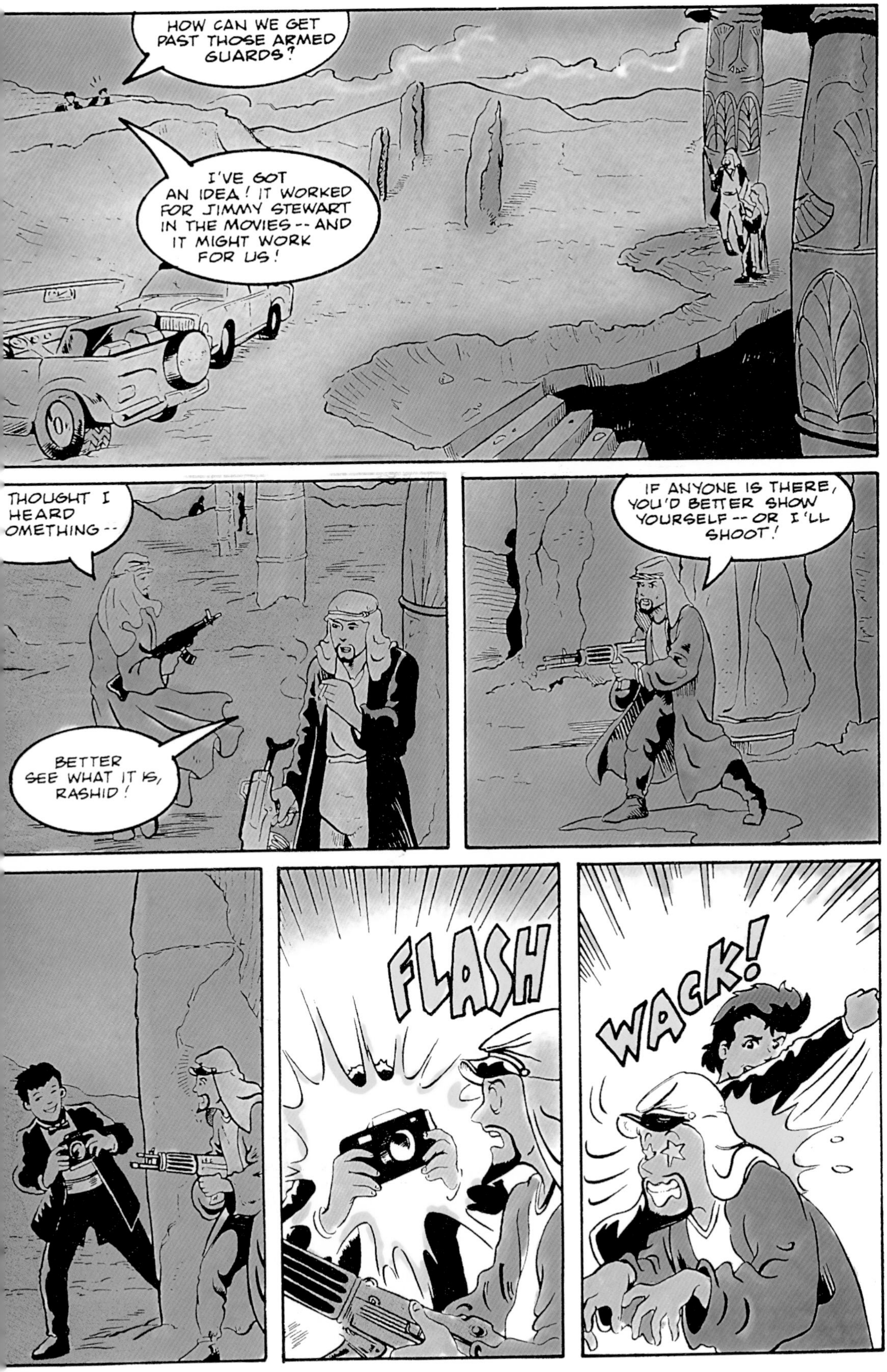
HOW CAN WE GET PAST THOSE ARMED GUARDS?
I'VE GOT AN IDEA! IT WORKED FOR JIMMY STEWART IN THE MOVIES -- AND IT MIGHT WORK FOR US!
THOUGHT I HEARD OMETHING --
BETTER SEE WHAT IT IS, RASHID!
IF ANYONE IS THERE, YOU'D BETTER SHOW YOURSELF -- OR I'LL SHOOT!
FLASH
WACK!

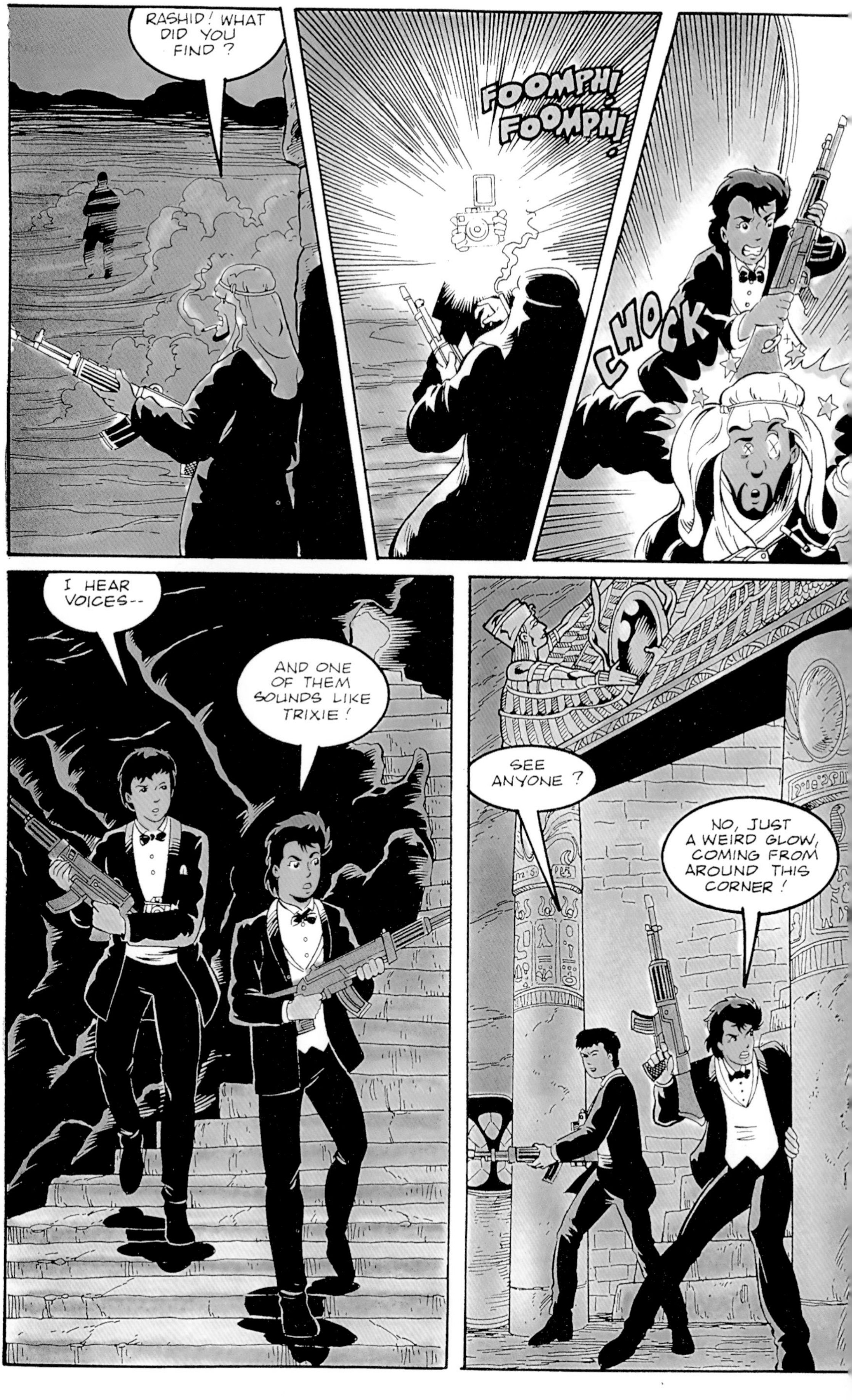
RASHID! WHAT DID YOU FIND ?
FOOMPH! FOOMPH!
CHOCK
I HEAR VOICES--
AND ONE OF THEM SOUNDS LIKE TRIXIE!
SEE ANYONE ?
NO, JUST A WEIRD GLOW, COMING FROM AROUND THIS CORNER !

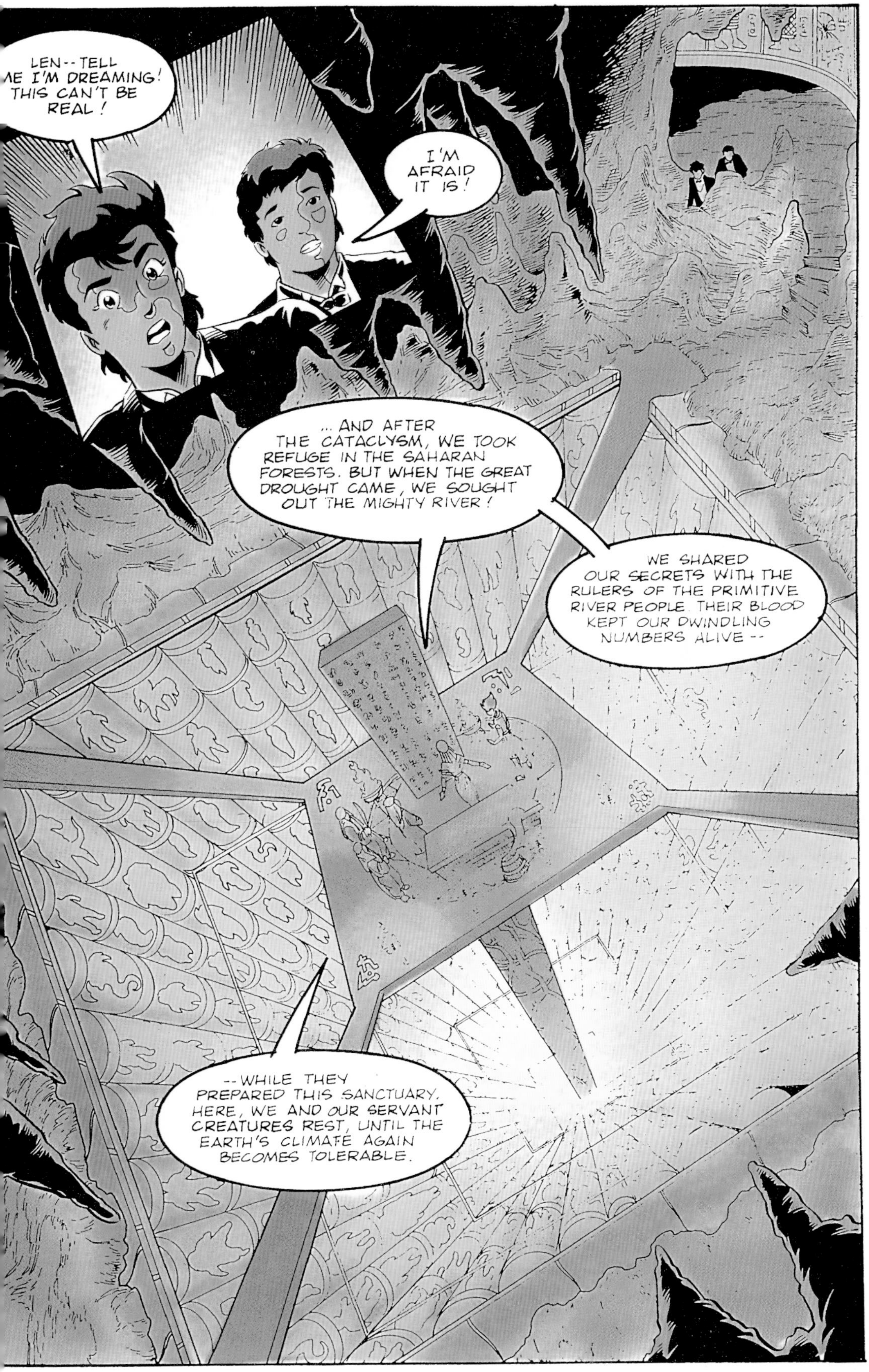
LEN--TELL ME I'M DREAMING! THIS CAN'T BE REAL!
I'M AFRAID IT IS!
...AND AFTER THE CATACLYSM, WE TOOK REFUGE IN THE SAHARAN FORESTS. BUT WHEN THE GREAT DROUGHT CAME, WE SOUGHT OUT THE MIGHTY RIVER!
WE SHARED OUR SECRETS WITH THE RULERS OF THE PRIMITIVE RIVER PEOPLE. THEIR BLOOD KEPT OUR DWINDLING NUMBERS ALIVE--
--WHILE THEY PREPARED THIS SANCTUARY. HERE, WE AND OUR SERVANT CREATURES REST, UNTIL THE EARTH'S CLIMATE AGAIN BECOMES TOLERABLE.

SO-- THE PYRAMIDS AND MUMMIES WERE JUST CRUDE ATTEMPTS BY MY ANCESTORS TO EMULATE THE ATLANTIANS!

WHEN THE TIME IS RIGHT, THE DESCENDANTS OF THE RIVER PEOPLE WILL KNOW A GREAT PRINCESS--

--AND HER *BLOOD* WILL BEGIN OUR REVIVAL. GREAT POWER AND WEALTH WILL B GIVEN TO THOSE WHO SERVE US, AS IT WAS TO THE PHARA

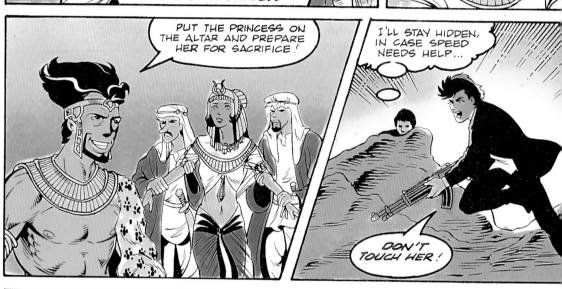

PUT THE PRINCESS ON THE ALTAR AND PREPARE HER FOR SACRIFICE!

I'LL STAY HIDDEN, IN CASE SPEED NEEDS HELP...

DON'T TOUCH HER!

STOP HIM! I NEED ONLY MOMENTS TO COMPLETE THE INCANTATION AND PERFORM THE SACRIFICE!

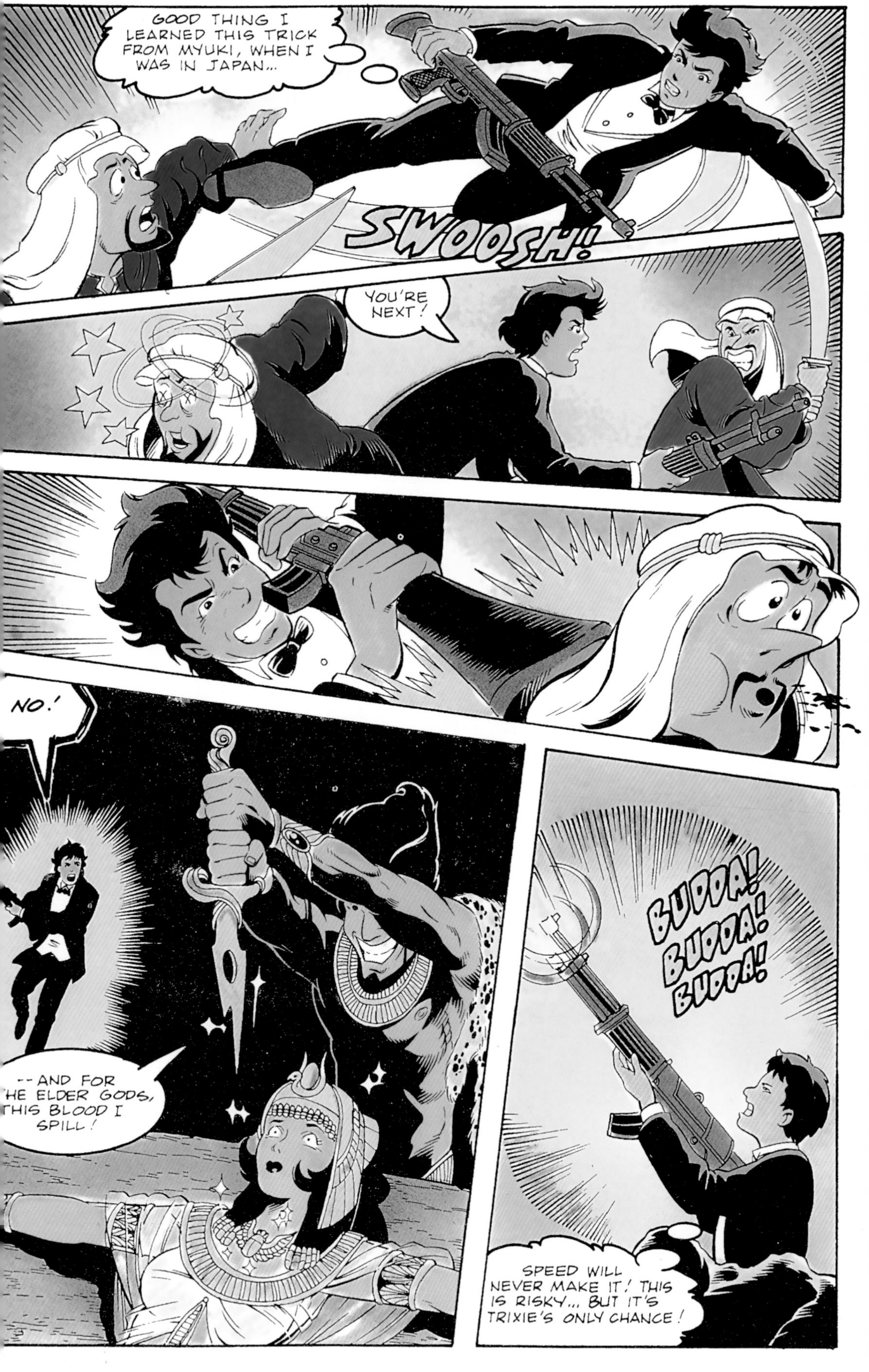
GOOD THING I LEARNED THIS TRICK FROM MYUKI, WHEN I WAS IN JAPAN...
SWOOSH!
YOU'RE NEXT!
NO!
--AND FOR THE ELDER GODS, THIS BLOOD I SPILL!
BUDDA! BUDDA! BUDDA!
SPEED WILL NEVER MAKE IT! THIS IS RISKY... BUT IT'S TRIXIE'S ONLY CHANCE!

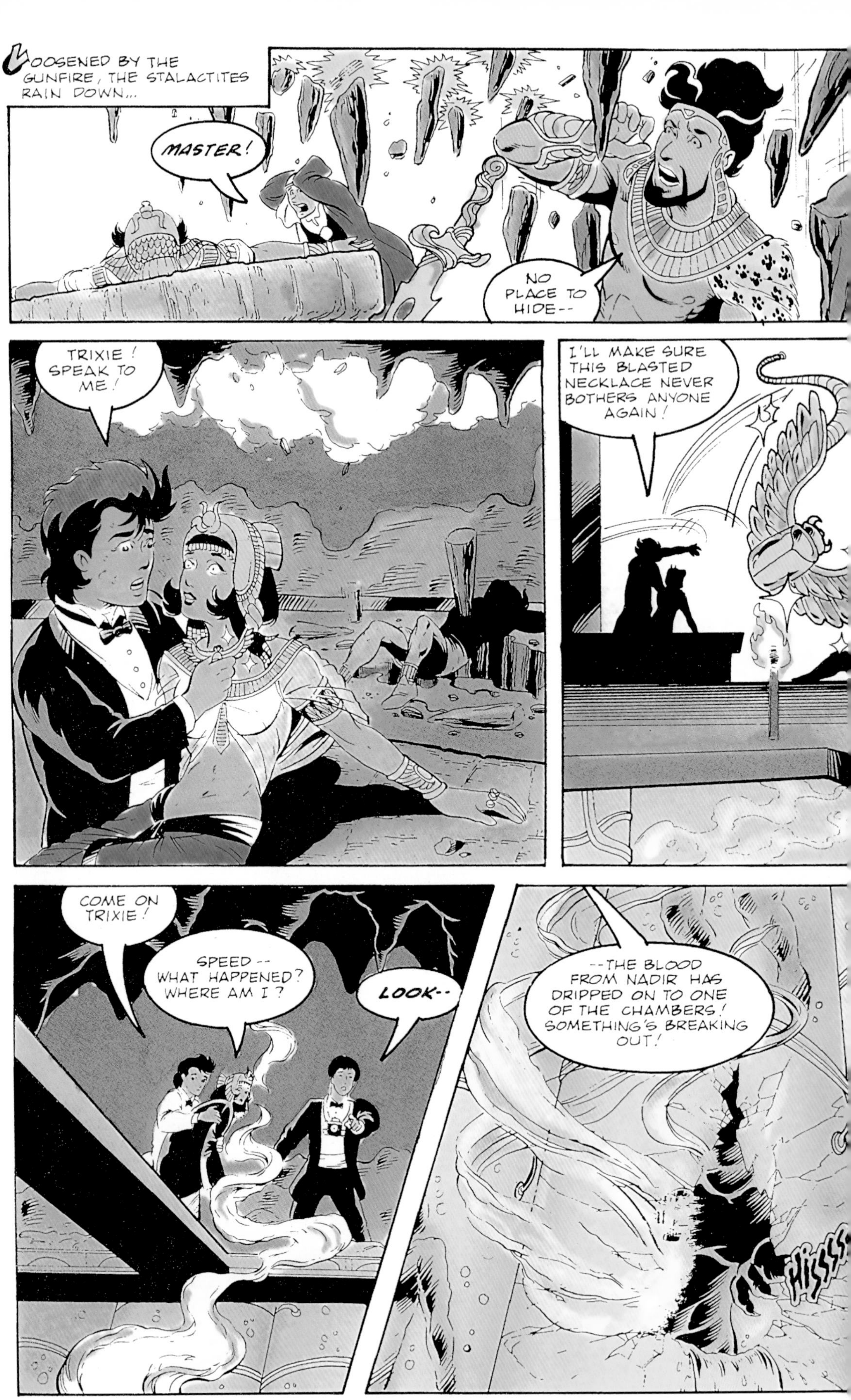
LOOSENED BY THE GUNFIRE, THE STALACTITES RAIN DOWN...
MASTER!
NO PLACE TO HIDE--
TRIXIE! SPEAK TO ME!
I'LL MAKE SURE THIS BLASTED NECKLACE NEVER BOTHERS ANYONE AGAIN!
COME ON TRIXIE!
SPEED-- WHAT HAPPENED? WHERE AM I?
LOOK--
--THE BLOOD FROM NADIR HAS DRIPPED ON TO ONE OF THE CHAMBERS! SOMETHING'S BREAKING OUT!
HISSSS

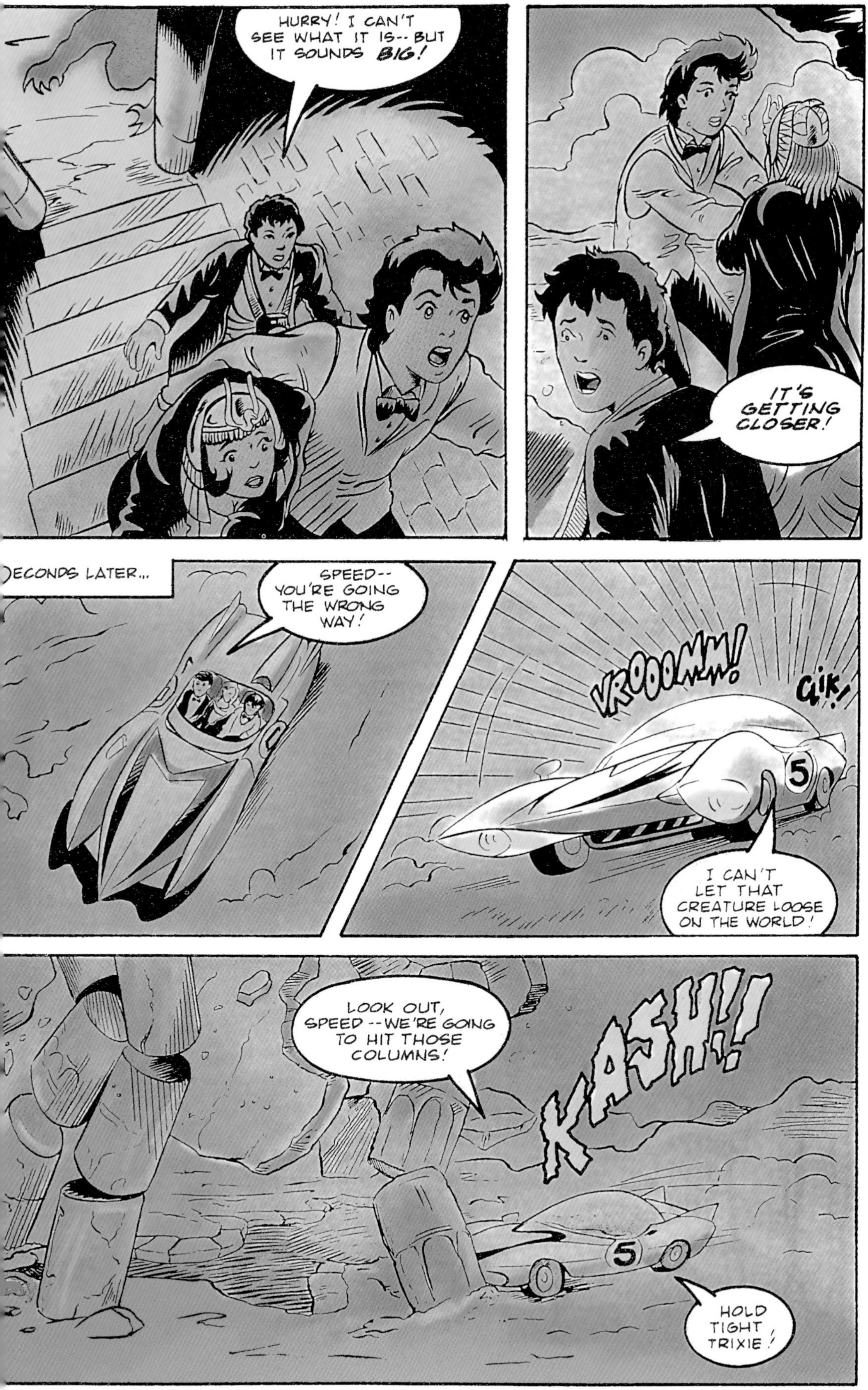
HURRY! I CAN'T SEE WHAT IT IS-- BUT IT SOUNDS BIG!
IT'S GETTING CLOSER!
SECONDS LATER...
SPEED-- YOU'RE GOING THE WRONG WAY!
VROOOMM!
GIK!
I CAN'T LET THAT CREATURE LOOSE ON THE WORLD!
LOOK OUT, SPEED --WE'RE GOING TO HIT THOSE COLUMNS!
KASH!!
HOLD TIGHT, TRIXIE!

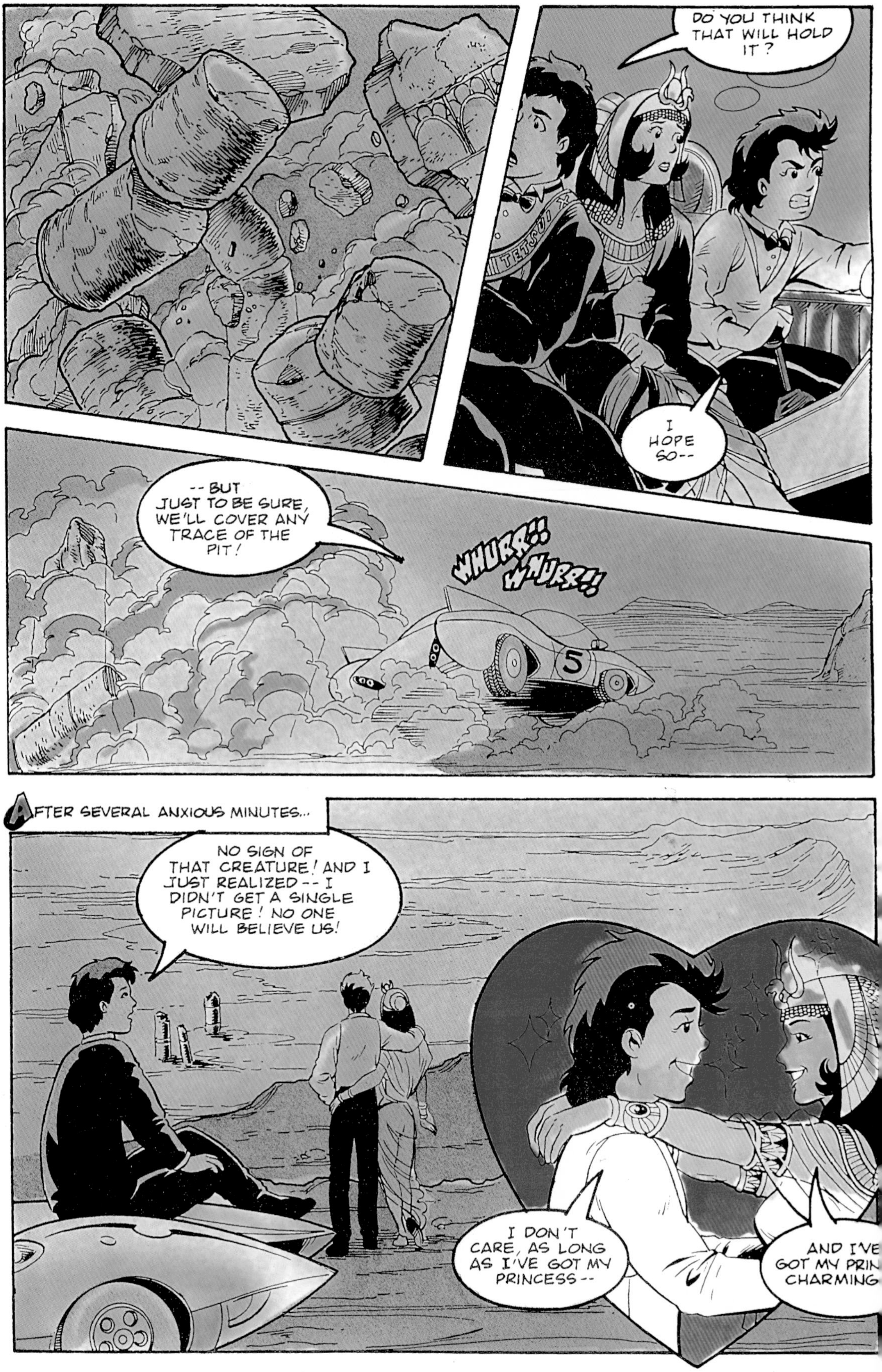
DO YOU THINK THAT WILL HOLD IT?
I HOPE SO--
--BUT JUST TO BE SURE, WE'LL COVER ANY TRACE OF THE PIT!
WHURR!! WHURR!!
AFTER SEVERAL ANXIOUS MINUTES...
NO SIGN OF THAT CREATURE! AND I JUST REALIZED -- I DIDN'T GET A SINGLE PICTURE! NO ONE WILL BELIEVE US!
I DON'T CARE, AS LONG AS I'VE GOT MY PRINCESS--
AND I'VE GOT MY PRIN CHARMING

VWROOM

Speed Racer #16

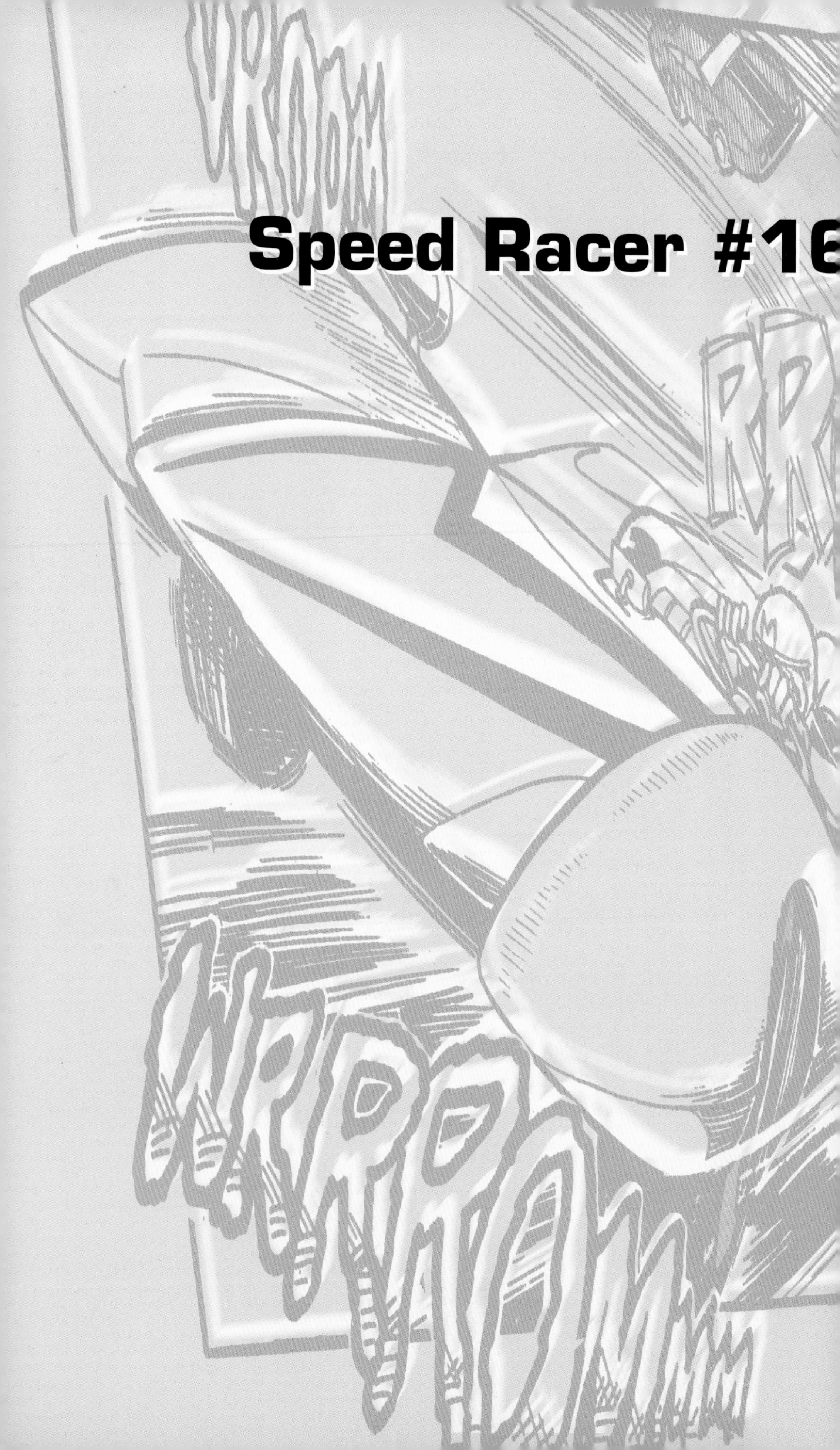

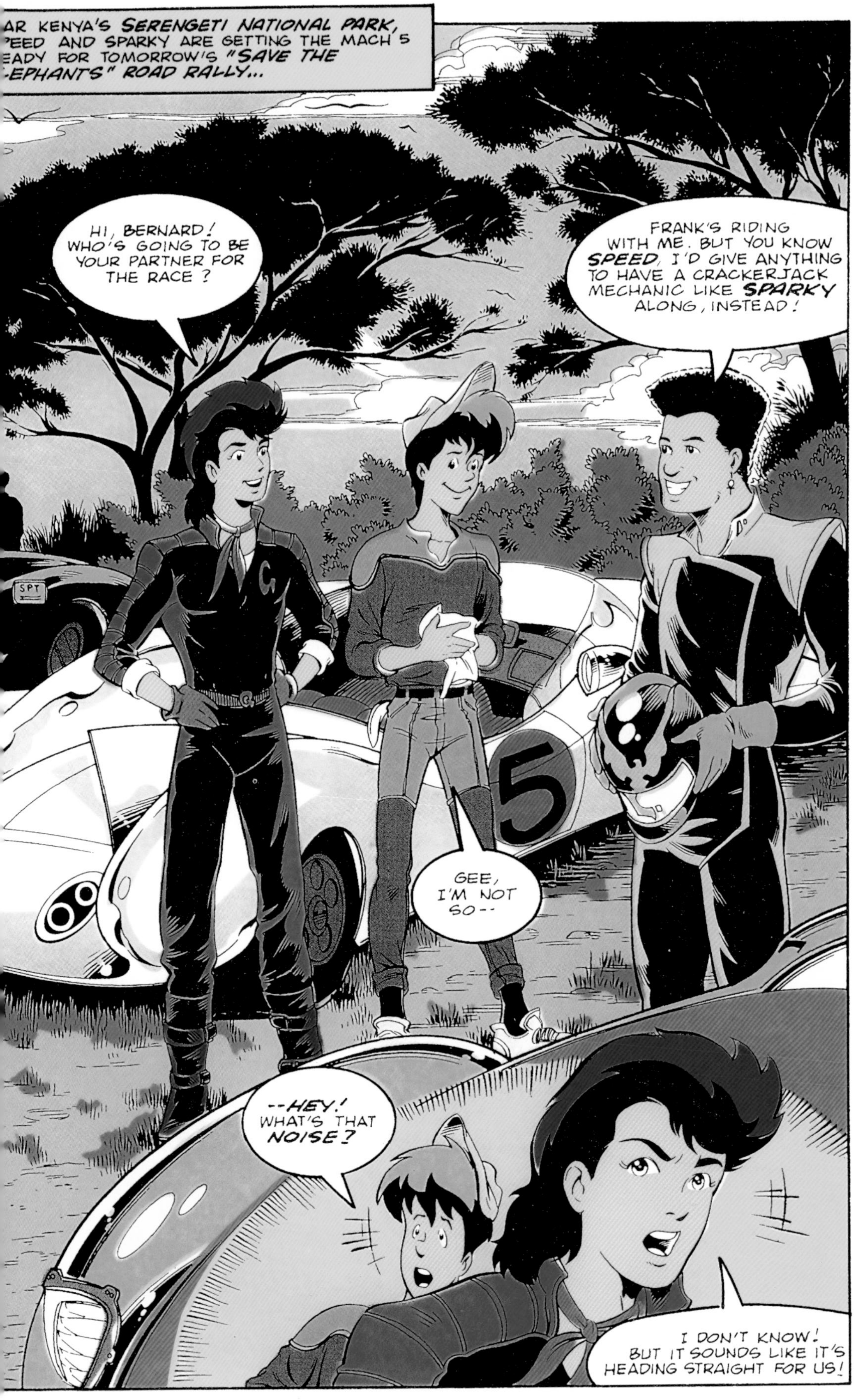
AR KENYA'S SERENGETI NATIONAL PARK, PEED AND SPARKY ARE GETTING THE MACH 5 EADY FOR TOMORROW'S "SAVE THE EPHANTS" ROAD RALLY...
HI, BERNARD! WHO'S GOING TO BE YOUR PARTNER FOR THE RACE?
FRANK'S RIDING WITH ME. BUT YOU KNOW SPEED, I'D GIVE ANYTHING TO HAVE A CRACKERJACK MECHANIC LIKE SPARKY ALONG, INSTEAD!
GEE, I'M NOT SO--
--HEY! WHAT'S THAT NOISE?
I DON'T KNOW! BUT IT SOUNDS LIKE IT'S HEADING STRAIGHT FOR US!

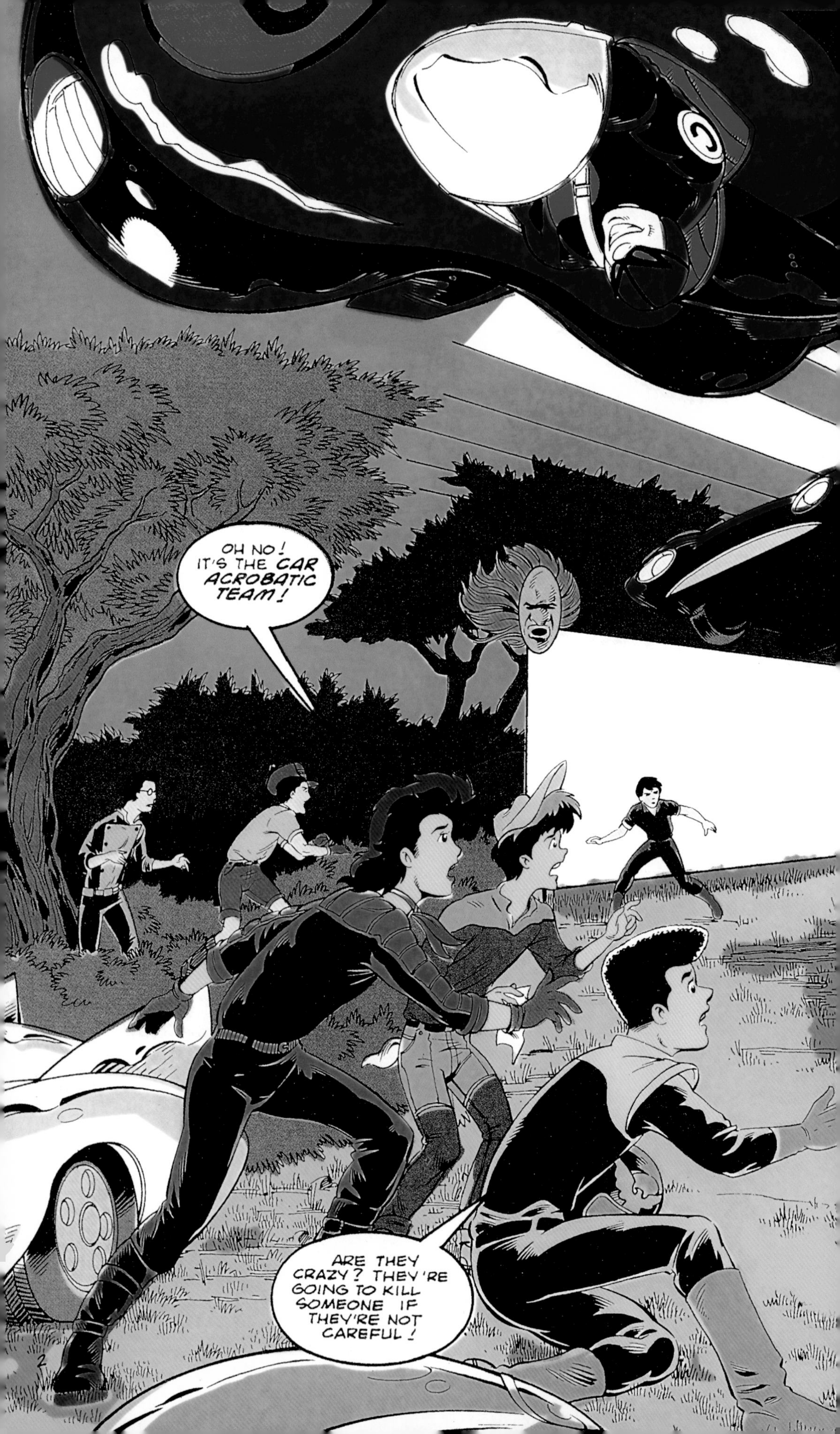
OH NO! IT'S THE CAR ACROBATIC TEAM!
ARE THEY CRAZY? THEY'RE GOING TO KILL SOMEONE IF THEY'RE NOT CAREFUL!

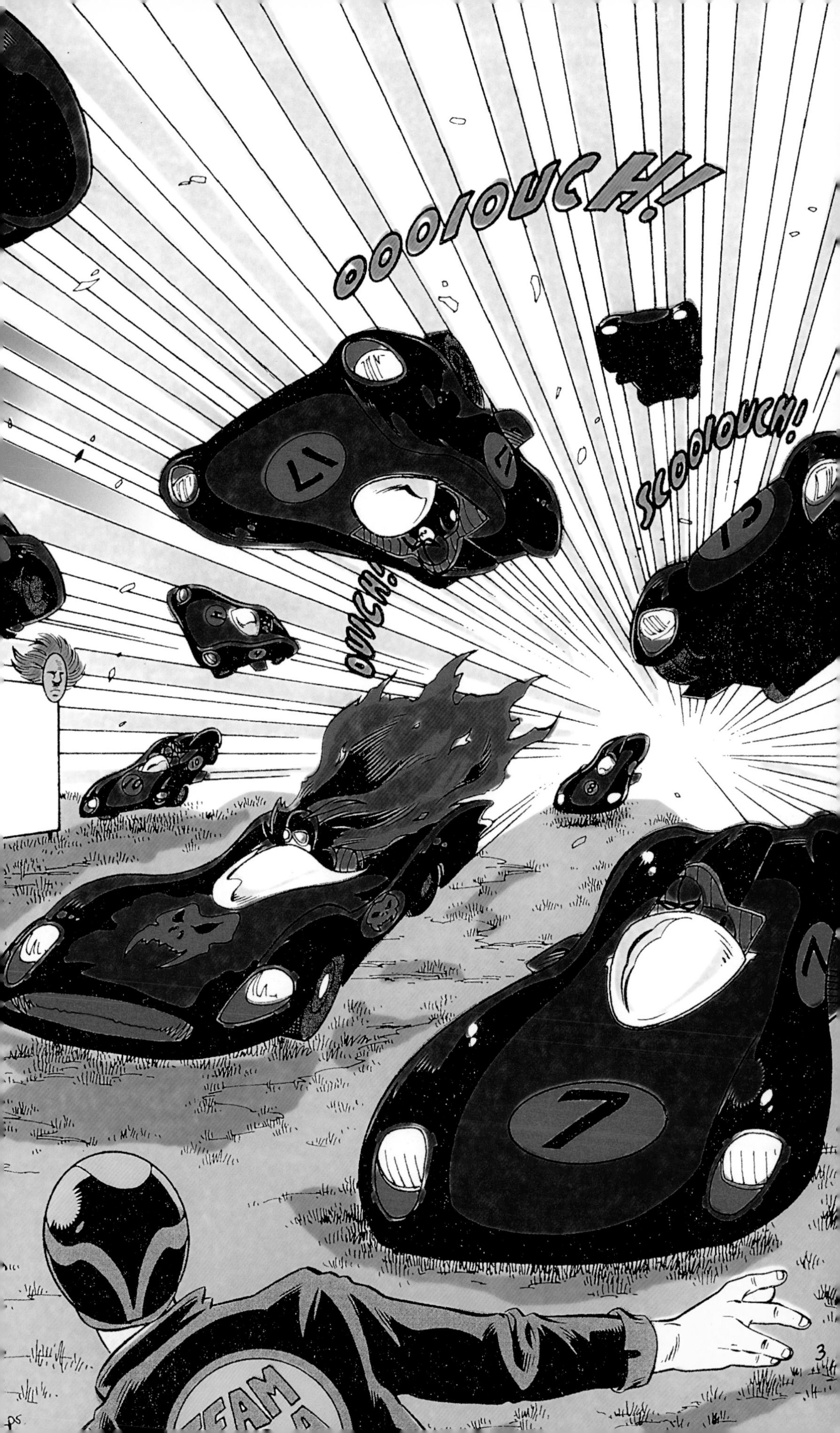
OOOIOUCH!!
SCOOIOUCH!
OUCH!
TEAM

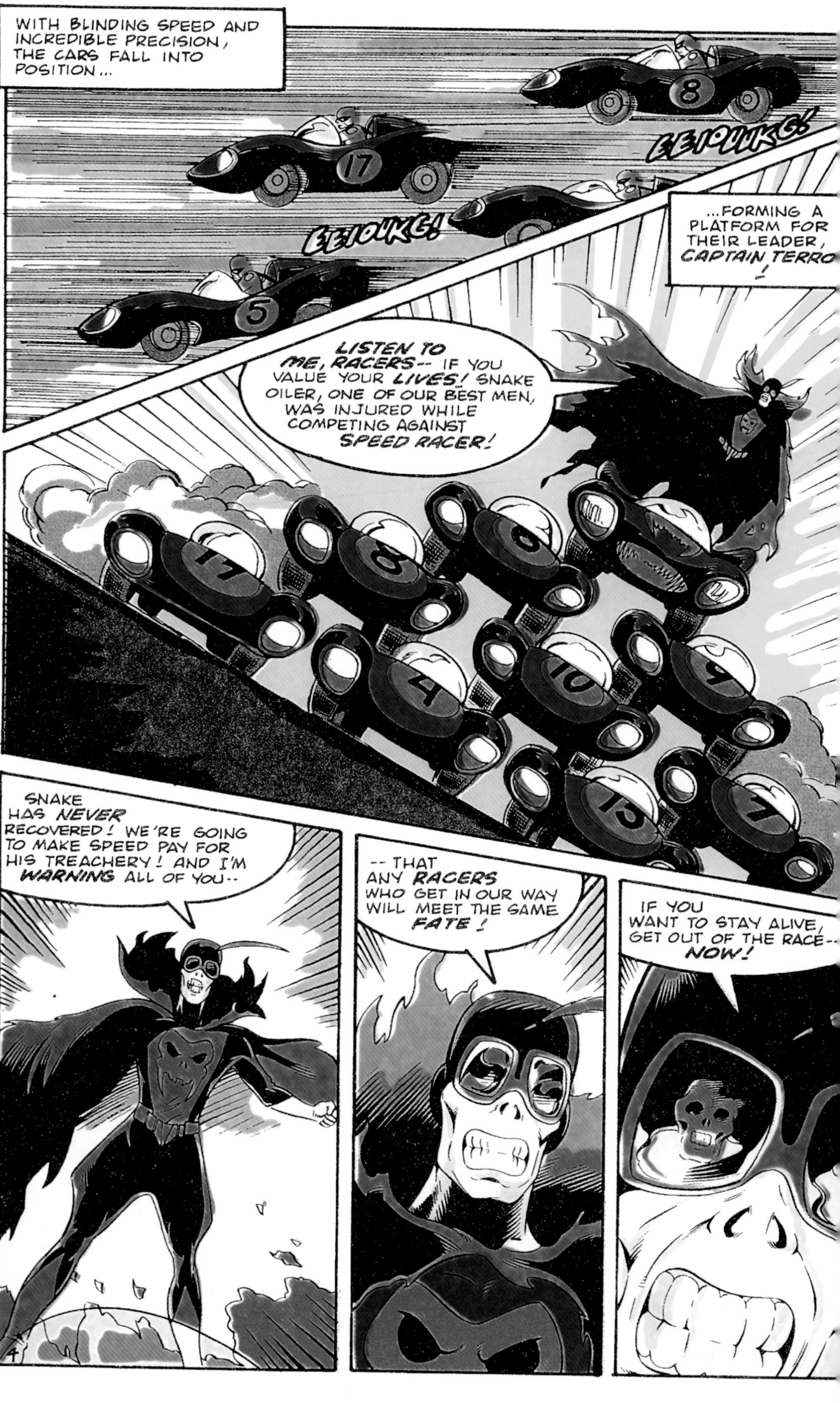

WITH BLINDING SPEED AND INCREDIBLE PRECISION, THE CARS FALL INTO POSITION...
EEIOUKG!
EEIOUKG!
...FORMING A PLATFORM FOR THEIR LEADER, CAPTAIN TERRO
LISTEN TO ME, RACERS-- IF YOU VALUE YOUR LIVES! SNAKE OILER, ONE OF OUR BEST MEN, WAS INJURED WHILE COMPETING AGAINST SPEED RACER!
SNAKE HAS NEVER RECOVERED! WE'RE GOING TO MAKE SPEED PAY FOR HIS TREACHERY! AND I'M WARNING ALL OF YOU--
--THAT ANY RACERS WHO GET IN OUR WAY WILL MEET THE SAME FATE!
IF YOU WANT TO STAY ALIVE, GET OUT OF THE RACE-- NOW!

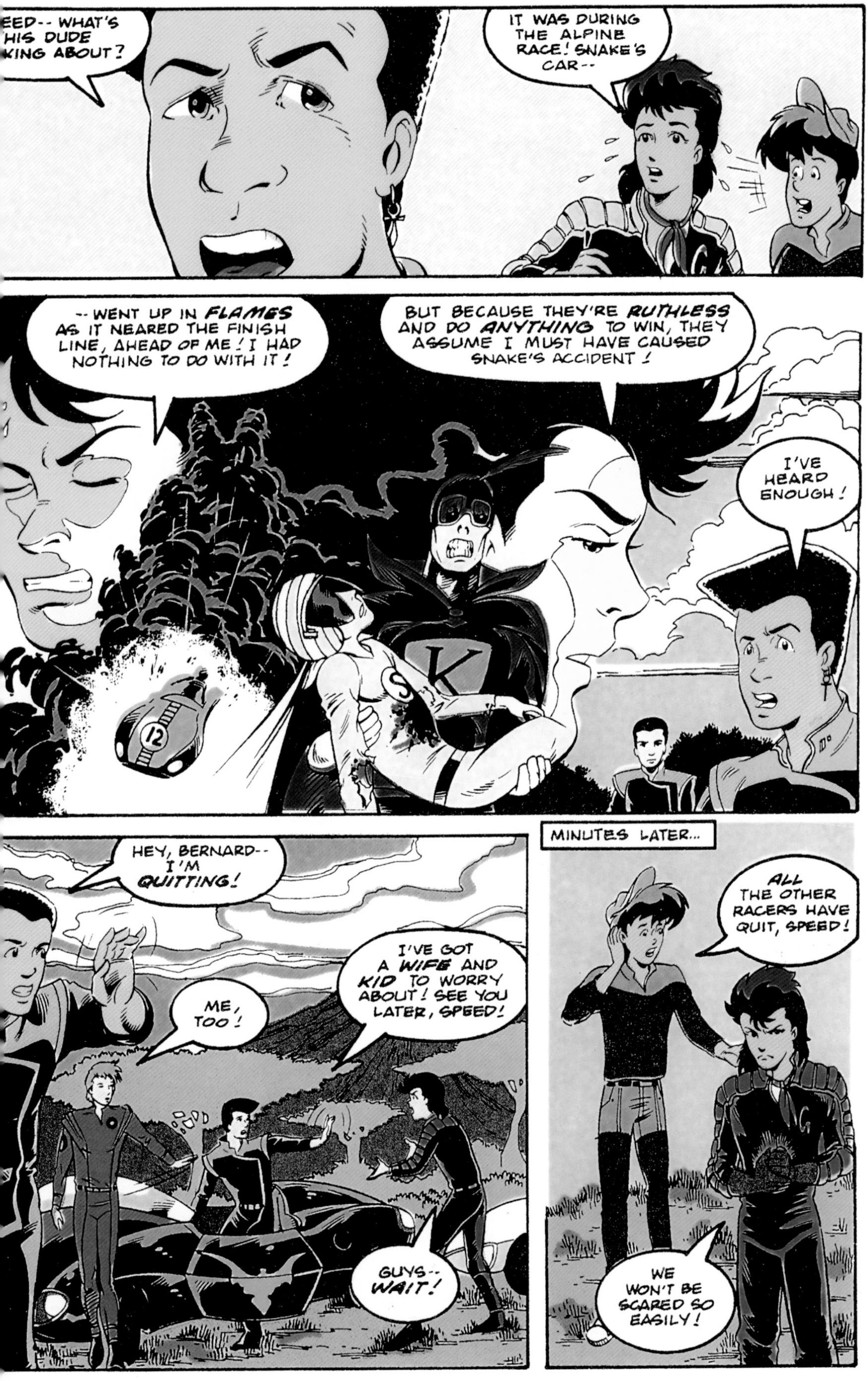

EED-- WHAT'S
HIS DUDE
KING ABOUT?
IT WAS DURING THE ALPINE RACE! SNAKE'S CAR--
--WENT UP IN FLAMES AS IT NEARED THE FINISH LINE, AHEAD OF ME! I HAD NOTHING TO DO WITH IT!
BUT BECAUSE THEY'RE RUTHLESS AND DO ANYTHING TO WIN, THEY ASSUME I MUST HAVE CAUSED SNAKE'S ACCIDENT!
I'VE HEARD ENOUGH!
HEY, BERNARD-- I'M QUITTING!
ME, TOO!
I'VE GOT A WIFE AND KID TO WORRY ABOUT! SEE YOU LATER, SPEED!
GUYS-- WAIT!
MINUTES LATER...
ALL THE OTHER RACERS HAVE QUIT, SPEED!
WE WON'T BE SCARED SO EASILY!

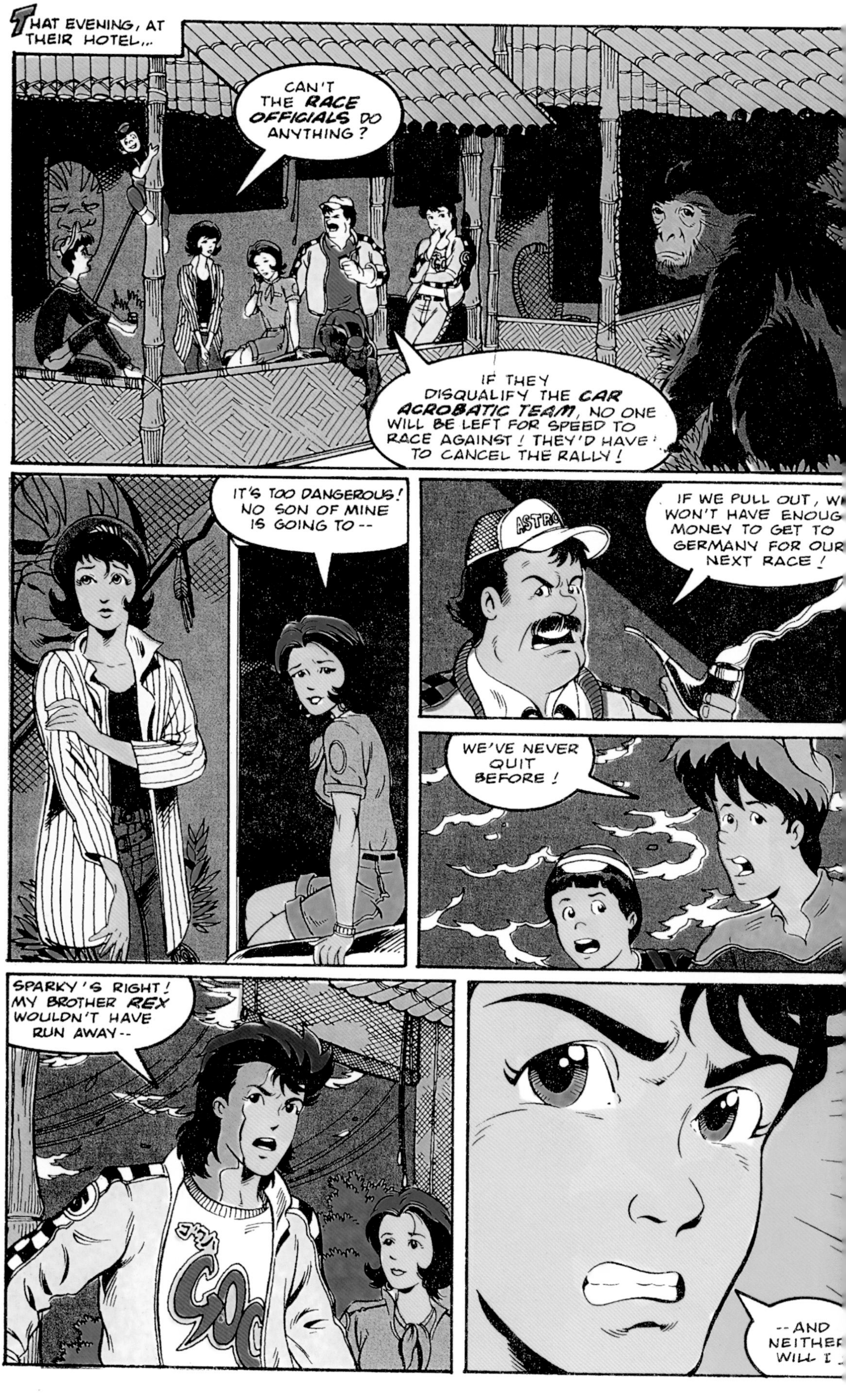

THAT EVENING, AT THEIR HOTEL...
CAN'T THE RACE OFFICIALS DO ANYTHING?
IF THEY DISQUALIFY THE CAR ACROBATIC TEAM, NO ONE WILL BE LEFT FOR SPEED TO RACE AGAINST! THEY'D HAVE TO CANCEL THE RALLY!
IT'S TOO DANGEROUS! NO SON OF MINE IS GOING TO --
ASTRO
IF WE PULL OUT, W WON'T HAVE ENOUG MONEY TO GET TO GERMANY FOR OUR NEXT RACE!
WE'VE NEVER QUIT BEFORE!
SPARKY'S RIGHT! MY BROTHER REX WOULDN'T HAVE RUN AWAY --
-- AND NEITHER WILL I.

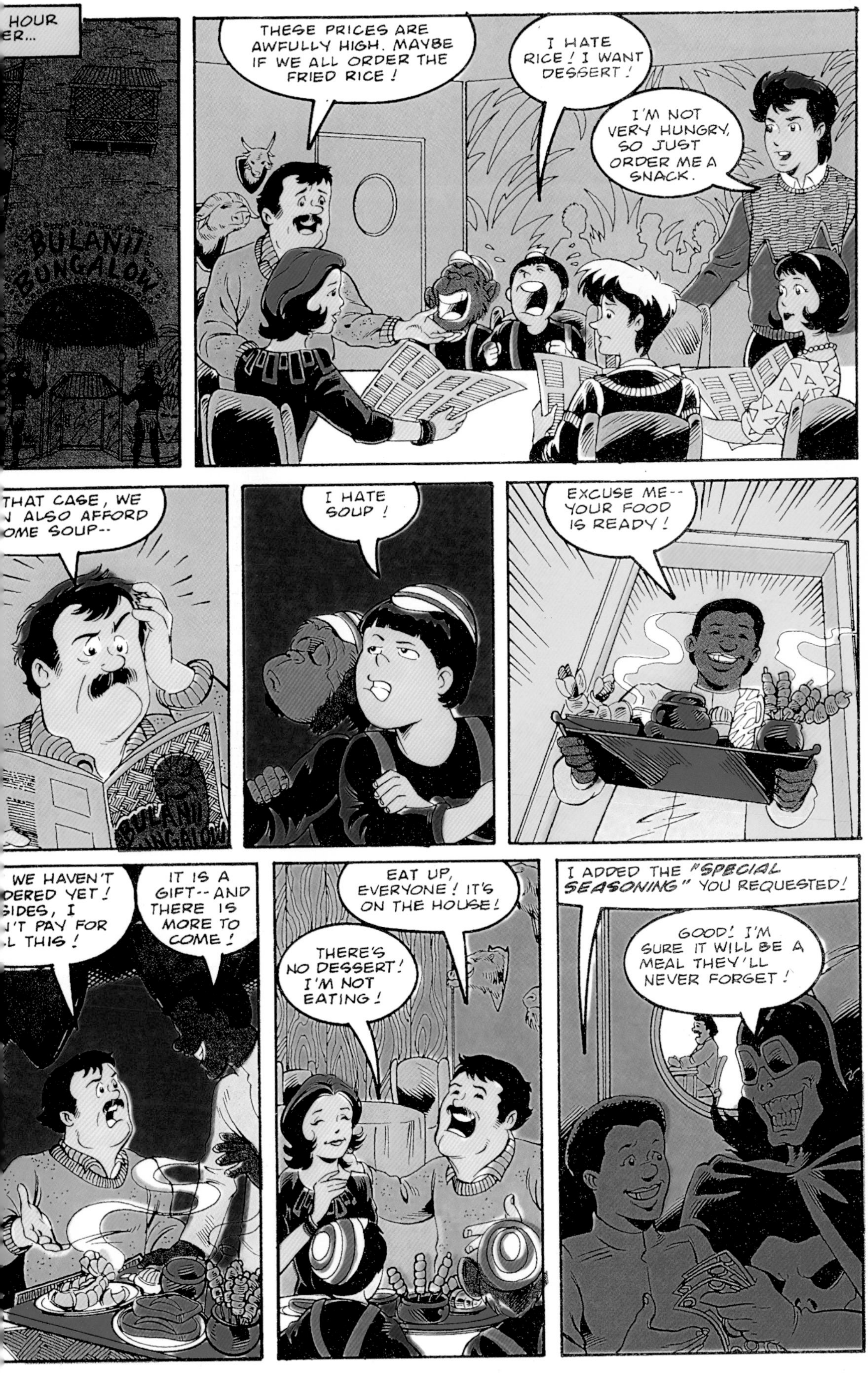
HOUR
ER...
THESE PRICES ARE AWFULLY HIGH. MAYBE IF WE ALL ORDER THE FRIED RICE!
I HATE RICE! I WANT DESSERT!
I'M NOT VERY HUNGRY, SO JUST ORDER ME A SNACK.
BULANJI BUNGALOW
THAT CASE, WE
N ALSO AFFORD
OME SOUP--
I HATE SOUP!
EXCUSE ME-- YOUR FOOD IS READY!
WE HAVEN'T
DERED YET!
SIDES, I
N'T PAY FOR
L THIS!
IT IS A GIFT--AND THERE IS MORE TO COME!
EAT UP, EVERYONE! IT'S ON THE HOUSE!
THERE'S NO DESSERT! I'M NOT EATING!
I ADDED THE "SPECIAL SEASONING" YOU REQUESTED!
GOOD! I'M SURE IT WILL BE A MEAL THEY'LL NEVER FORGET!

AT MIDNIGHT, AS A THUNDERSTORM BUILDS...

FEEL THE POWER OF THE RISING STORM! LET THE STRENGTH OF THE ELEMENTS FLOW INTO YOUR BODIES!

REMEMBER WE MUST DO MORE TH JUST WIN THE RACE TO RE GAIN OUR HONOR! WE MU MAKE SPEED *SUFFER* FO WHAT HE DID TO SNAKE

SPEED WILL BE IN NO CONDITION TO RACE TOMORROW -- BUT HE WILL NO DOUBT FEEL *HONOR BOUND* TO COMPETE!

SHOULD WE KILL HIM, IF WE GET THE CHANCE?

JUST MAKE IT A SLOW DEAT CRUSHER! A VERY SLOW DEAT

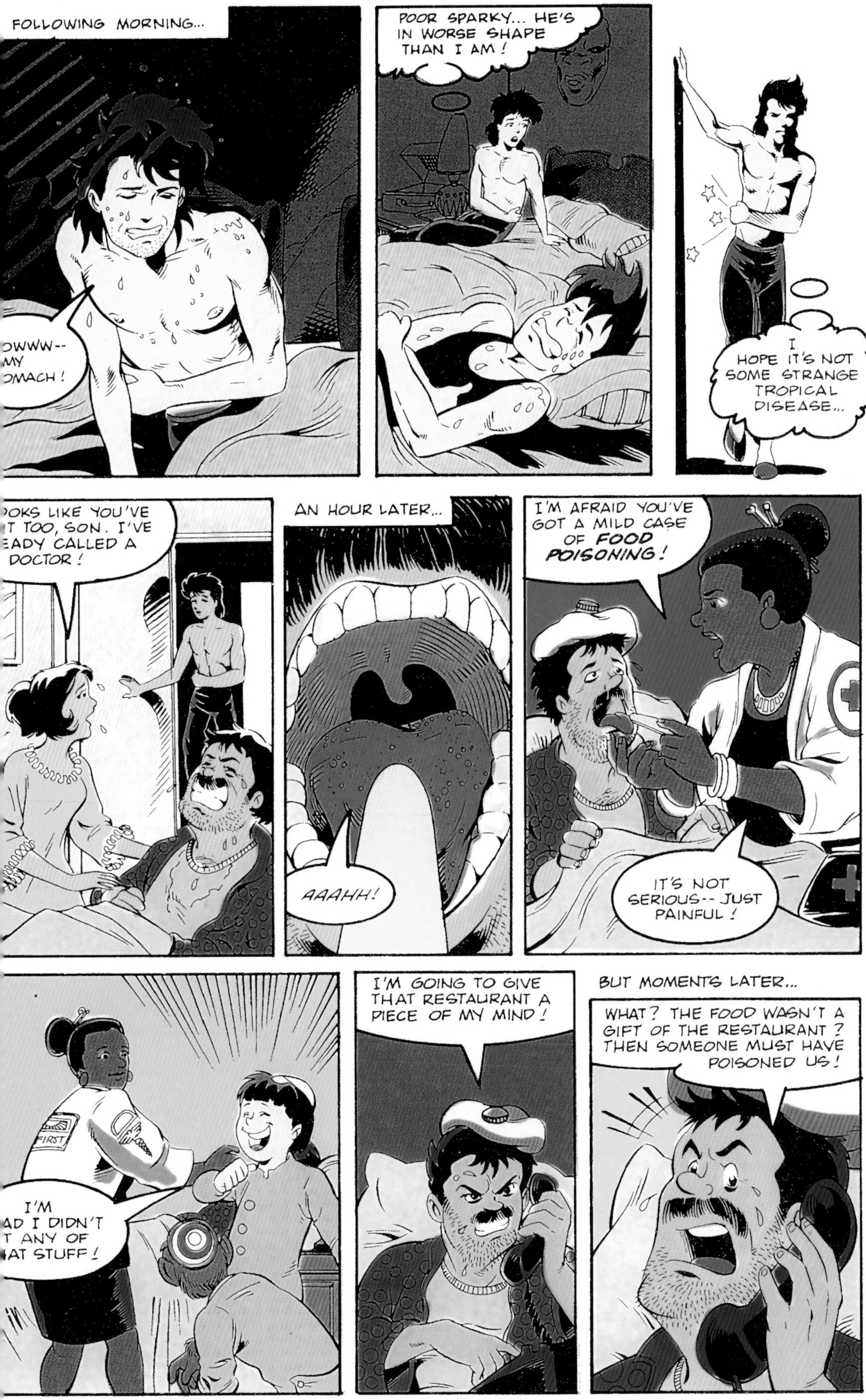
FOLLOWING MORNING...
OWWW-- MY OMACH!
POOR SPARKY... HE'S IN WORSE SHAPE THAN I AM!
I HOPE IT'S NOT SOME STRANGE TROPICAL DISEASE...
OOKS LIKE YOU'VE T TOO, SON. I'VE EADY CALLED A DOCTOR!
AN HOUR LATER...
AAAHH!
I'M AFRAID YOU'VE GOT A MILD CASE OF FOOD POISONING!
IT'S NOT SERIOUS-- JUST PAINFUL!
FIRST
I'M AD I DIDN'T T ANY OF AT STUFF!
I'M GOING TO GIVE THAT RESTAURANT A PIECE OF MY MIND!
BUT MOMENTS LATER...
WHAT? THE FOOD WASN'T A GIFT OF THE RESTAURANT? THEN SOMEONE MUST HAVE POISONED US!

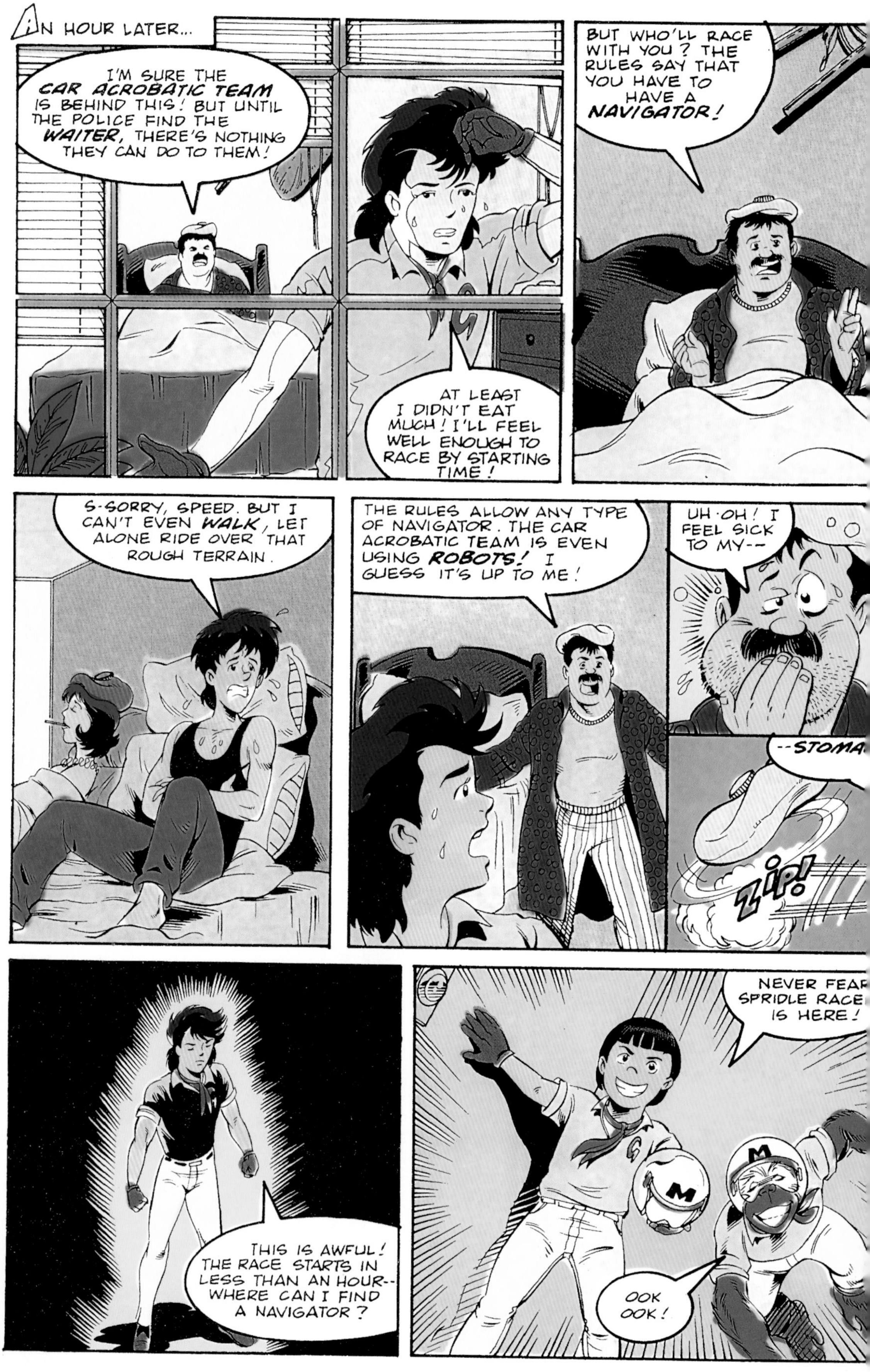

AN HOUR LATER...
I'M SURE THE CAR ACROBATIC TEAM IS BEHIND THIS! BUT UNTIL THE POLICE FIND THE WAITER, THERE'S NOTHING THEY CAN DO TO THEM!
AT LEAST I DIDN'T EAT MUCH! I'LL FEEL WELL ENOUGH TO RACE BY STARTING TIME!
BUT WHO'LL RACE WITH YOU? THE RULES SAY THAT YOU HAVE TO HAVE A NAVIGATOR!
S-SORRY, SPEED. BUT I CAN'T EVEN WALK, LET ALONE RIDE OVER THAT ROUGH TERRAIN.
THE RULES ALLOW ANY TYPE OF NAVIGATOR. THE CAR ACROBATIC TEAM IS EVEN USING ROBOTS! I GUESS IT'S UP TO ME!
UH-OH! I FEEL SICK TO MY--
--STOMA
ZIP!
THIS IS AWFUL! THE RACE STARTS IN LESS THAN AN HOUR-- WHERE CAN I FIND A NAVIGATOR?
NEVER FEAR SPRIDLE RACE IS HERE!
OOK OOK!

BUT SPRIDLE, YOU'RE TOO YOUNG!

IT'S MUCH TOO *DANGEROUS!*

YOU DON'T REALIZE HOW RUTHLESS THEY ARE!

YES I DO!

DON'T YOU REMEMBER HOW CHIM CHIM AND I FACED UP TO THEM BEFORE?

SPRIDLE'S RIGHT! AND BESIDES-- HE'S OUR ONLY HOPE!

CAPTAIN TERROR-- I KNOW THAT YOU'RE RESPONSIBLE FOR WHAT HAPPENED LAST NIGHT!

EVERY MAN CONDEMNED TO DEATH IS ENTITLED TO ONE LAST, MEMORABLE MEAL! I SEE THAT YOU'VE RECOVERED FROM YOURS!

YOU DON'T SCARE ME! AND I'M GOING TO WIN-- FAIR AND SQUARE!

WITH A *CHILD* AS YOUR NAVIGATOR? I DON'T THINK SO!

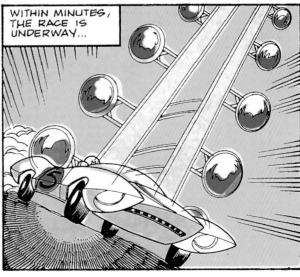

WITHIN MINUTES, THE RACE IS UNDERWAY...

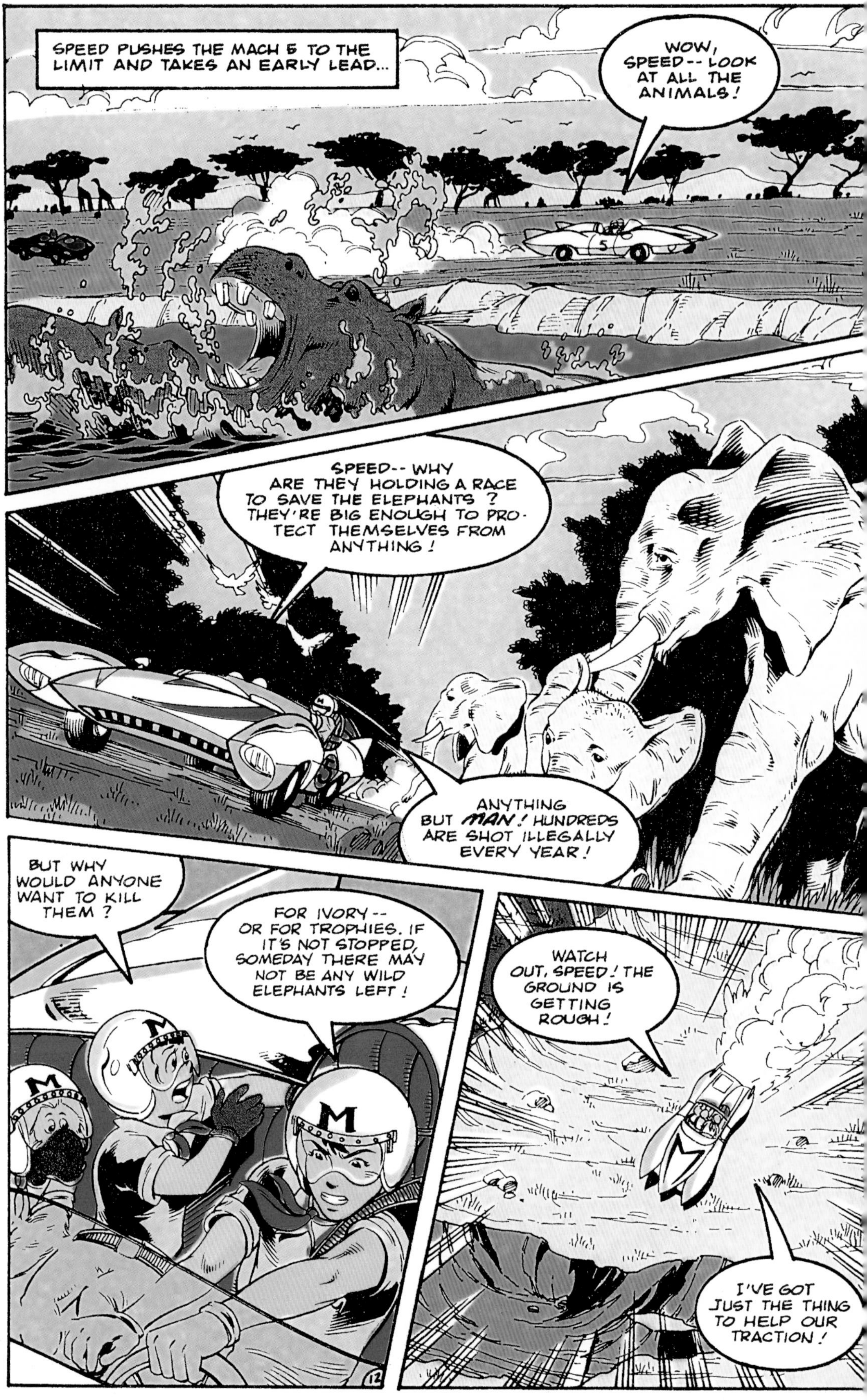
SPEED PUSHES THE MACH 5 TO THE LIMIT AND TAKES AN EARLY LEAD...
WOW, SPEED-- LOOK AT ALL THE ANIMALS!
SPEED-- WHY ARE THEY HOLDING A RACE TO SAVE THE ELEPHANTS? THEY'RE BIG ENOUGH TO PROTECT THEMSELVES FROM ANYTHING!
ANYTHING BUT MAN! HUNDREDS ARE SHOT ILLEGALLY EVERY YEAR!
BUT WHY WOULD ANYONE WANT TO KILL THEM?
FOR IVORY-- OR FOR TROPHIES. IF IT'S NOT STOPPED, SOMEDAY THERE MAY NOT BE ANY WILD ELEPHANTS LEFT!
WATCH OUT, SPEED! THE GROUND IS GETTING ROUGH!
I'VE GOT JUST THE THING TO HELP OUR TRACTION!
12

CLICK
YUNK!
YUNK!
YUNK!
ODDENLY...
WHERE DID THEY COME FROM?
EED STEERS AWAY FROM
E CARS TO AVOID A
LLISION...
SKREEEE!
THEY RAN US OFF THE ROAD ON PURPOSE! WHAT ARE THEY UP TO?
LL LET MY
BOT TAKE OVER
RIVING... SO I
AN LET SPEED
OW WHAT HE'S IN FOR!
CLICK!
DRIVING FUNCTION ASSUMED.

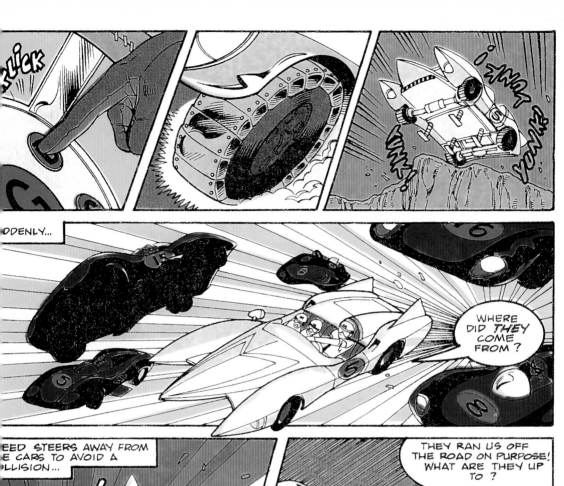

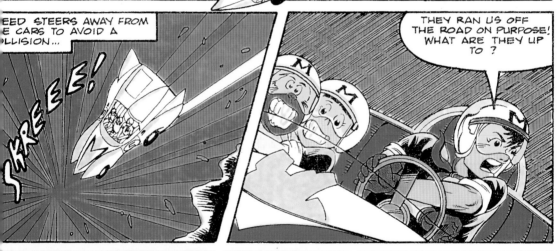

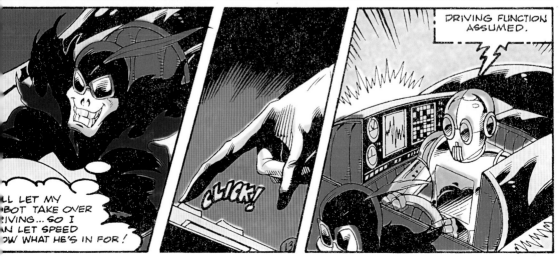

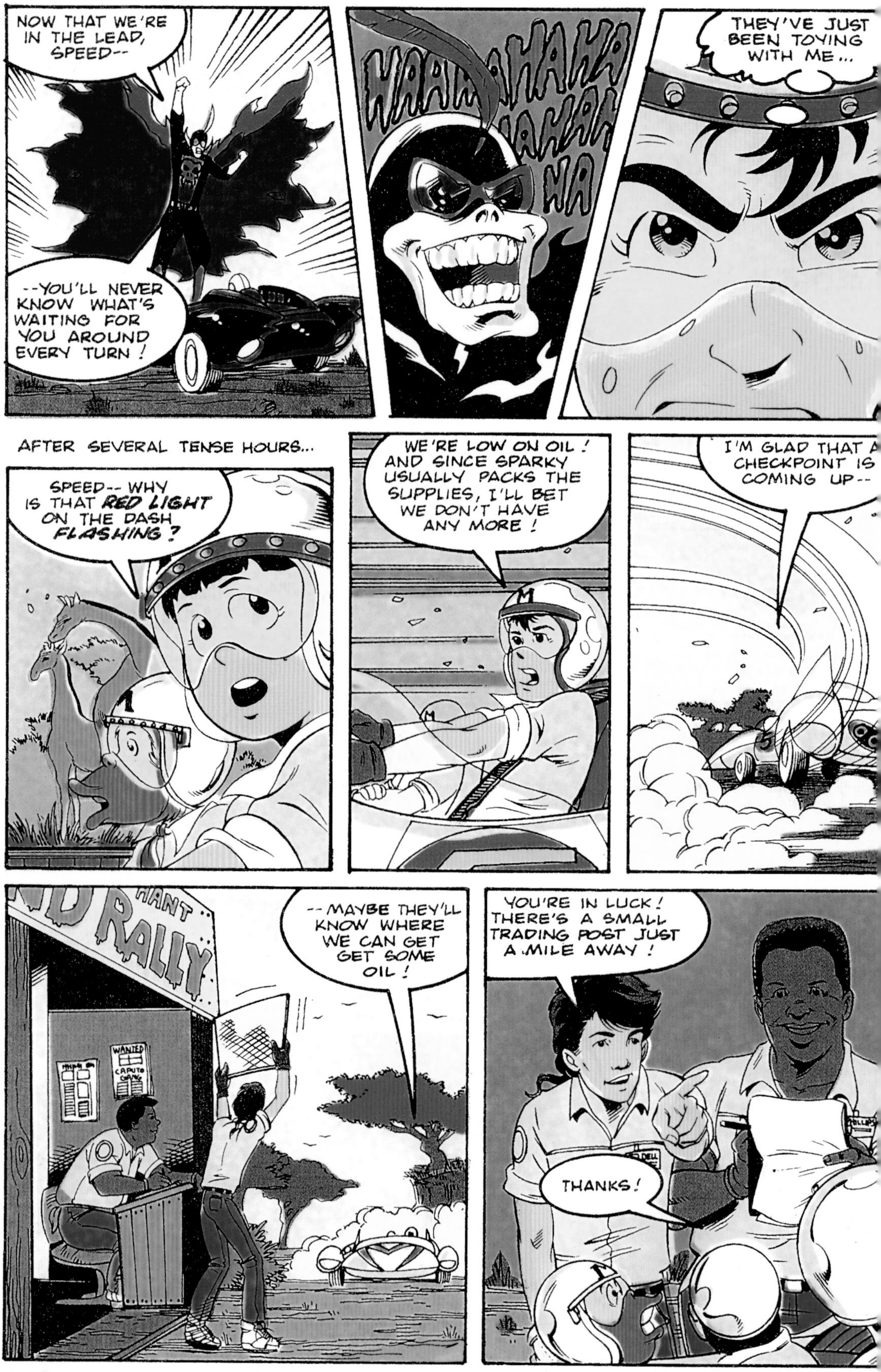
NOW THAT WE'RE IN THE LEAD, SPEED--
--YOU'LL NEVER KNOW WHAT'S WAITING FOR YOU AROUND EVERY TURN!
WAHAHAHAHA HAHAHA HA
THEY'VE JUST BEEN TOYING WITH ME...
AFTER SEVERAL TENSE HOURS...
SPEED-- WHY IS THAT RED LIGHT ON THE DASH FLASHING?
WE'RE LOW ON OIL! AND SINCE SPARKY USUALLY PACKS THE SUPPLIES, I'LL BET WE DON'T HAVE ANY MORE!
I'M GLAD THAT A CHECKPOINT IS COMING UP--
--MAYBE THEY'LL KNOW WHERE WE CAN GET GET SOME OIL!
WANTED CAPUTO GANG
YOU'RE IN LUCK! THERE'S A SMALL TRADING POST JUST A MILE AWAY!
THANKS!

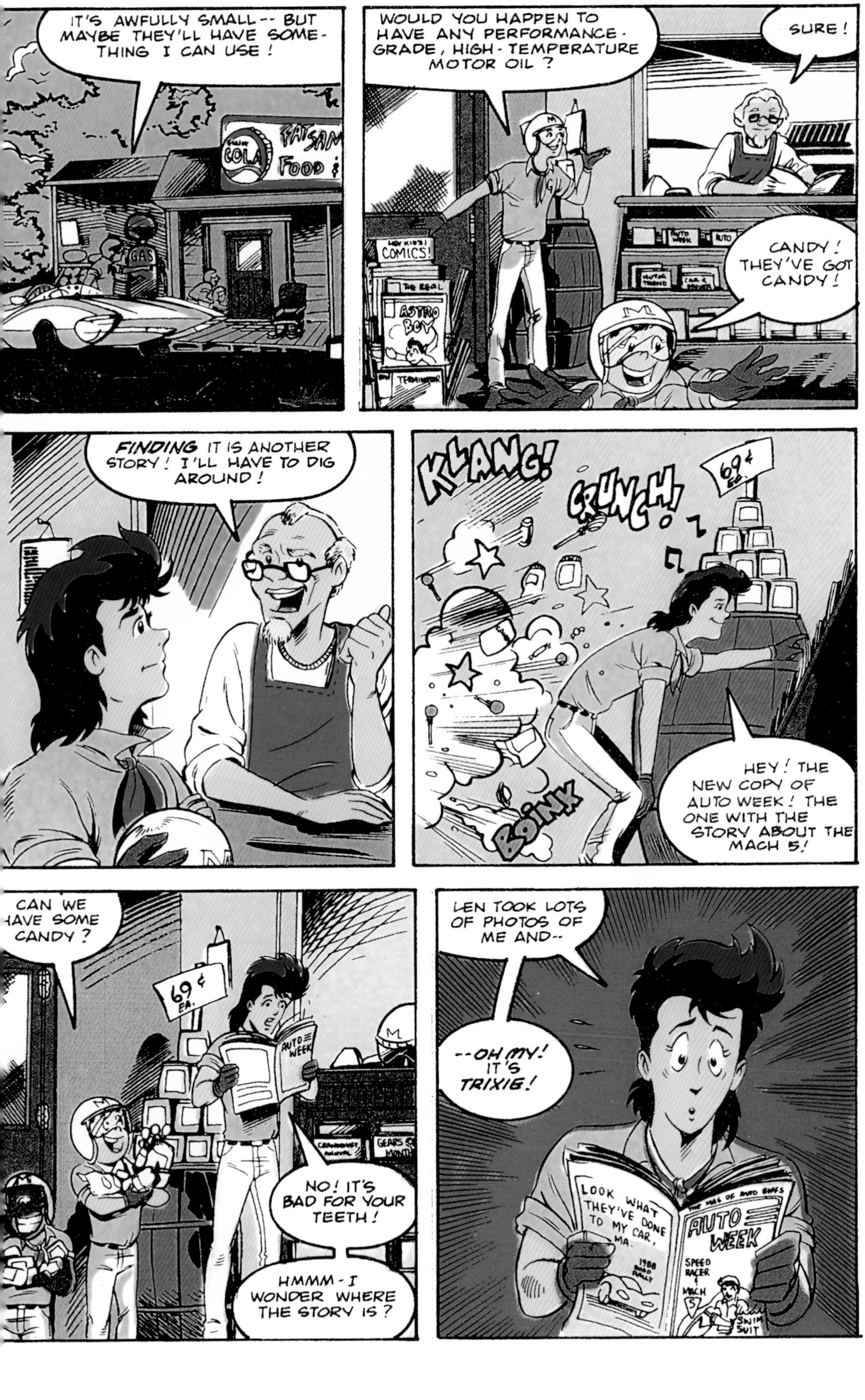
IT'S AWFULLY SMALL-- BUT MAYBE THEY'LL HAVE SOME-THING I CAN USE!
COLA
FOOD
GAS
WOULD YOU HAPPEN TO HAVE ANY PERFORMANCE-GRADE, HIGH-TEMPERATURE MOTOR OIL?
SURE!
COMICS!
ASTRO BOY
CANDY! THEY'VE GOT CANDY!
FINDING IT IS ANOTHER STORY! I'LL HAVE TO DIG AROUND!
KLANG!
CRUNCH!
69¢ EA.
BOINK
HEY! THE NEW COPY OF AUTO WEEK! THE ONE WITH THE STORY ABOUT THE MACH 5!
CAN WE HAVE SOME CANDY?
69¢ EA.
AUTO WEEK
NO! IT'S BAD FOR YOUR TEETH!
HMMM-I WONDER WHERE THE STORY IS?
LEN TOOK LOTS OF PHOTOS OF ME AND--
--OH MY! IT'S TRIXIE!
LOOK WHAT THEY'VE DONE TO MY CAR, MA.
AUTO WEEK
SPEED RACER & MACH 5
SWIM SUIT

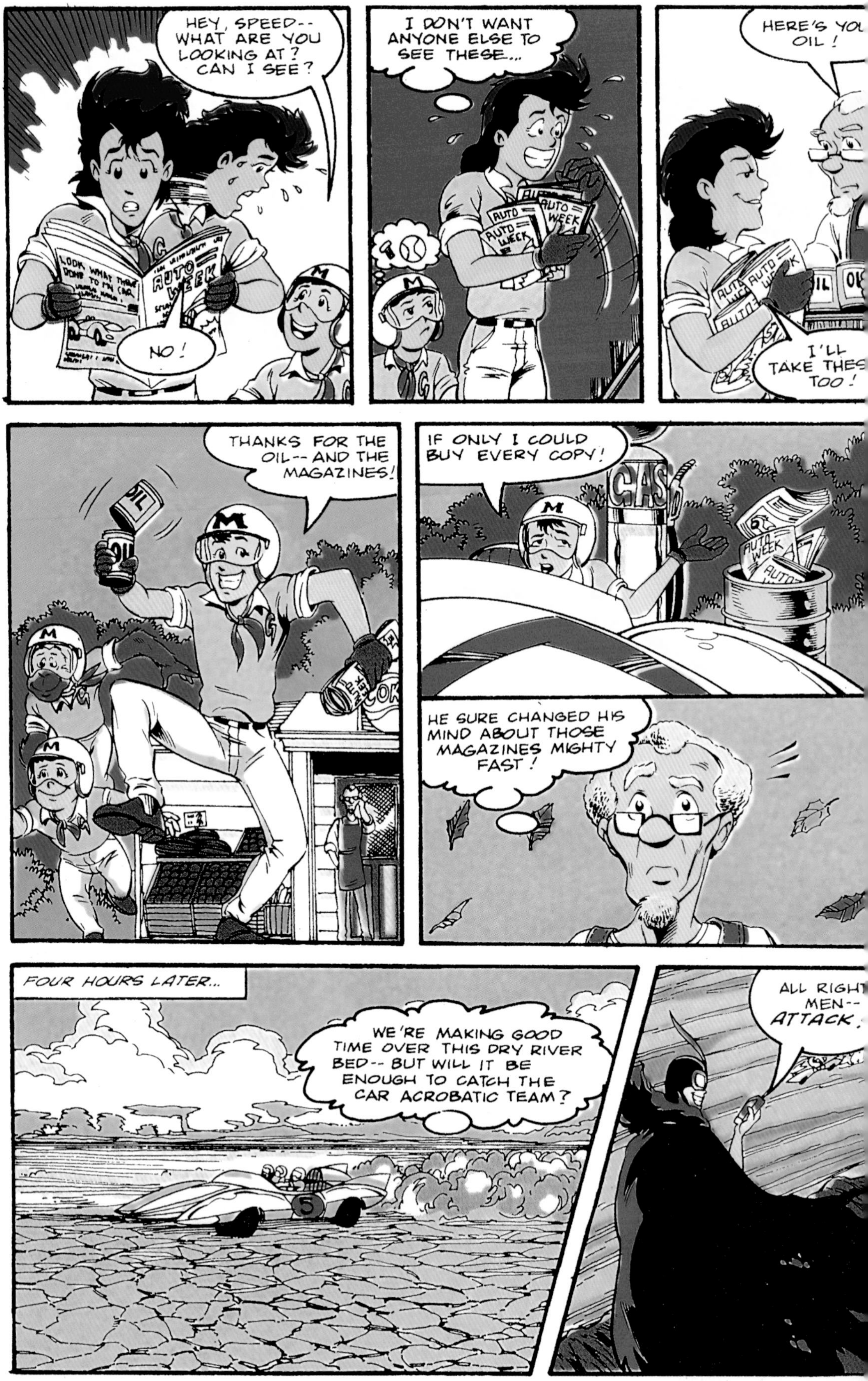
HEY, SPEED-- WHAT ARE YOU LOOKING AT? CAN I SEE?
NO!
AUTO WEEK
I DON'T WANT ANYONE ELSE TO SEE THESE...
AUTO WEEK
HERE'S YOU OIL!
I'LL TAKE THES TOO!
THANKS FOR THE OIL-- AND THE MAGAZINES!
OIL
IF ONLY I COULD BUY EVERY COPY!
GAS
AUTO WEEK
HE SURE CHANGED HIS MIND ABOUT THOSE MAGAZINES MIGHTY FAST!
FOUR HOURS LATER...
WE'RE MAKING GOOD TIME OVER THIS DRY RIVER BED-- BUT WILL IT BE ENOUGH TO CATCH THE CAR ACROBATIC TEAM?
ALL RIGHT MEN-- ATTACK!

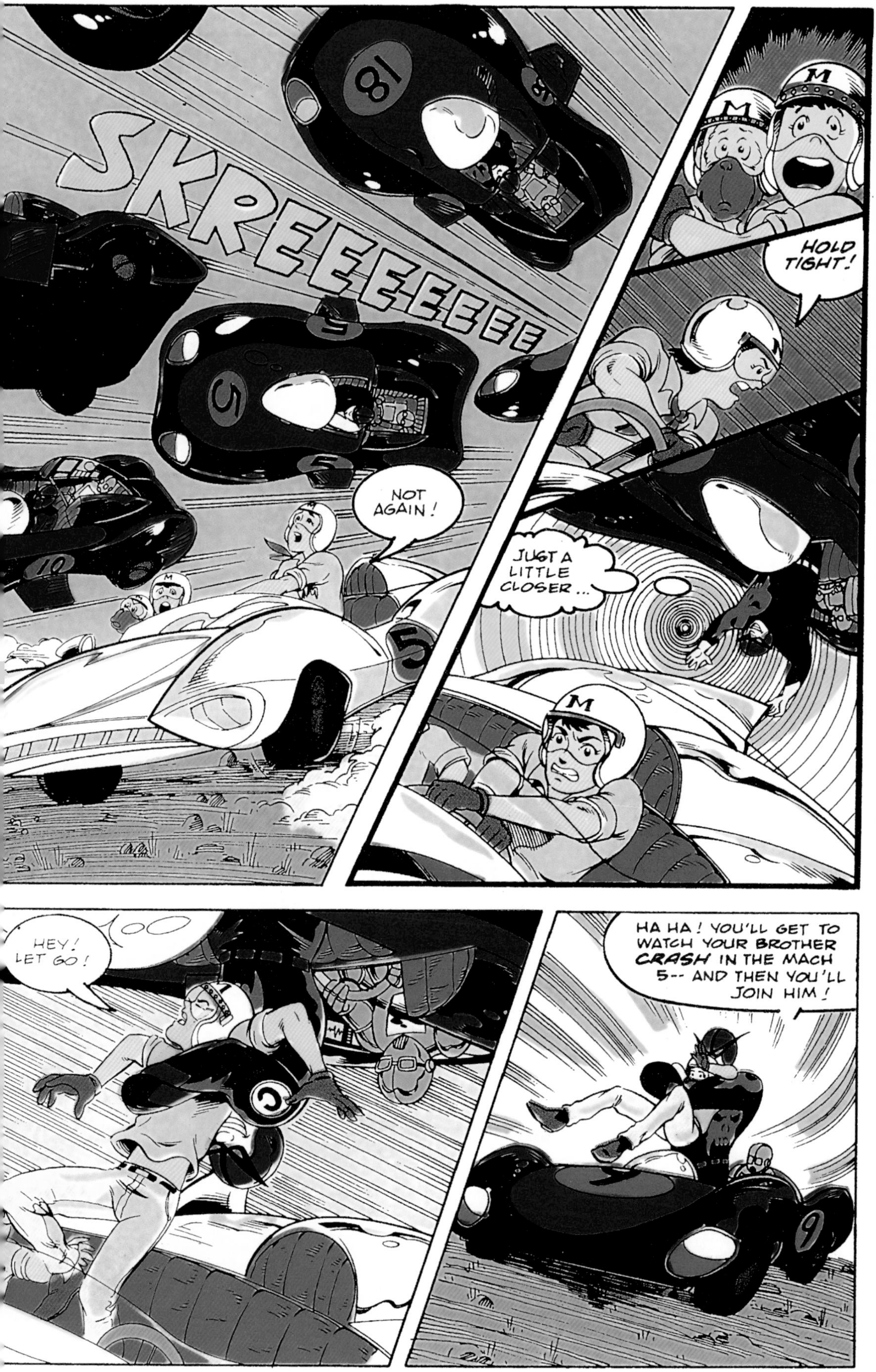
SKREEEEEEEE
NOT AGAIN!
HOLD TIGHT!
JUST A LITTLE CLOSER...
HEY! LET GO!
HA HA! YOU'LL GET TO WATCH YOUR BROTHER CRASH IN THE MACH 5-- AND THEN YOU'LL JOIN HIM!

BUT SPRIDLE AND CHIM-CHIM AREN'T COMPLETELY HELPLESS...

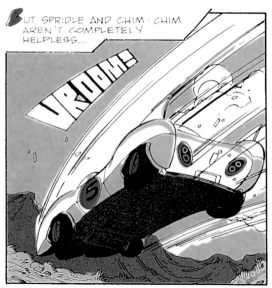

VROOM!

HIT THE GAS, CHIM-CHIM! WE'VE GOT TO SAVE SPEED!

OOK-OOK!

SPRIDLE WON'T BE ABLE TO CONTROL THE MACH 5 FOR LONG... I'D BETTER MOVE FAST!

HEY!

I'M GLAD REX TAUGHT ME THAT FLIP, ALL THOSE YEARS AGO...

GRRRR!!

OOOFF!

WAK!

SPRIDLE! TRY TO GET JUST A LITTLE CLOSER!
I'M AFRAID I'LL CRASH!
HERE GOES!
I'LL TAKE OVER, NOW!
OH NO! WE'RE GOING TO HIT CAPTAIN TERROR'S CAR, UNLESS I HIT THE JUMPER'S IN TIME!
YUNK
YUNK
UUUGGHH! WHAT'S ALL THIS GLOP?
SPLUNK!
QUICKSAND! WE MUST BE OVER AN UNDERGROUND RIVER!

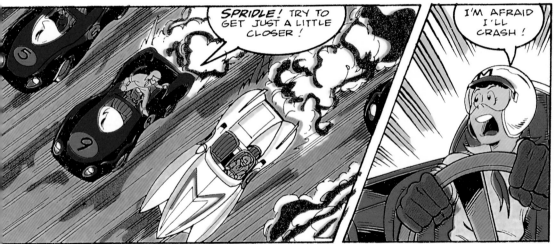

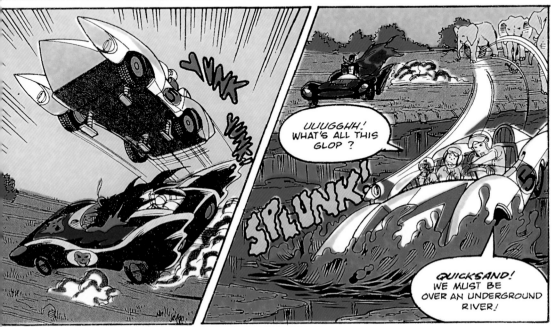

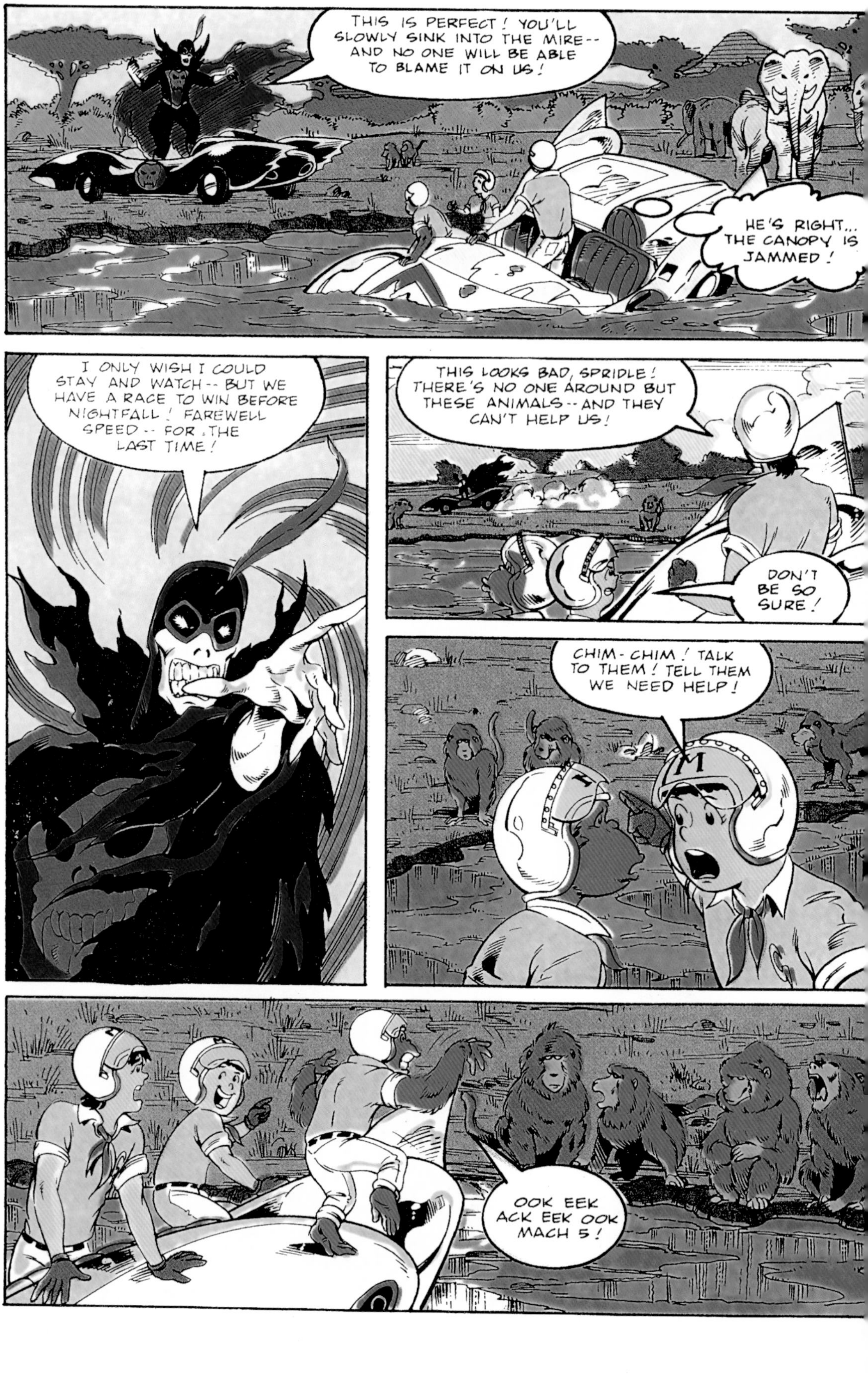
THIS IS PERFECT! YOU'LL SLOWLY SINK INTO THE MIRE-- AND NO ONE WILL BE ABLE TO BLAME IT ON US!
HE'S RIGHT... THE CANOPY IS JAMMED!
I ONLY WISH I COULD STAY AND WATCH-- BUT WE HAVE A RACE TO WIN BEFORE NIGHTFALL! FAREWELL SPEED-- FOR THE LAST TIME!
THIS LOOKS BAD, SPRIDLE! THERE'S NO ONE AROUND BUT THESE ANIMALS--AND THEY CAN'T HELP US!
DON'T BE SO SURE!
CHIM-CHIM! TALK TO THEM! TELL THEM WE NEED HELP!
OOK EEK ACK EEK OOK MACH 5!

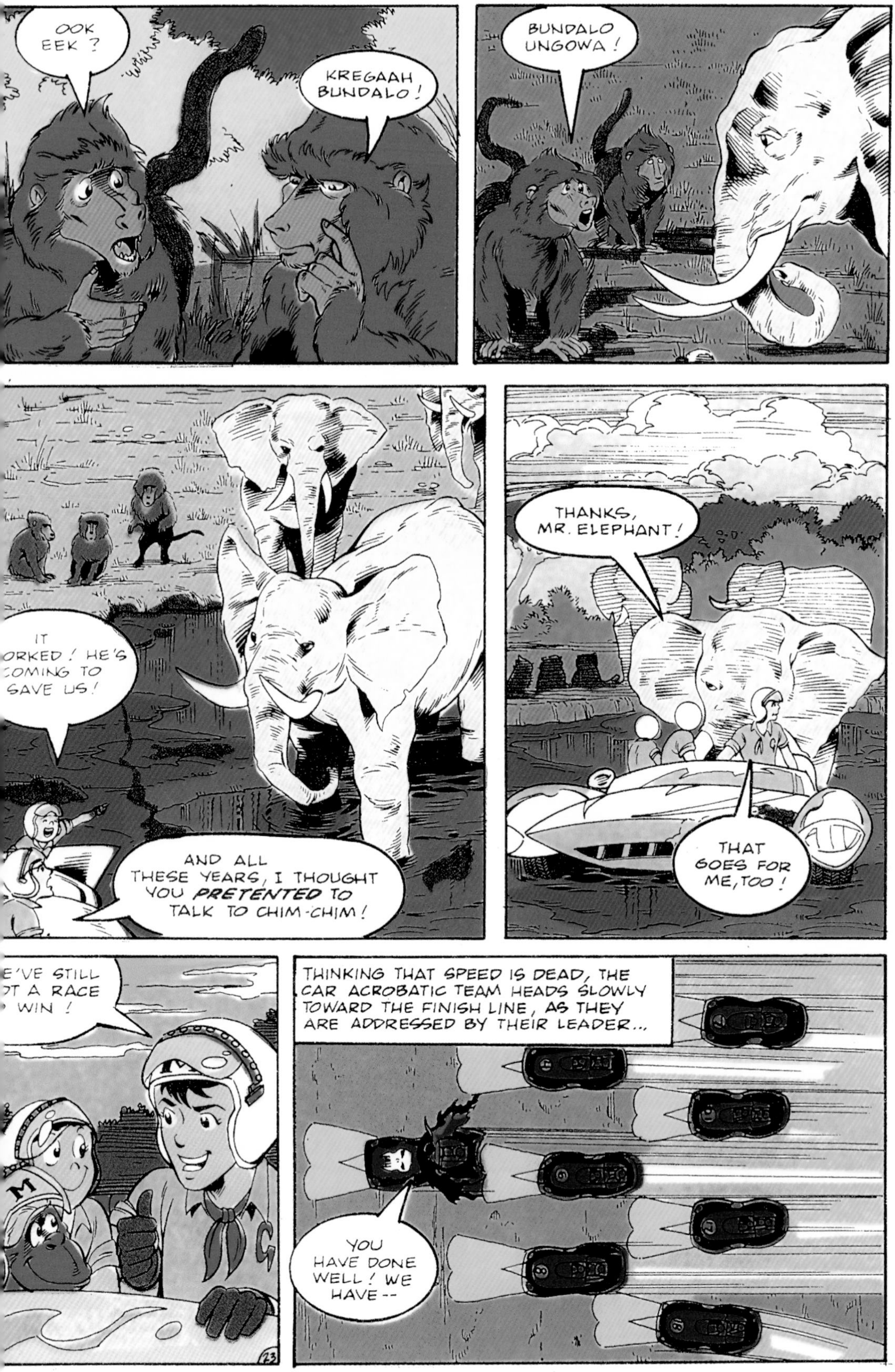
OOK EEK ?
KREGAAH BUNDALO !
BUNDALO UNGOWA !
IT ORKED ! HE'S COMING TO SAVE US !
AND ALL THESE YEARS, I THOUGHT YOU *PRETENTED* TO TALK TO CHIM-CHIM !
THANKS, MR. ELEPHANT !
THAT GOES FOR ME, TOO !
E'VE STILL OT A RACE WIN !
23
THINKING THAT SPEED IS DEAD, THE CAR ACROBATIC TEAM HEADS SLOWLY TOWARD THE FINISH LINE, AS THEY ARE ADDRESSED BY THEIR LEADER...
YOU HAVE DONE WELL ! WE HAVE --

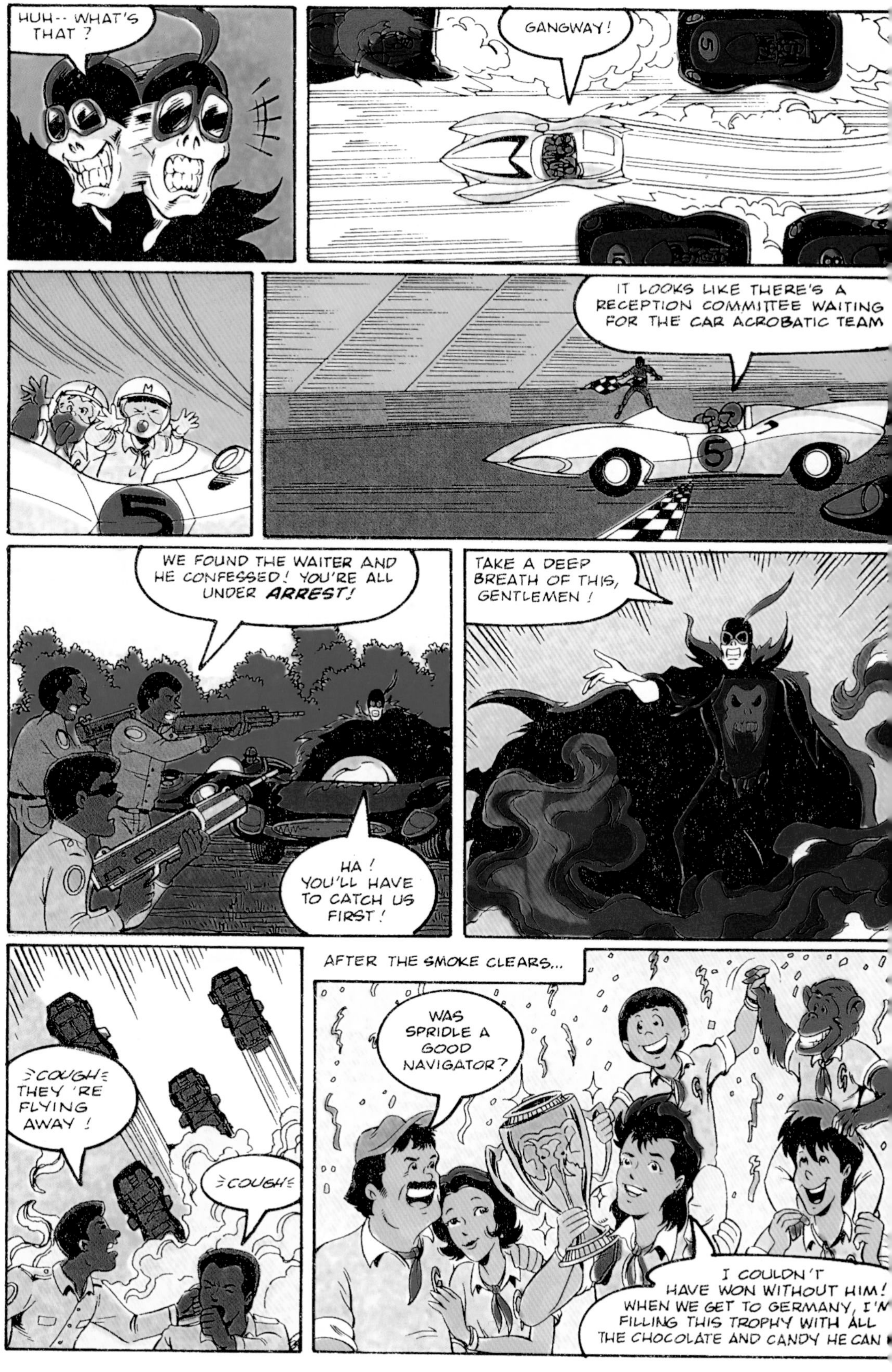
HUH-- WHAT'S THAT ?
GANGWAY!
IT LOOKS LIKE THERE'S A RECEPTION COMMITTEE WAITING FOR THE CAR ACROBATIC TEAM
WE FOUND THE WAITER AND HE CONFESSED! YOU'RE ALL UNDER ARREST!
HA! YOU'LL HAVE TO CATCH US FIRST!
TAKE A DEEP BREATH OF THIS, GENTLEMEN!
COUGH THEY'RE FLYING AWAY!
COUGH
AFTER THE SMOKE CLEARS...
WAS SPRIDLE A GOOD NAVIGATOR?
I COULDN'T HAVE WON WITHOUT HIM! WHEN WE GET TO GERMANY, I'M FILLING THIS TROPHY WITH ALL THE CHOCOLATE AND CANDY HE CAN

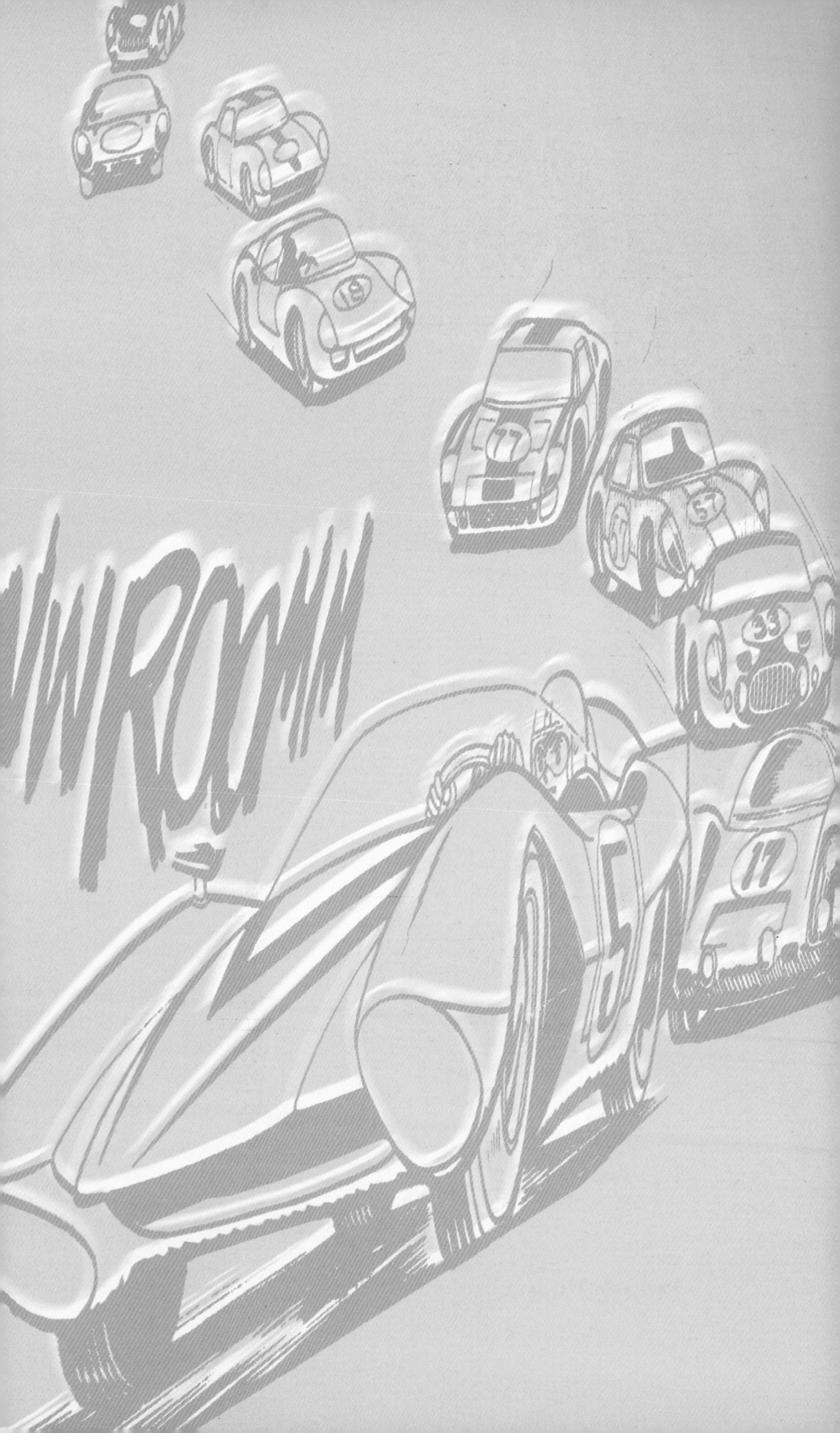

Speed Racer #17

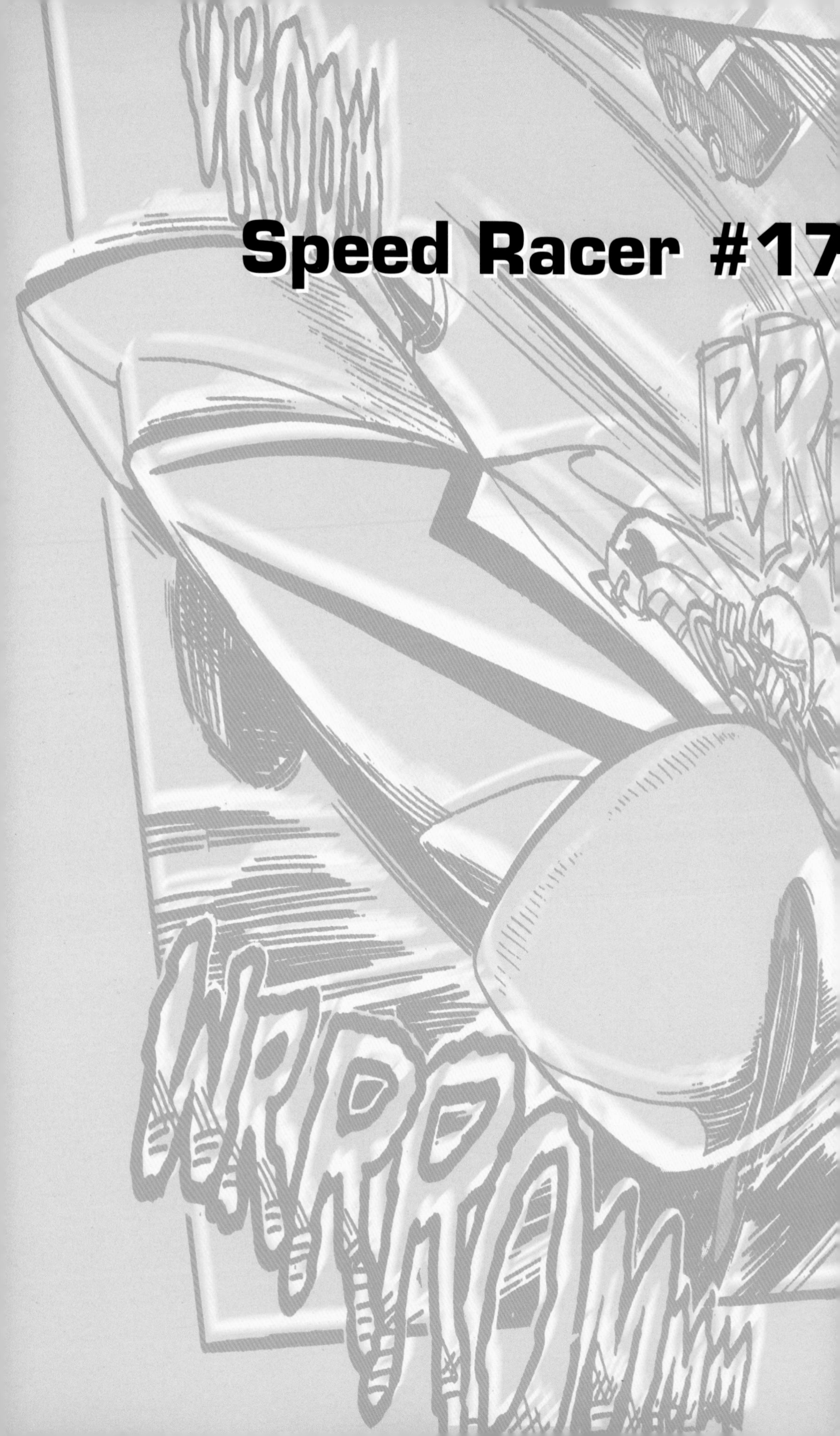

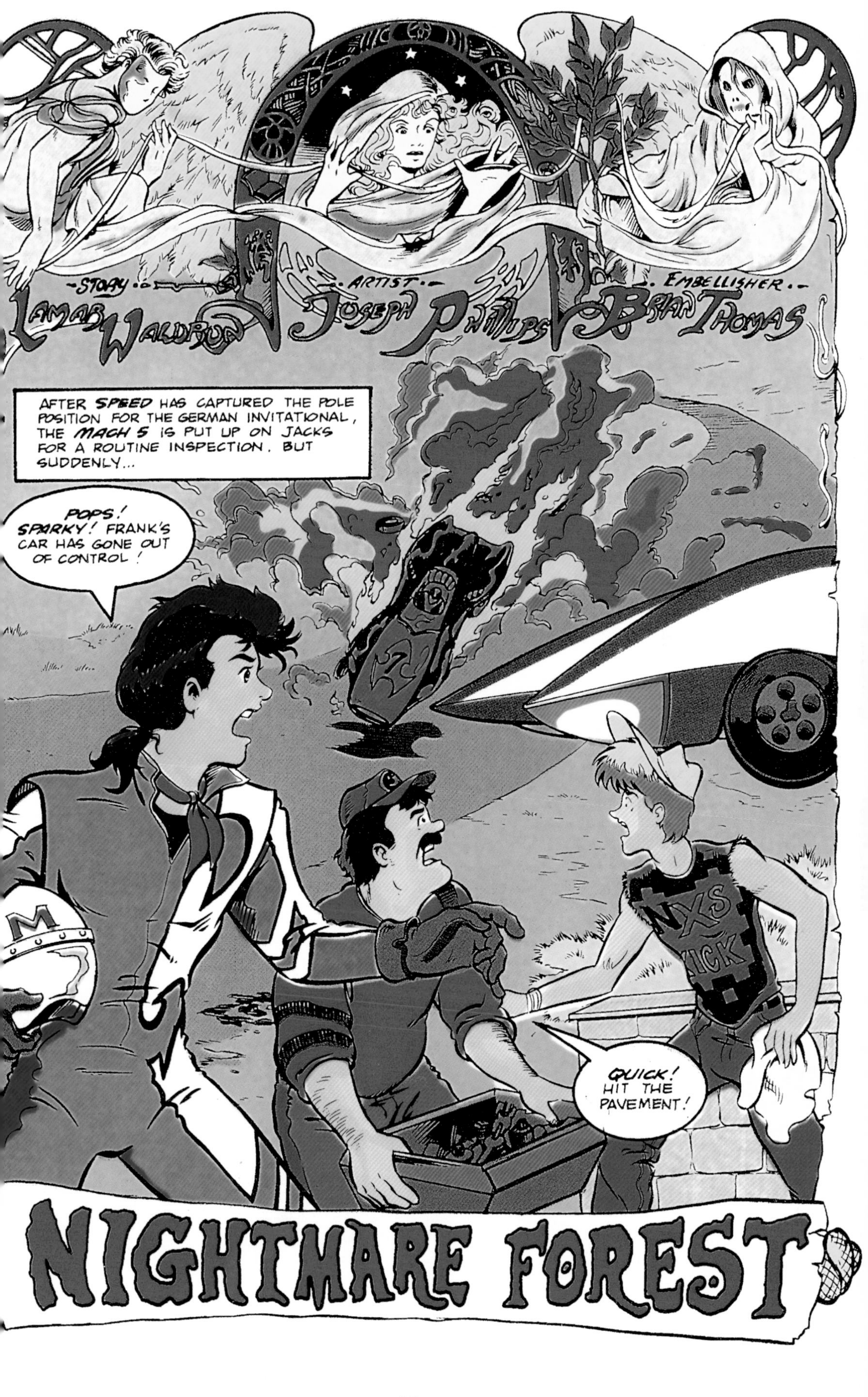
STORY LAMAR WALDRON
ARTIST JOSEPH PHILLIPS
EMBELLISHER BRIAN THOMAS
AFTER SPEED HAS CAPTURED THE POLE POSITION FOR THE GERMAN INVITATIONAL, THE MACH 5 IS PUT UP ON JACKS FOR A ROUTINE INSPECTION. BUT SUDDENLY...
POPS! SPARKY! FRANK'S CAR HAS GONE OUT OF CONTROL!
QUICK! HIT THE PAVEMENT!
NIGHTMARE FOREST

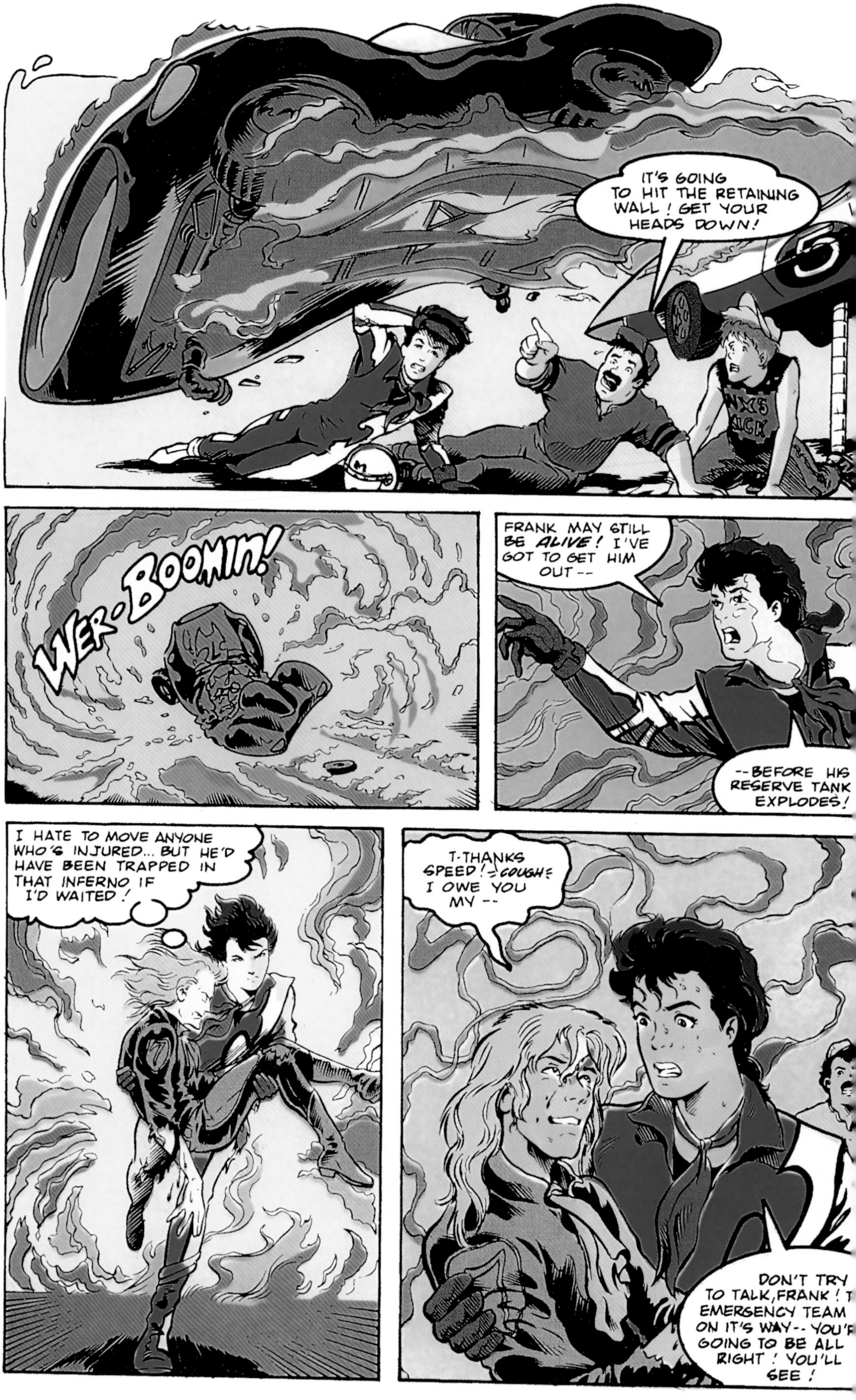
IT'S GOING TO HIT THE RETAINING WALL! GET YOUR HEADS DOWN!
WER-BOOMM!
FRANK MAY STILL BE *ALIVE*! I'VE GOT TO GET HIM OUT --
--BEFORE HIS RESERVE TANK EXPLODES!
I HATE TO MOVE ANYONE WHO'S INJURED... BUT HE'D HAVE BEEN TRAPPED IN THAT INFERNO IF I'D WAITED!
T-THANKS SPEED! =COUGH= I OWE YOU MY --
DON'T TRY TO TALK, FRANK! T EMERGENCY TEAM ON IT'S WAY-- YOU'R GOING TO BE ALL RIGHT! YOU'LL SEE!

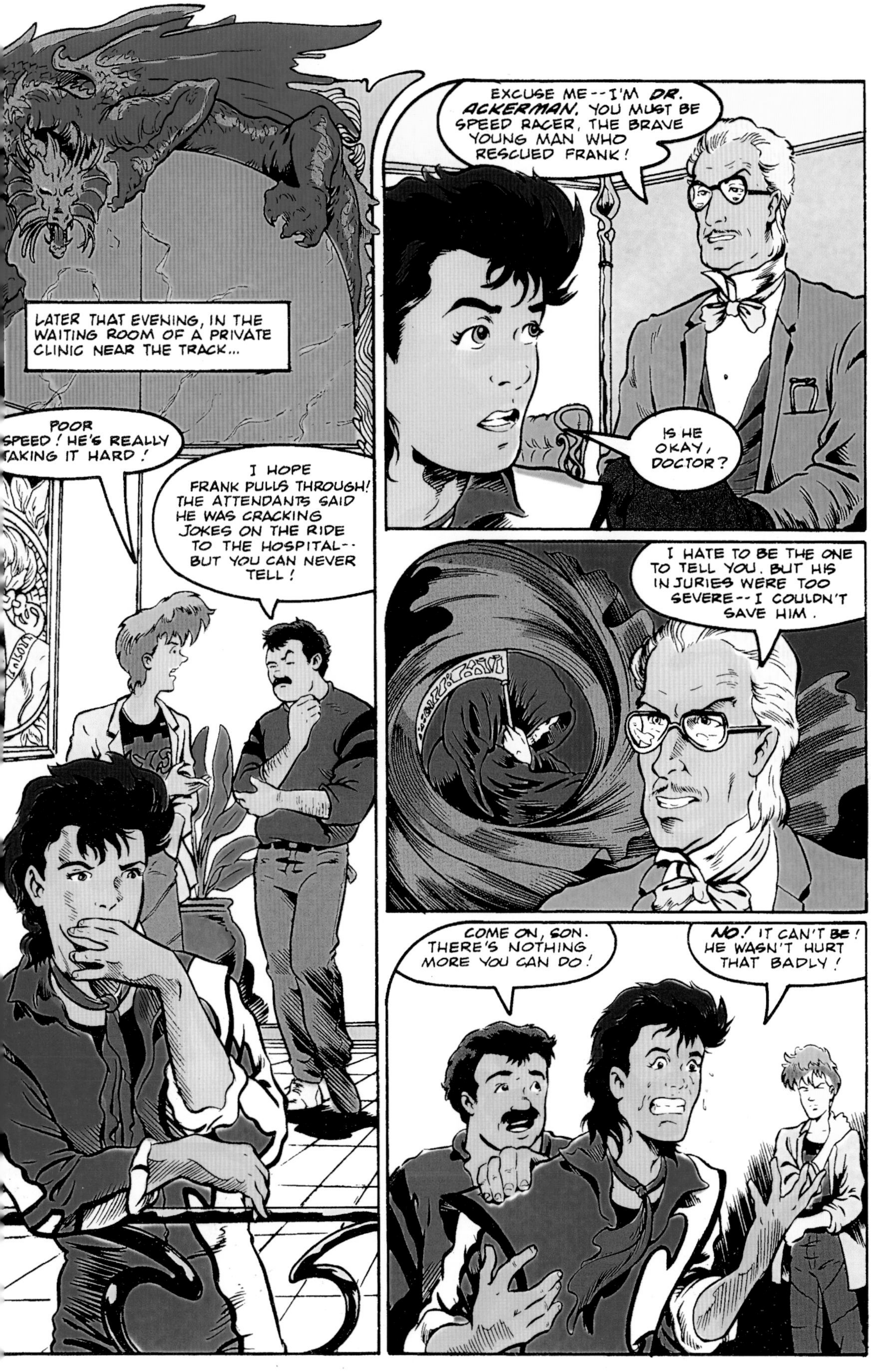

LATER THAT EVENING, IN THE WAITING ROOM OF A PRIVATE CLINIC NEAR THE TRACK...
POOR SPEED! HE'S REALLY TAKING IT HARD!
I HOPE FRANK PULLS THROUGH! THE ATTENDANTS SAID HE WAS CRACKING JOKES ON THE RIDE TO THE HOSPITAL-- BUT YOU CAN NEVER TELL!
EXCUSE ME--I'M DR. ACKERMAN. YOU MUST BE SPEED RACER, THE BRAVE YOUNG MAN WHO RESCUED FRANK!
IS HE OKAY, DOCTOR?
I HATE TO BE THE ONE TO TELL YOU. BUT HIS INJURIES WERE TOO SEVERE--I COULDN'T SAVE HIM.
COME ON, SON. THERE'S NOTHING MORE YOU CAN DO!
NO! IT CAN'T BE! HE WASN'T HURT THAT BADLY!

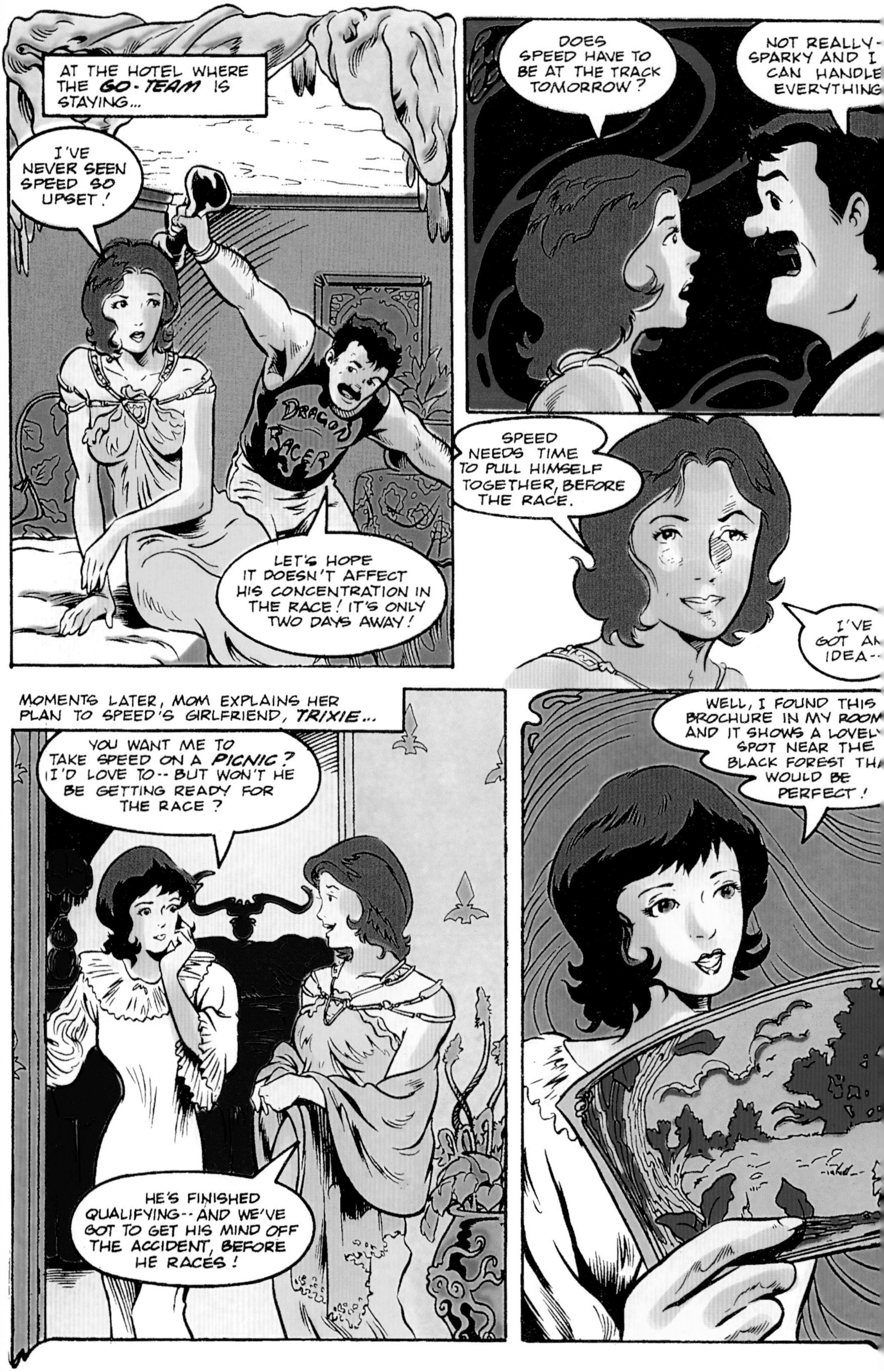

AT THE HOTEL WHERE THE GO-TEAM IS STAYING...
I'VE NEVER SEEN SPEED SO UPSET!
DRAGON RACER
LET'S HOPE IT DOESN'T AFFECT HIS CONCENTRATION IN THE RACE! IT'S ONLY TWO DAYS AWAY!
DOES SPEED HAVE TO BE AT THE TRACK TOMORROW?
NOT REALLY-- SPARKY AND I CAN HANDLE EVERYTHING
SPEED NEEDS TIME TO PULL HIMSELF TOGETHER, BEFORE THE RACE.
I'VE GOT AN IDEA--
MOMENTS LATER, MOM EXPLAINS HER PLAN TO SPEED'S GIRLFRIEND, TRIXIE...
YOU WANT ME TO TAKE SPEED ON A PICNIC? I'D LOVE TO-- BUT WON'T HE BE GETTING READY FOR THE RACE?
HE'S FINISHED QUALIFYING-- AND WE'VE GOT TO GET HIS MIND OFF THE ACCIDENT, BEFORE HE RACES!
WELL, I FOUND THIS BROCHURE IN MY ROOM AND IT SHOWS A LOVELY SPOT NEAR THE BLACK FOREST THAT WOULD BE PERFECT!

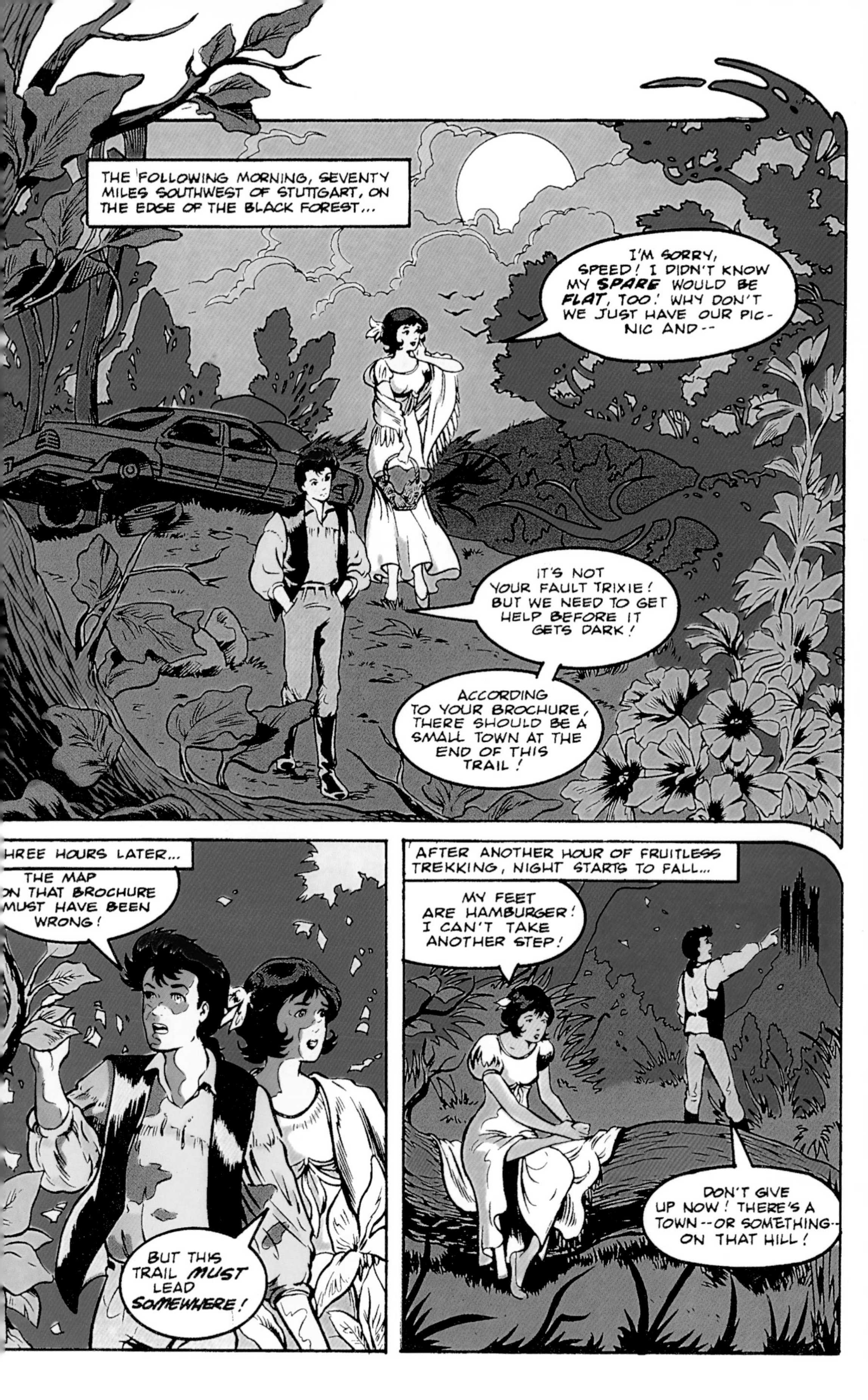
THE FOLLOWING MORNING, SEVENTY MILES SOUTHWEST OF STUTTGART, ON THE EDGE OF THE BLACK FOREST...
I'M SORRY, SPEED! I DIDN'T KNOW MY SPARE WOULD BE FLAT, TOO! WHY DON'T WE JUST HAVE OUR PIC-NIC AND--
IT'S NOT YOUR FAULT TRIXIE! BUT WE NEED TO GET HELP BEFORE IT GETS DARK!
ACCORDING TO YOUR BROCHURE, THERE SHOULD BE A SMALL TOWN AT THE END OF THIS TRAIL!
HREE HOURS LATER...
THE MAP ON THAT BROCHURE MUST HAVE BEEN WRONG!
BUT THIS TRAIL MUST LEAD SOMEWHERE!
AFTER ANOTHER HOUR OF FRUITLESS TREKKING, NIGHT STARTS TO FALL...
MY FEET ARE HAMBURGER! I CAN'T TAKE ANOTHER STEP!
DON'T GIVE UP NOW! THERE'S A TOWN--OR SOMETHING--ON THAT HILL!

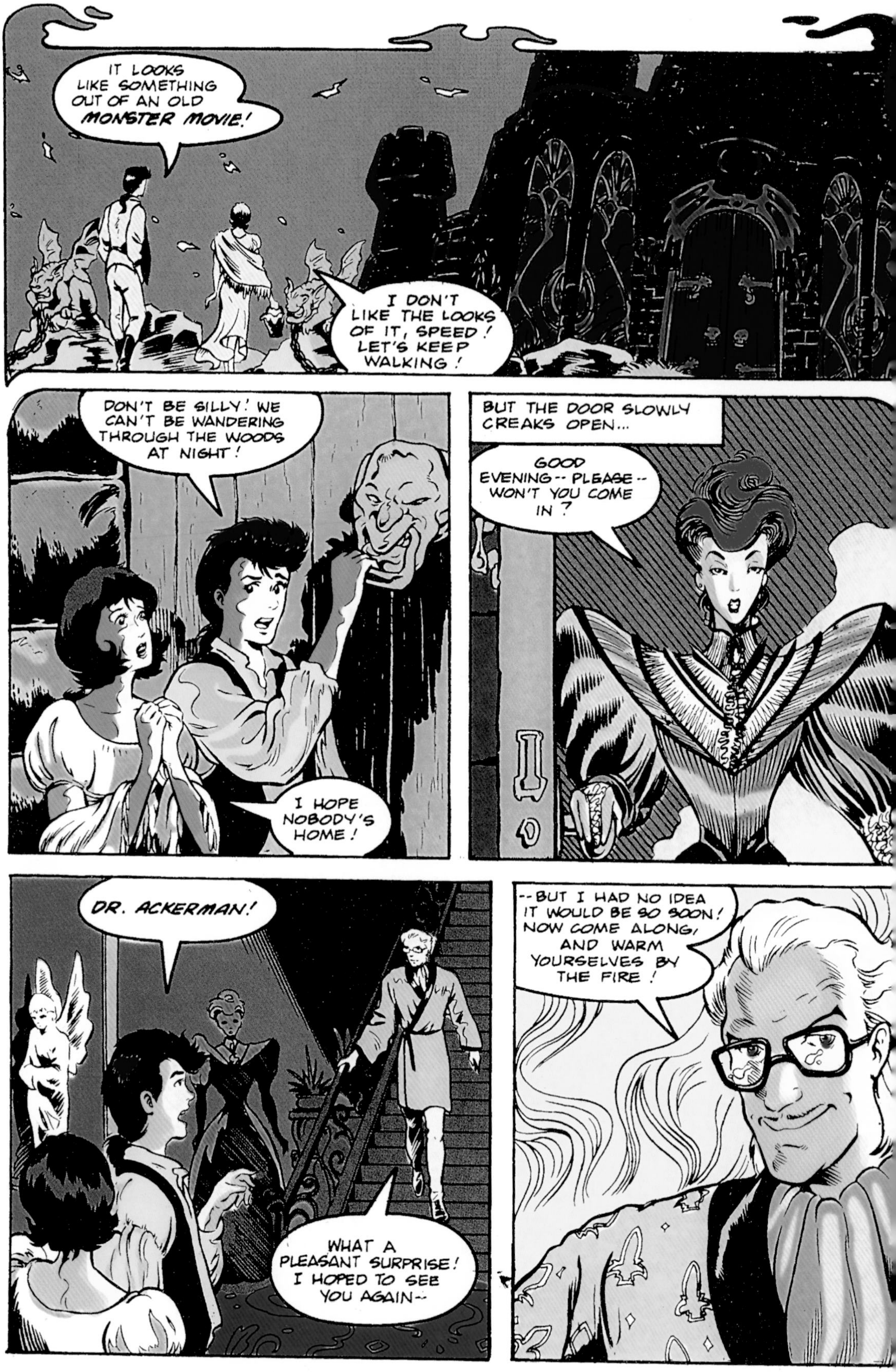

IT LOOKS LIKE SOMETHING OUT OF AN OLD MONSTER MOVIE!
I DON'T LIKE THE LOOKS OF IT, SPEED! LET'S KEEP WALKING!
DON'T BE SILLY! WE CAN'T BE WANDERING THROUGH THE WOODS AT NIGHT!
I HOPE NOBODY'S HOME!
BUT THE DOOR SLOWLY CREAKS OPEN...
GOOD EVENING-- PLEASE-- WON'T YOU COME IN?
DR. ACKERMAN!
WHAT A PLEASANT SURPRISE! I HOPED TO SEE YOU AGAIN--
--BUT I HAD NO IDEA IT WOULD BE SO SOON! NOW COME ALONG, AND WARM YOURSELVES BY THE FIRE!

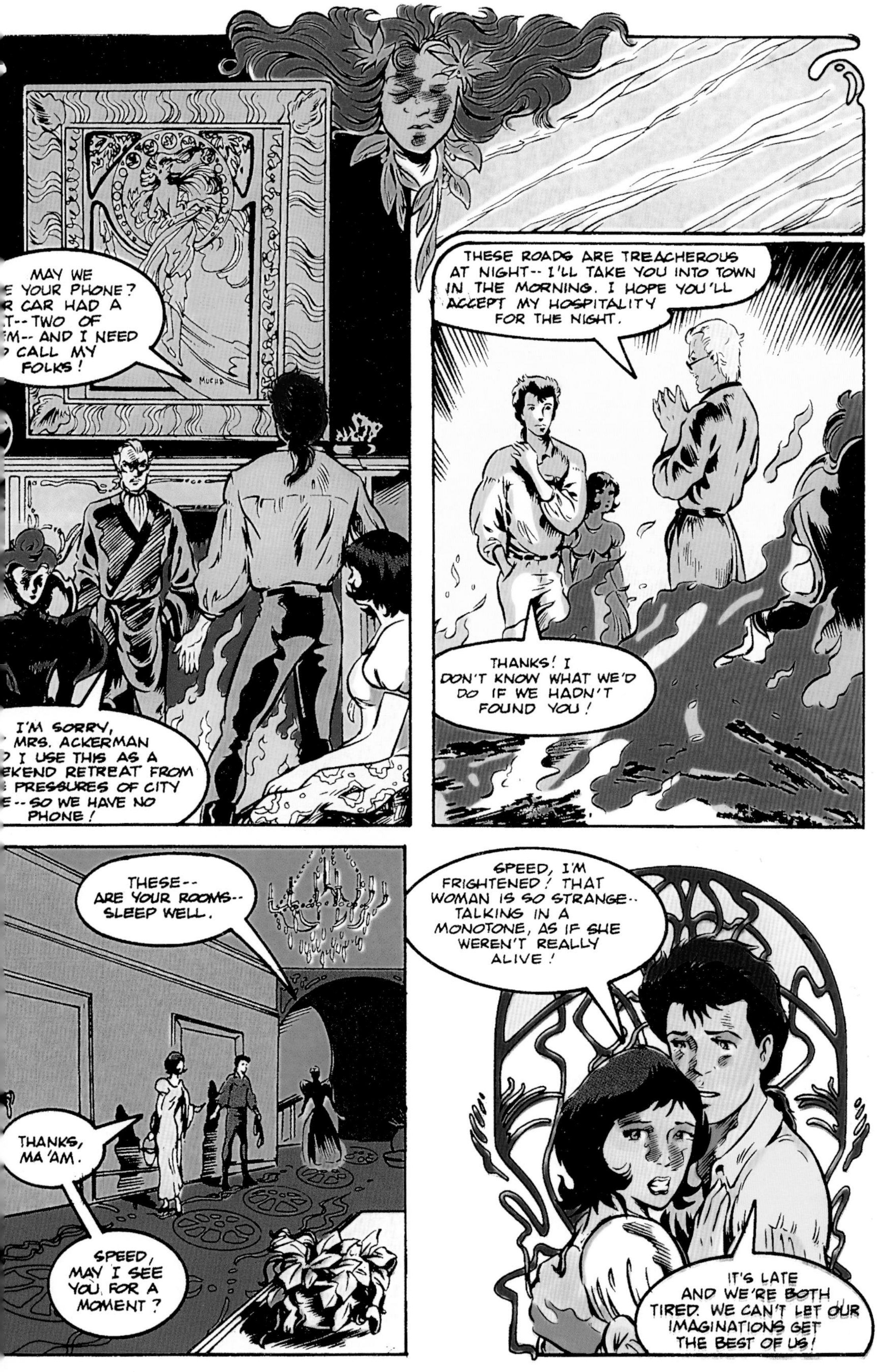

MAY WE
E YOUR PHONE?
R CAR HAD A
T-- TWO OF
EM-- AND I NEED
D CALL MY
FOLKS!
MUCHA
I'M SORRY,
MRS. ACKERMAN
D I USE THIS AS A
EKEND RETREAT FROM
E PRESSURES OF CITY
E-- SO WE HAVE NO
PHONE!
THESE ROADS ARE TREACHEROUS AT NIGHT-- I'LL TAKE YOU INTO TOWN IN THE MORNING. I HOPE YOU'LL ACCEPT MY HOSPITALITY FOR THE NIGHT.
THANKS! I DON'T KNOW WHAT WE'D DO IF WE HADN'T FOUND YOU!
THESE-- ARE YOUR ROOMS-- SLEEP WELL.
THANKS, MA'AM.
SPEED, MAY I SEE YOU FOR A MOMENT?
SPEED, I'M FRIGHTENED! THAT WOMAN IS SO STRANGE-- TALKING IN A MONOTONE, AS IF SHE WEREN'T REALLY ALIVE!
IT'S LATE AND WE'RE BOTH TIRED. WE CAN'T LET OUR IMAGINATIONS GET THE BEST OF US!

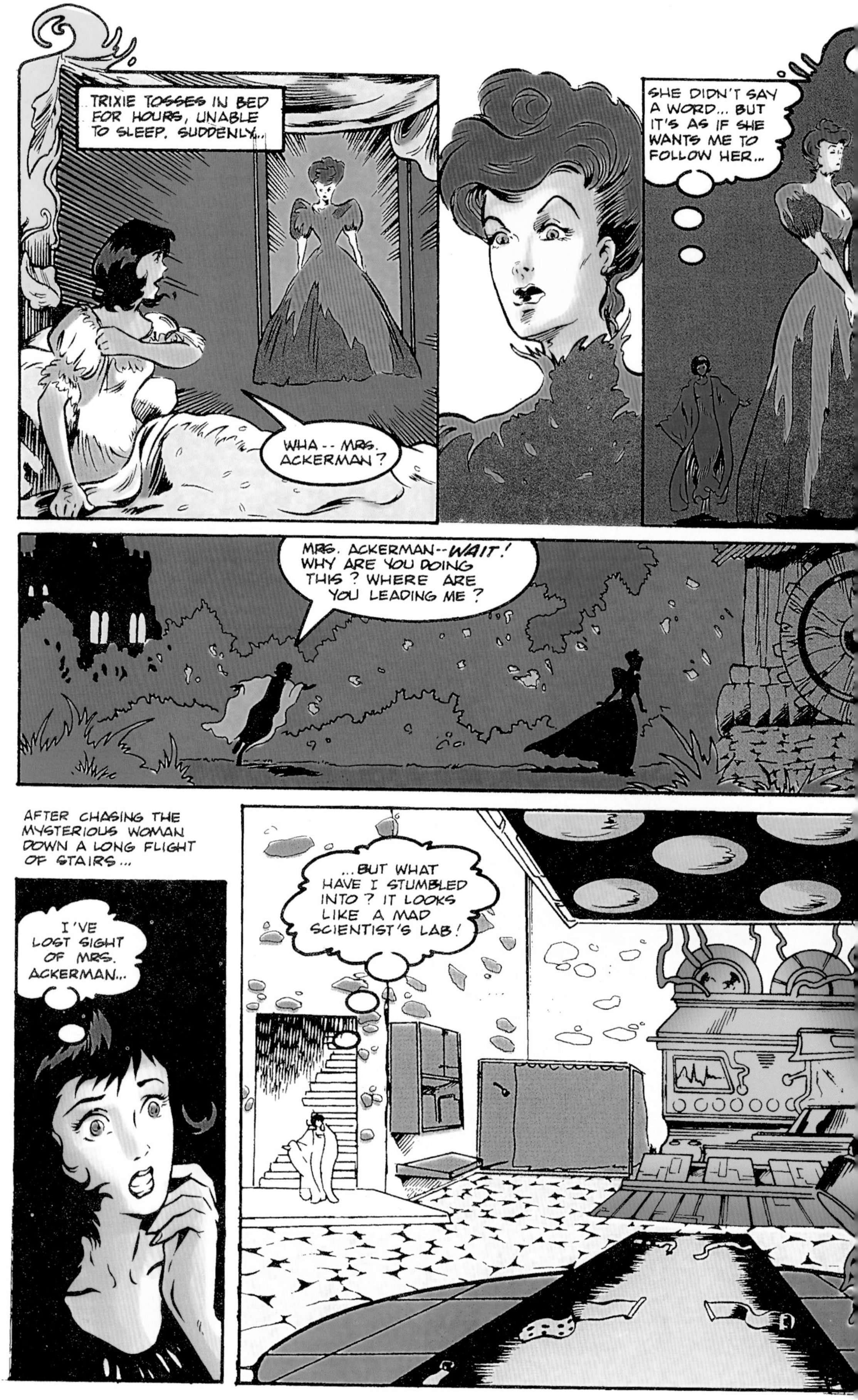

TRIXIE TOSSES IN BED FOR HOURS, UNABLE TO SLEEP. SUDDENLY...
WHA -- MRS. ACKERMAN?
SHE DIDN'T SAY A WORD... BUT IT'S AS IF SHE WANTS ME TO FOLLOW HER...
MRS. ACKERMAN--WAIT! WHY ARE YOU DOING THIS? WHERE ARE YOU LEADING ME?
AFTER CHASING THE MYSTERIOUS WOMAN DOWN A LONG FLIGHT OF STAIRS...
I'VE LOST SIGHT OF MRS. ACKERMAN...
...BUT WHAT HAVE I STUMBLED INTO? IT LOOKS LIKE A MAD SCIENTIST'S LAB!

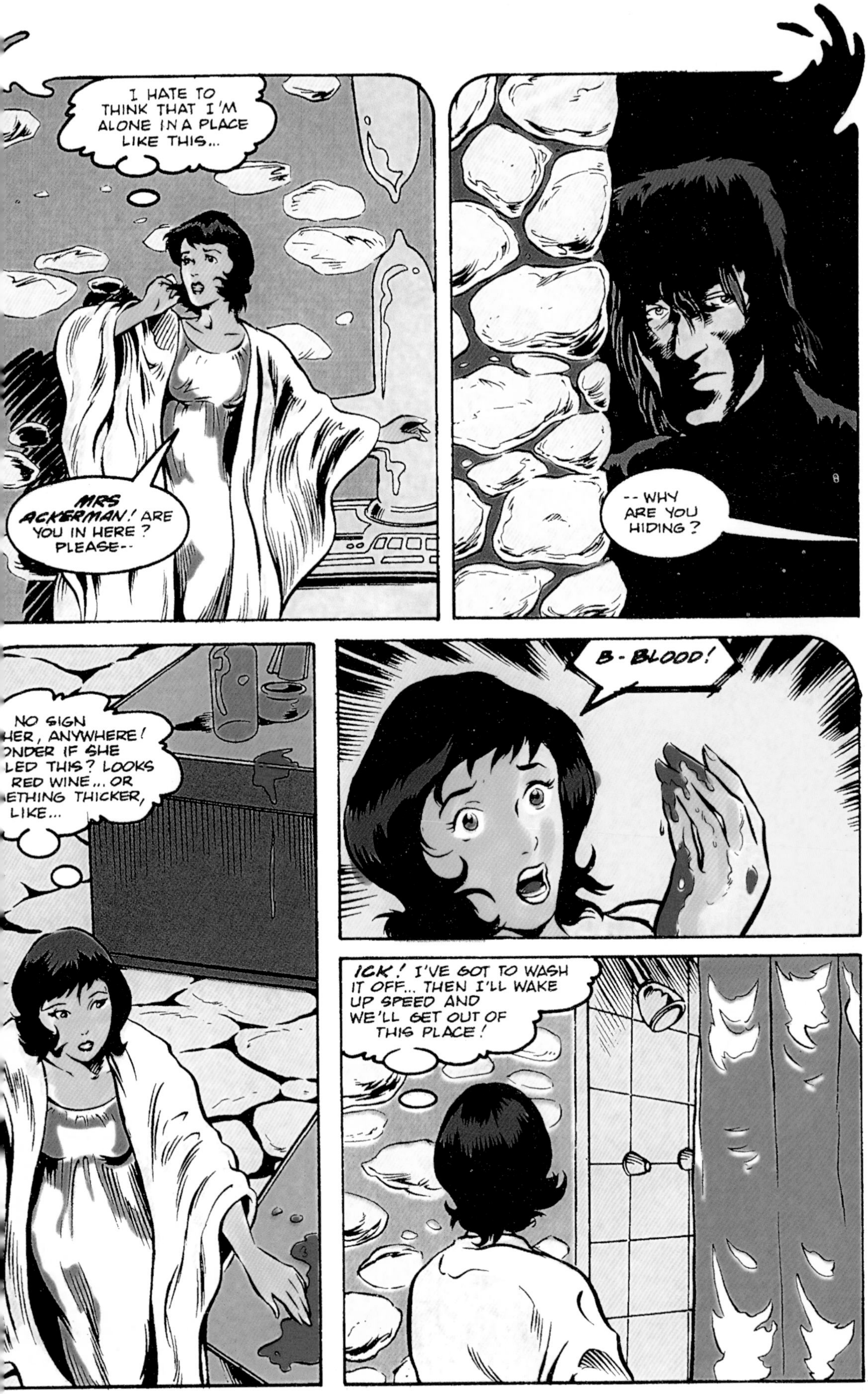

I HATE TO THINK THAT I'M ALONE IN A PLACE LIKE THIS...
MRS ACKERMAN! ARE YOU IN HERE? PLEASE--
--WHY ARE YOU HIDING?
NO SIGN HER, ANYWHERE! ONDER IF SHE LED THIS? LOOKS RED WINE... OR ETHING THICKER, LIKE...
B-BLOOD!
ICK! I'VE GOT TO WASH IT OFF... THEN I'LL WAKE UP SPEED AND WE'LL GET OUT OF THIS PLACE!

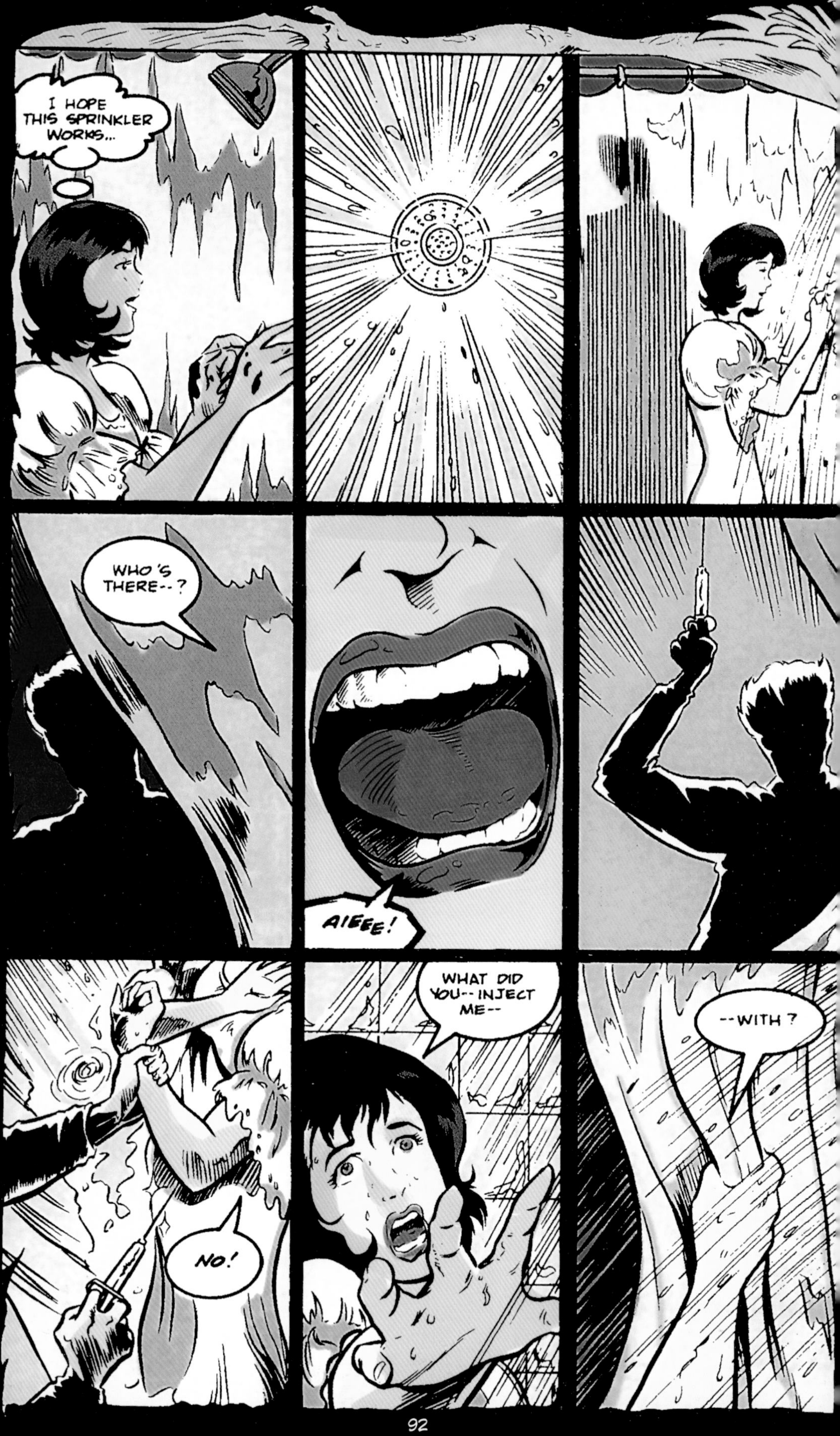
I HOPE THIS SPRINKLER WORKS...
WHO'S THERE--?
AIEEE!
NO!
WHAT DID YOU--INJECT ME--
--WITH?

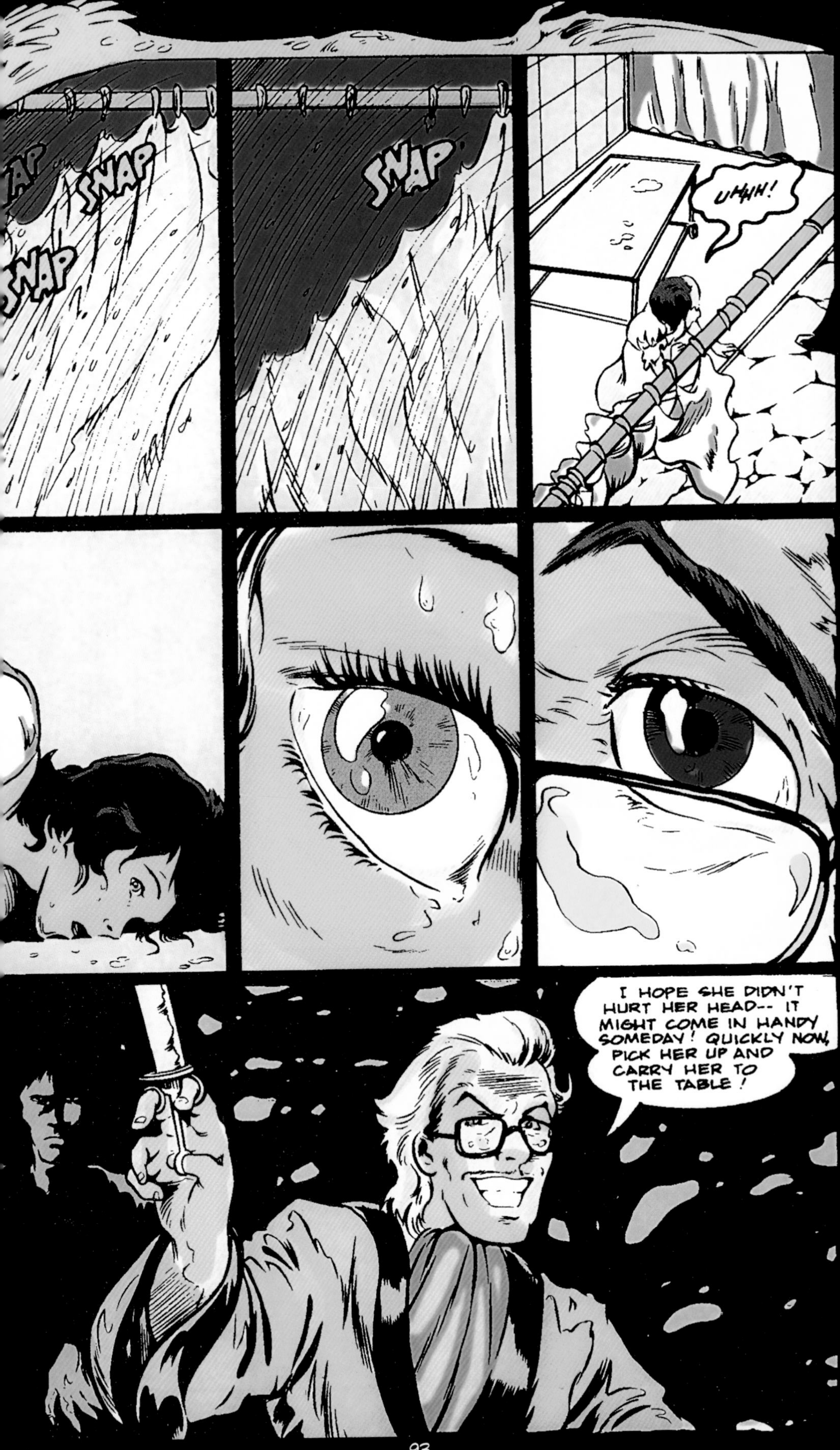
SNAP
SNAP
SNAP
UHHH!
I HOPE SHE DIDN'T HURT HER HEAD-- IT MIGHT COME IN HANDY SOMEDAY! QUICKLY NOW, PICK HER UP AND CARRY HER TO THE TABLE!

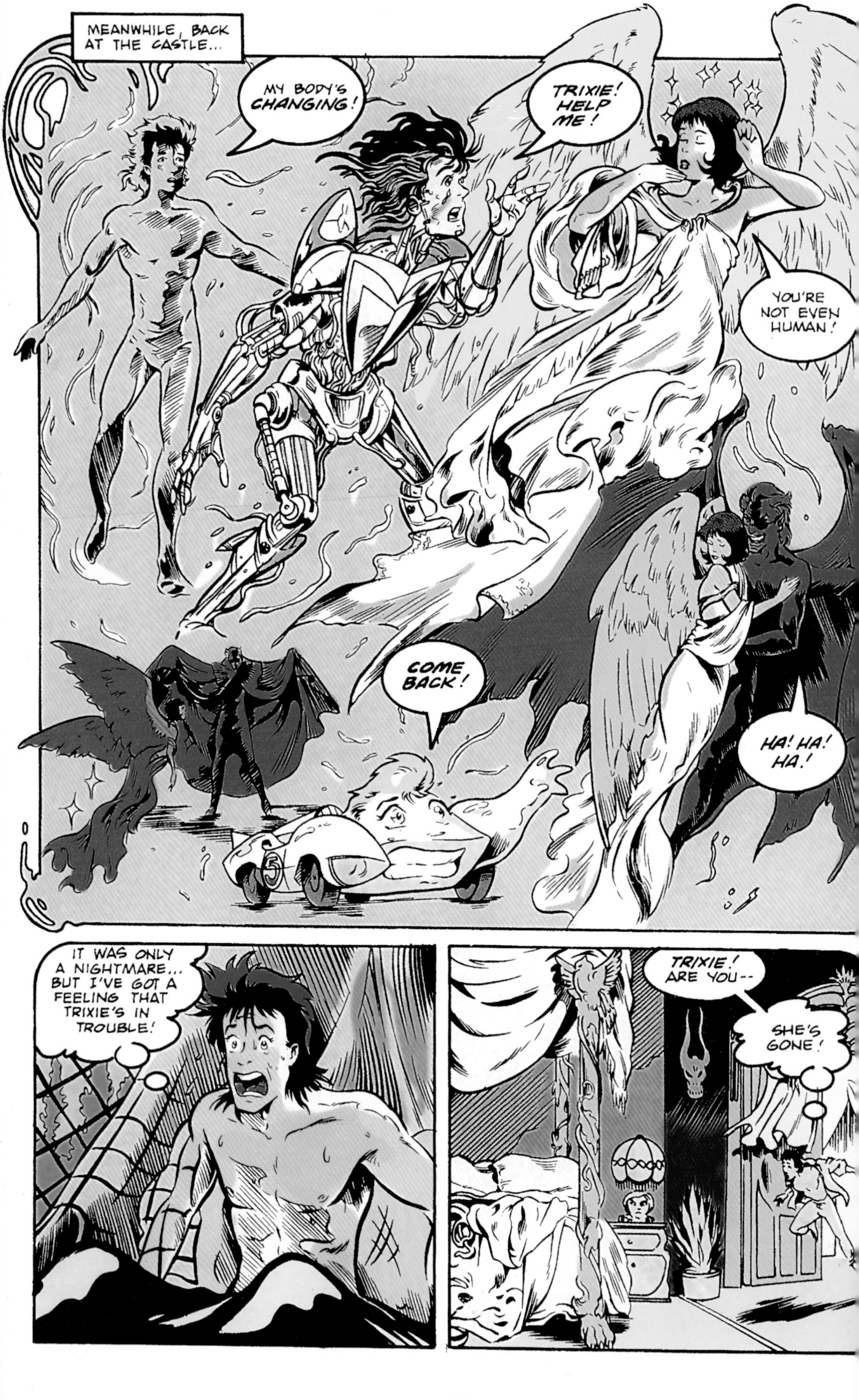
MEANWHILE, BACK AT THE CASTLE...
MY BODY'S CHANGING!
TRIXIE! HELP ME!
YOU'RE NOT EVEN HUMAN!
COME BACK!
HA! HA! HA!
IT WAS ONLY A NIGHTMARE... BUT I'VE GOT A FEELING THAT TRIXIE'S IN TROUBLE!
TRIXIE! ARE YOU--
SHE'S GONE!

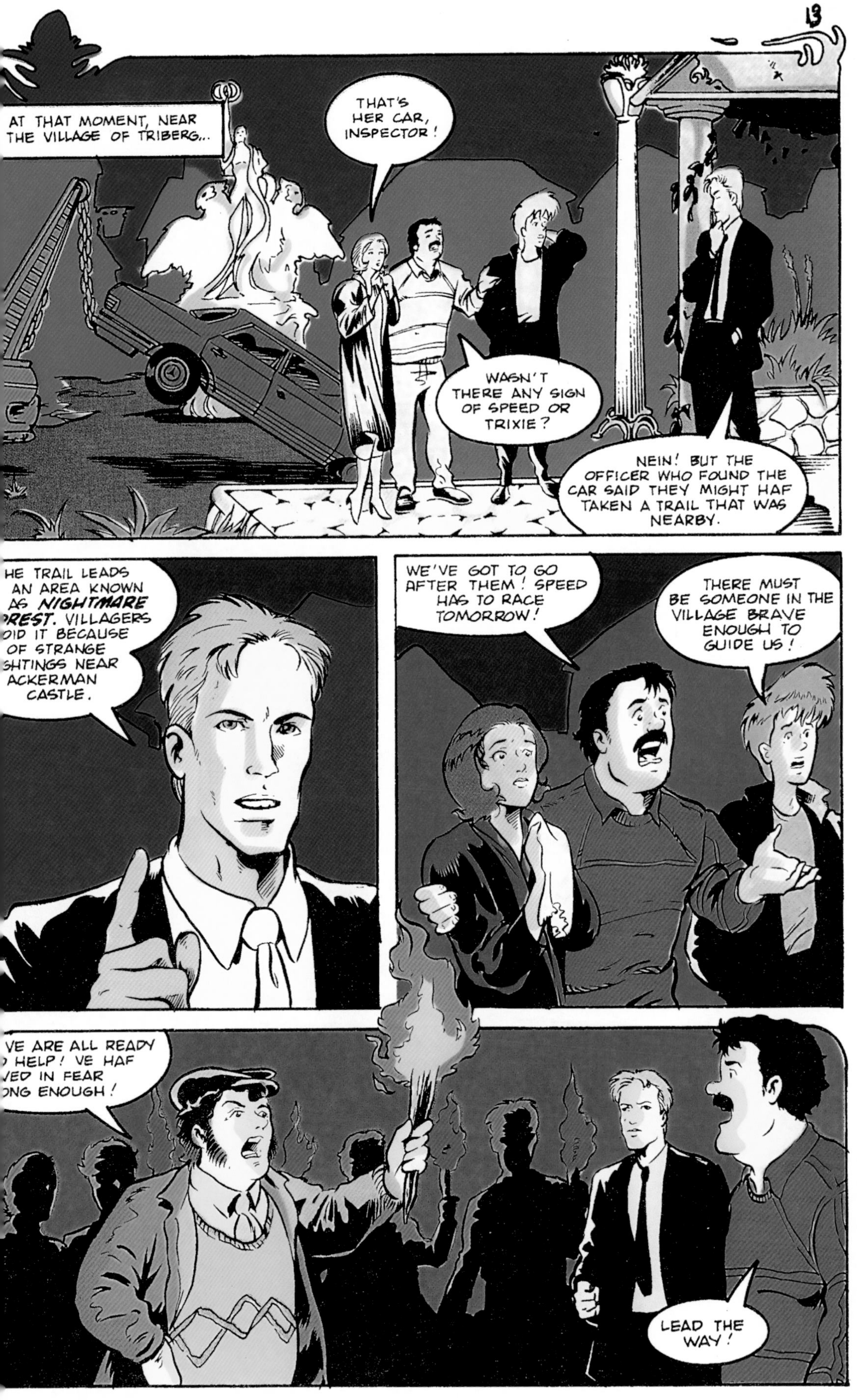

13
AT THAT MOMENT, NEAR THE VILLAGE OF TRIBERG...
THAT'S HER CAR, INSPECTOR!
WASN'T THERE ANY SIGN OF SPEED OR TRIXIE?
NEIN! BUT THE OFFICER WHO FOUND THE CAR SAID THEY MIGHT HAF TAKEN A TRAIL THAT WAS NEARBY.
HE TRAIL LEADS AN AREA KNOWN AS NIGHTMARE OREST. VILLAGERS OID IT BECAUSE OF STRANGE GHTINGS NEAR ACKERMAN CASTLE.
WE'VE GOT TO GO AFTER THEM! SPEED HAS TO RACE TOMORROW!
THERE MUST BE SOMEONE IN THE VILLAGE BRAVE ENOUGH TO GUIDE US!
VE ARE ALL READY HELP! VE HAF VED IN FEAR ONG ENOUGH!
LEAD THE WAY!

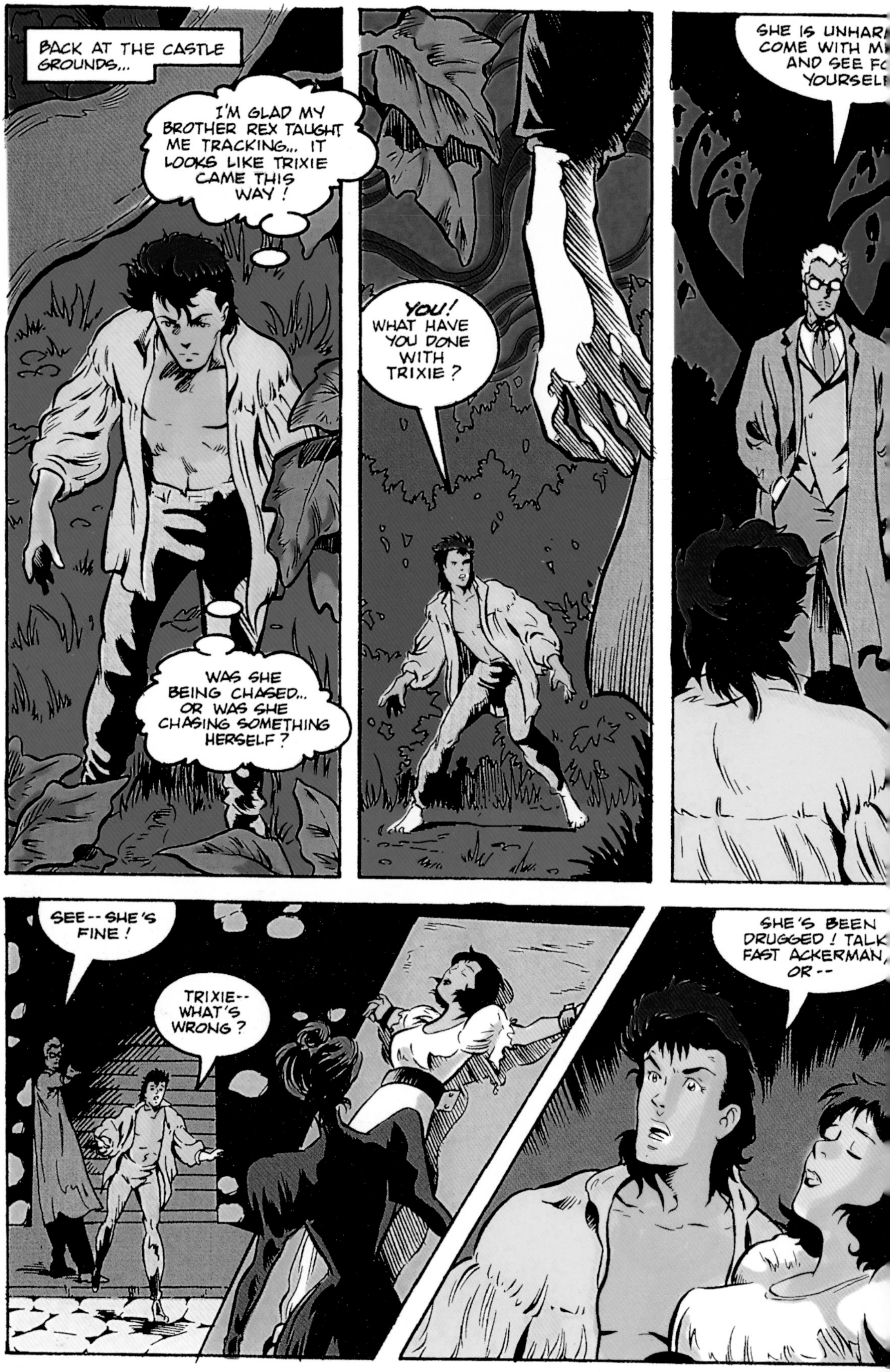
BACK AT THE CASTLE GROUNDS...
I'M GLAD MY BROTHER REX TAUGHT ME TRACKING... IT LOOKS LIKE TRIXIE CAME THIS WAY!
WAS SHE BEING CHASED... OR WAS SHE CHASING SOMETHING HERSELF?
YOU! WHAT HAVE YOU DONE WITH TRIXIE?
SHE IS UNHAR COME WITH M AND SEE F YOURSEL
SEE--SHE'S FINE!
TRIXIE--WHAT'S WRONG?
SHE'S BEEN DRUGGED! TALK FAST ACKERMAN, OR--

"--MY WIFE AND I WERE RESPECTED MEDICAL RESEARCHERS! WE HAD A FINE SON, RICHARD, WHO WANTED MORE THAN ANYTHING TO BE A RACE CAR DRIVER!"

--YOU'LL REGRET IT!

IT ALL BEGAN SEVERAL YEARS AGO. AT THAT TIME--

"BUT WHILE RICHARD AND I WERE SPEEDING DOWN THE AUTOBAHN TO HIS FIRST PROFESSIONAL RACE, OUR CAR BLEW A TIRE AND CRASHED!"

"RICHARD WAS KILLED, INSTANTLY! MY BODY WAS SHATTERED, AND I BARELY CLUNG TO LIFE!"

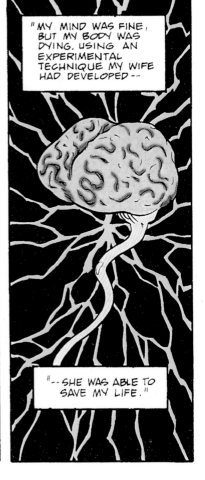

"MY MIND WAS FINE, BUT MY BODY WAS DYING. USING AN EXPERIMENTAL TECHNIQUE MY WIFE HAD DEVELOPED--

"--SHE WAS ABLE TO SAVE MY LIFE."

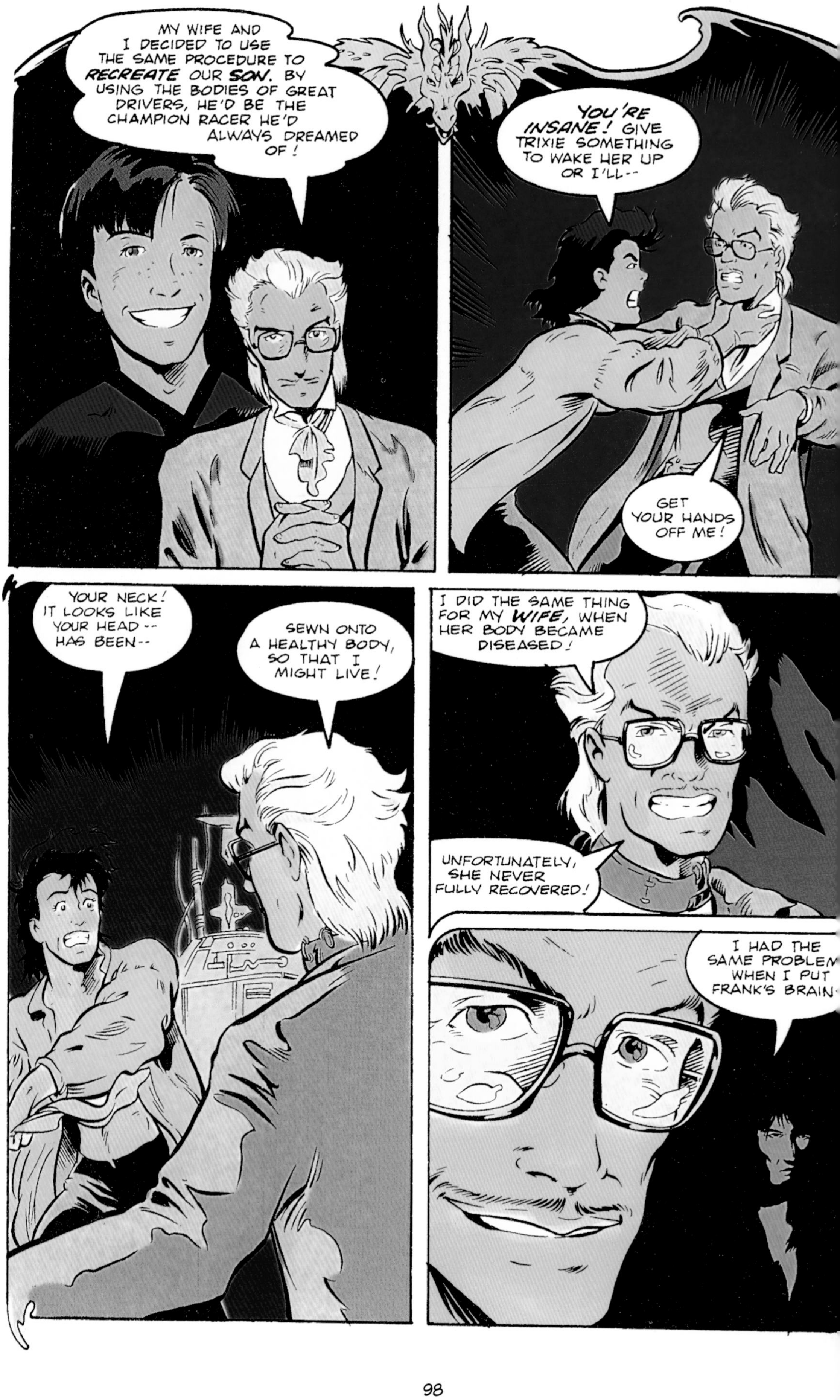
MY WIFE AND I DECIDED TO USE THE SAME PROCEDURE TO RECREATE OUR SON. BY USING THE BODIES OF GREAT DRIVERS, HE'D BE THE CHAMPION RACER HE'D ALWAYS DREAMED OF!
YOU'RE INSANE! GIVE TRIXIE SOMETHING TO WAKE HER UP OR I'LL--
GET YOUR HANDS OFF ME!
YOUR NECK! IT LOOKS LIKE YOUR HEAD-- HAS BEEN--
SEWN ONTO A HEALTHY BODY, SO THAT I MIGHT LIVE!
I DID THE SAME THING FOR MY WIFE, WHEN HER BODY BECAME DISEASED!
UNFORTUNATELY, SHE NEVER FULLY RECOVERED!
I HAD THE SAME PROBLEM WHEN I PUT FRANK'S BRAIN

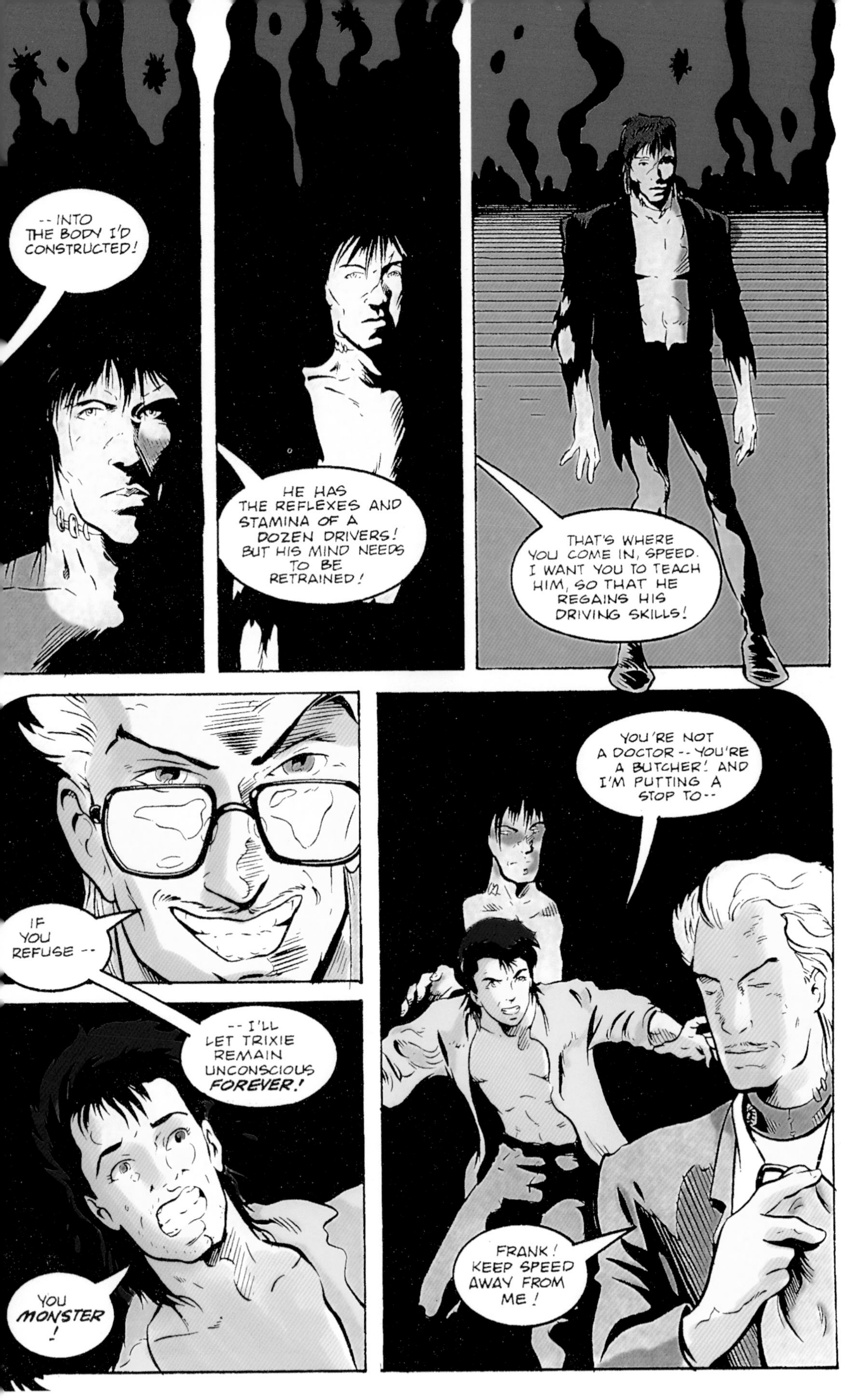
-- INTO THE BODY I'D CONSTRUCTED!
HE HAS THE REFLEXES AND STAMINA OF A DOZEN DRIVERS! BUT HIS MIND NEEDS TO BE RETRAINED!
THAT'S WHERE YOU COME IN, SPEED. I WANT YOU TO TEACH HIM, SO THAT HE REGAINS HIS DRIVING SKILLS!
IF YOU REFUSE --
-- I'LL LET TRIXIE REMAIN UNCONSCIOUS **FOREVER!**
YOU **MONSTER** !
YOU'RE NOT A DOCTOR -- YOU'RE A BUTCHER! AND I'M PUTTING A STOP TO --
FRANK! KEEP SPEED AWAY FROM ME!

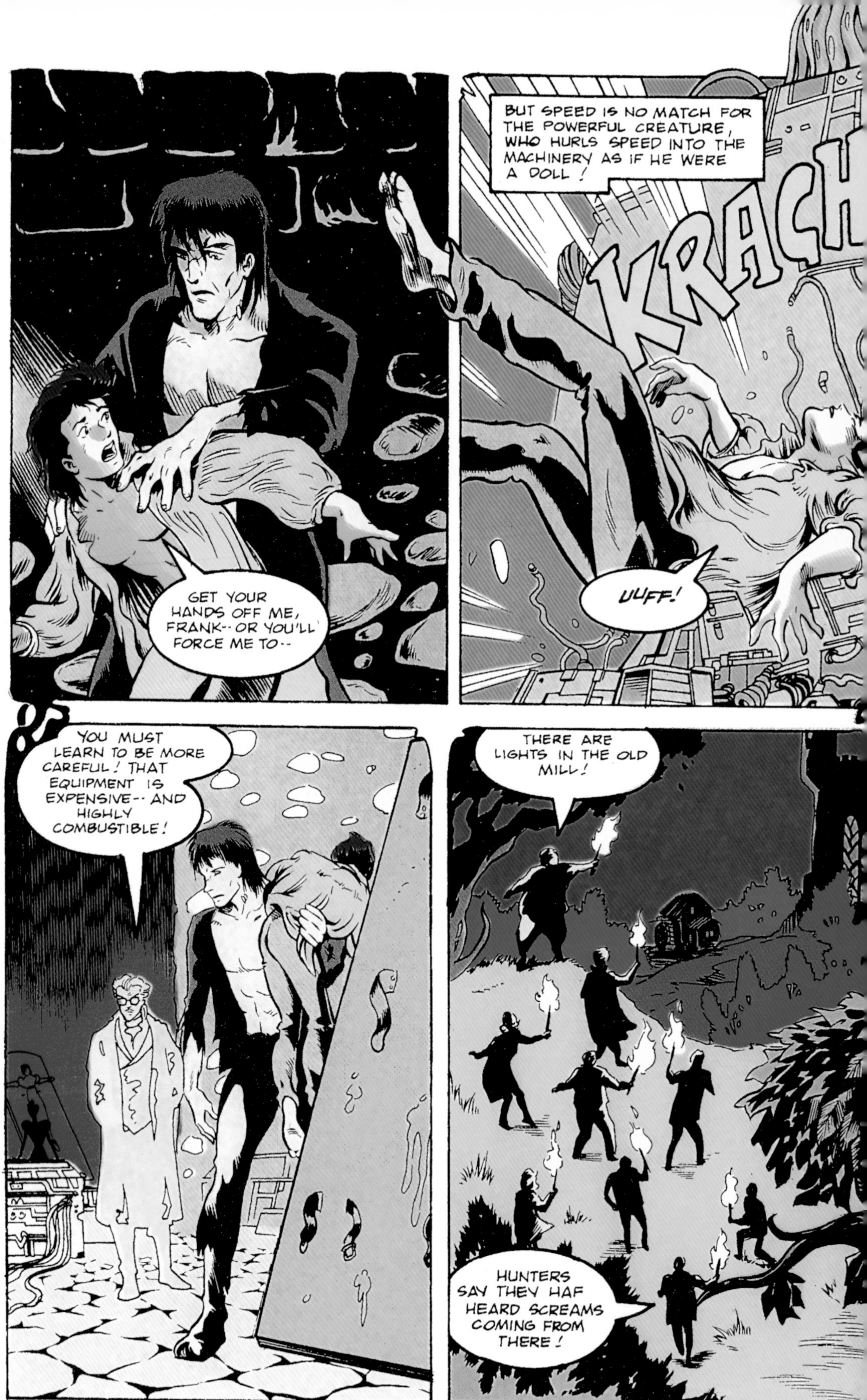
GET YOUR HANDS OFF ME, FRANK-- OR YOU'LL FORCE ME TO--
BUT SPEED IS NO MATCH FOR THE POWERFUL CREATURE, WHO HURLS SPEED INTO THE MACHINERY AS IF HE WERE A DOLL!
KRACH
UUFF!
YOU MUST LEARN TO BE MORE CAREFUL! THAT EQUIPMENT IS EXPENSIVE-- AND HIGHLY COMBUSTIBLE!
THERE ARE LIGHTS IN THE OLD MILL!
HUNTERS SAY THEY HAF HEARD SCREAMS COMING FROM THERE!

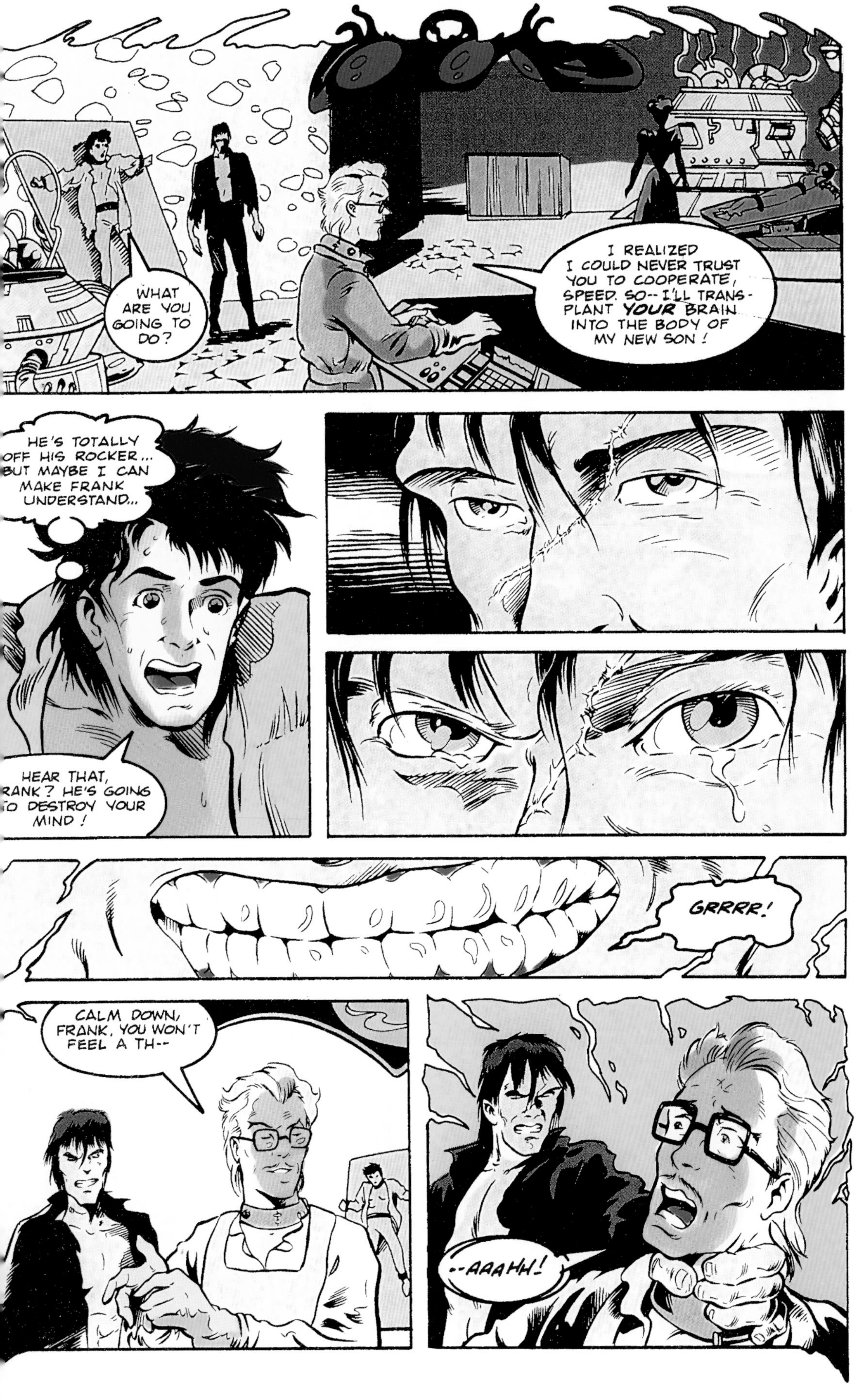
WHAT ARE YOU GOING TO DO?
I REALIZED I COULD NEVER TRUST YOU TO COOPERATE, SPEED. SO-- I'LL TRANS-PLANT YOUR BRAIN INTO THE BODY OF MY NEW SON!
HE'S TOTALLY OFF HIS ROCKER... BUT MAYBE I CAN MAKE FRANK UNDERSTAND...
HEAR THAT, FRANK? HE'S GOING TO DESTROY YOUR MIND!
GRRRR!
CALM DOWN, FRANK, YOU WON'T FEEL A TH--
--AAAHH!

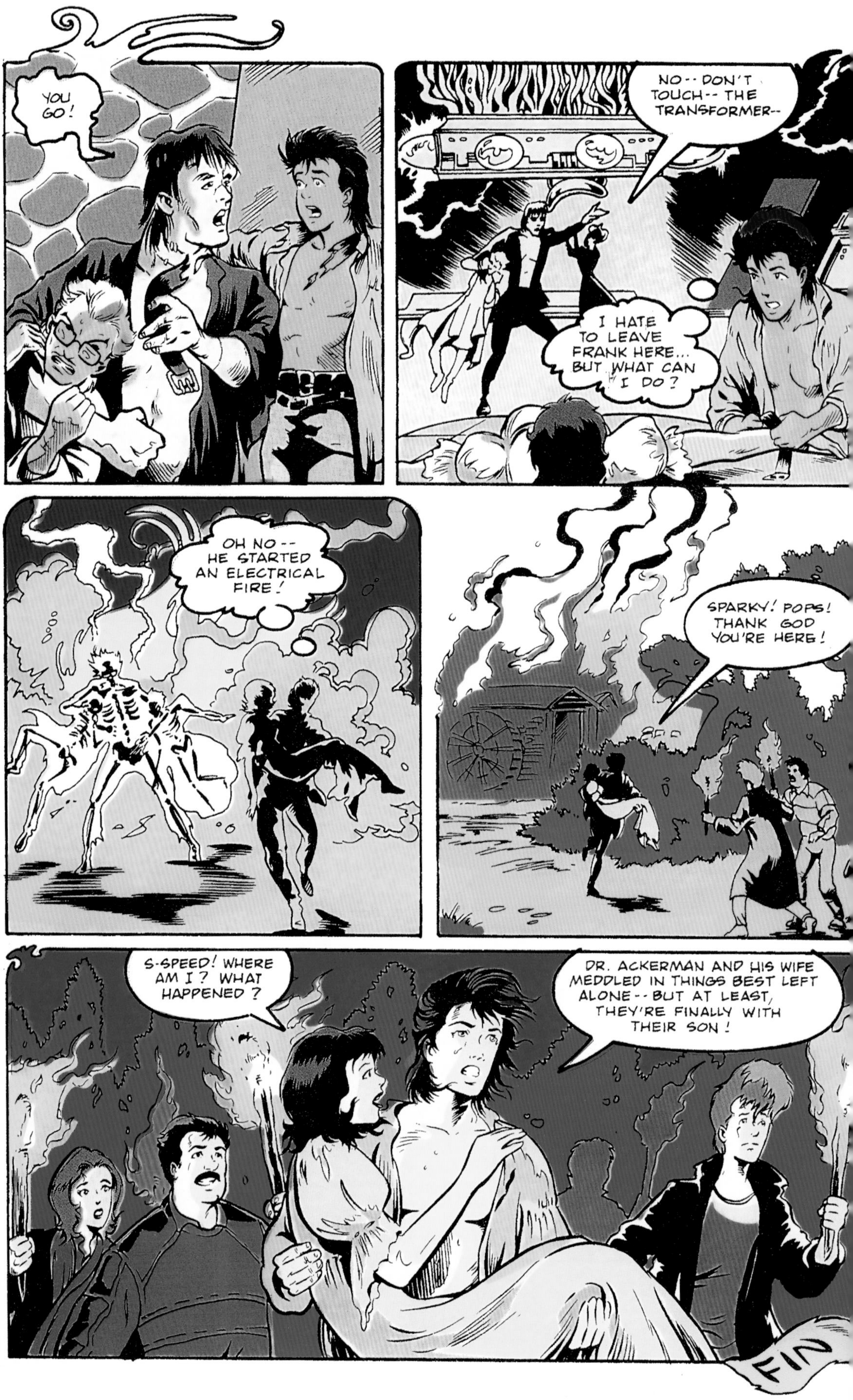
YOU GO!
NO--DON'T TOUCH--THE TRANSFORMER--
I HATE TO LEAVE FRANK HERE... BUT WHAT CAN I DO?
OH NO--HE STARTED AN ELECTRICAL FIRE!
SPARKY! POPS! THANK GOD YOU'RE HERE!
S-SPEED! WHERE AM I? WHAT HAPPENED?
DR. ACKERMAN AND HIS WIFE MEDDLED IN THINGS BEST LEFT ALONE--BUT AT LEAST, THEY'RE FINALLY WITH THEIR SON!
FIN

Speed Racer #18

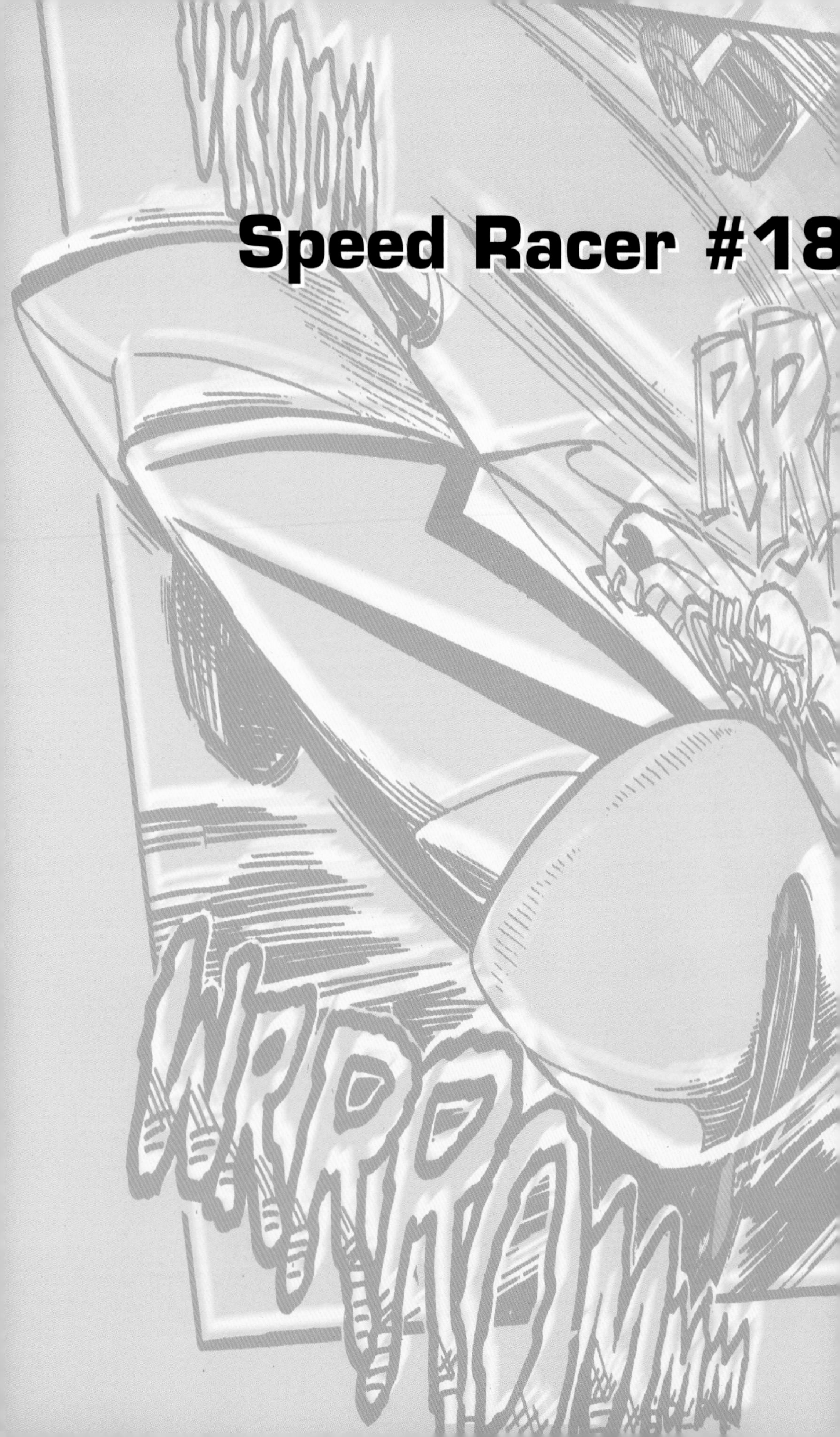

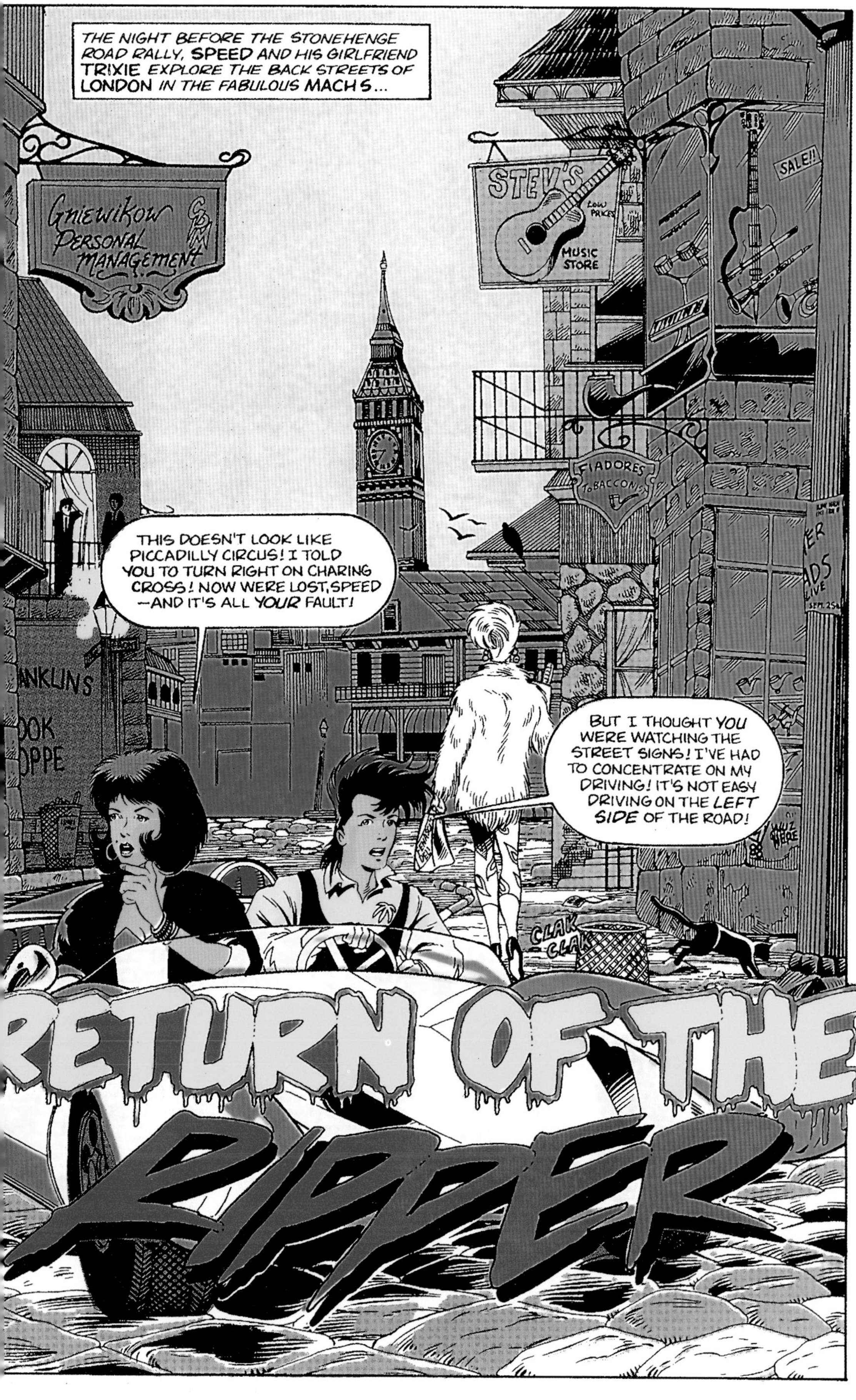
THE NIGHT BEFORE THE STONEHENGE ROAD RALLY, SPEED AND HIS GIRLFRIEND TRIXIE EXPLORE THE BACK STREETS OF LONDON IN THE FABULOUS MACH 5...
Gniewikow Personal Management
GPM
STEV'S
LOW PRICES
MUSIC STORE
SALE!!
FIADORES TOBACCONIST
THIS DOESN'T LOOK LIKE PICCADILLY CIRCUS! I TOLD YOU TO TURN RIGHT ON CHARING CROSS! NOW WERE LOST, SPEED --AND IT'S ALL YOUR FAULT!
BUT I THOUGHT YOU WERE WATCHING THE STREET SIGNS! I'VE HAD TO CONCENTRATE ON MY DRIVING! IT'S NOT EASY DRIVING ON THE LEFT SIDE OF THE ROAD!
CLAK CLAK
RETURN OF THE RIPPER

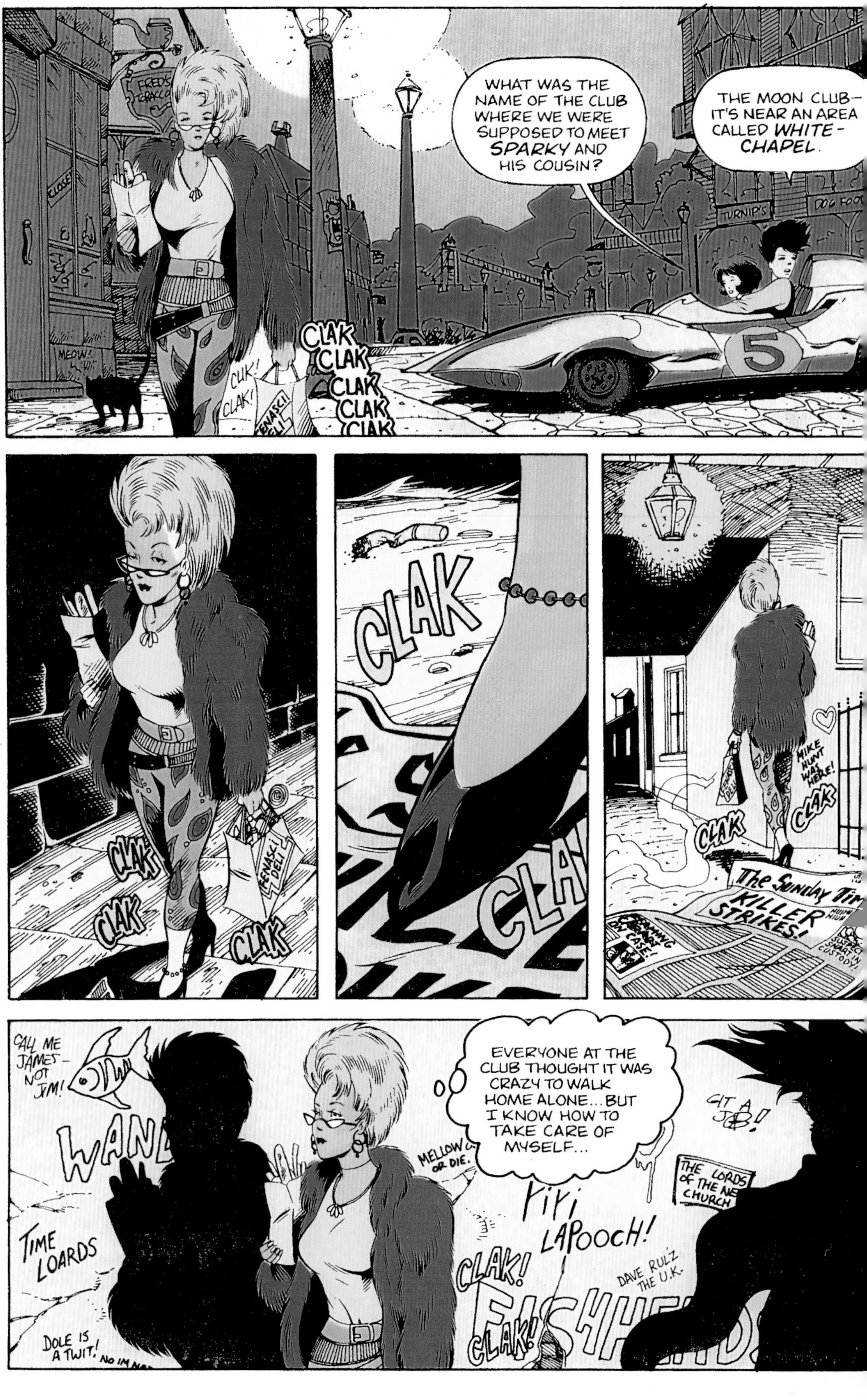
FRED'S TOBACCO
CLOSED
MEOW
WHAT WAS THE NAME OF THE CLUB WHERE WE WERE SUPPOSED TO MEET SPARKY AND HIS COUSIN?
THE MOON CLUB— IT'S NEAR AN AREA CALLED WHITE-CHAPEL.
TURNIP'S
DOG FOOD
CUK! CLAK!
CLAK CLAK CLAK CLAK CLAK
5
CLAK
CLAK
CLAK
CLAK
CLAK
MIKE HUNT WAS HERE!
CLAK
CLAK
The Sunday Tim
KILLER STRIKES!
CALL ME JAMES— NOT JIM!
WAN
TIME LOARDS
DOLE IS A TWIT!
MELLOW OR DIE.
EVERYONE AT THE CLUB THOUGHT IT WAS CRAZY TO WALK HOME ALONE... BUT I KNOW HOW TO TAKE CARE OF MYSELF...
GIT A JOB!
THE LORDS OF THE NE CHURCH
YIPI LAPOOCH!
CLAK!
CLAK!
DAVE RULZ THE U.K.

CLUMP CLUMP

SOUNDS LIKE I'M NOT ALONE... BUT IT'S PROBABLY JUST SOME BLOKE THAT'S HEADIN' HOME AFTER A HARD NIGHT AT THE PUB...

CLAK CLAK CLAK

CLUMP CLUM CLUMP!

WHOEVER IT IS, THEY'RE GETTING CLOSER! I'LL DUCK DOWN THAT ALLEY...

MIKE D. IS COOL!

OHN KIKI D.

DON'T TREAD ON ME?

J.D. ♥ L.F.

CLAK CLAK

...AND WAIT TILL THEY PASS!

CLACK CLACK CLACK CLACK CL

OT OT

I DON'T HEAR 'IM ANYMORE... GUESS I WAS GETTIN' WORKED UP OVER NOTHIN'...

NICK WAS HER

RODINO RULE

XMS

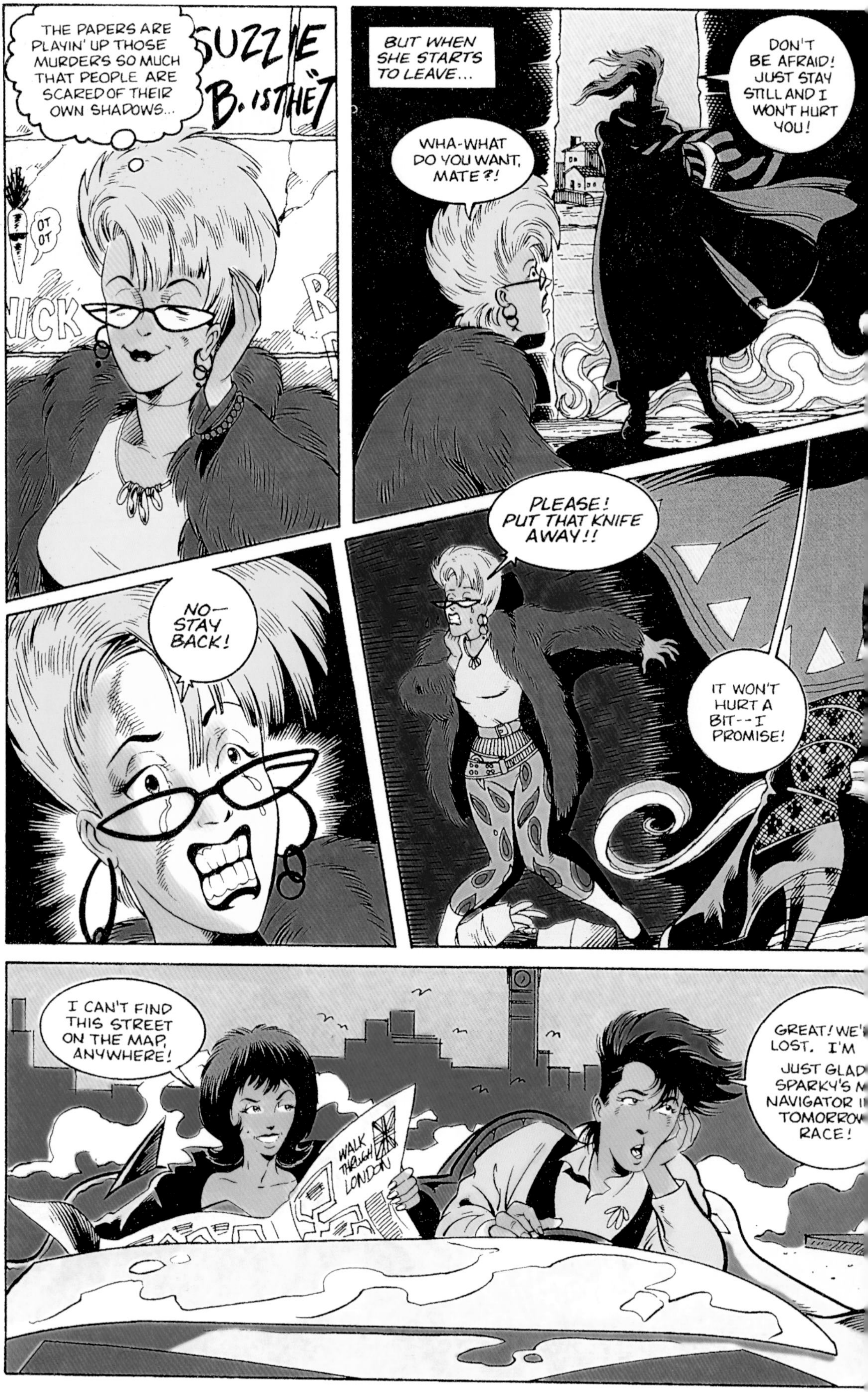
THE PAPERS ARE PLAYIN' UP THOSE MURDERS SO MUCH THAT PEOPLE ARE SCARED OF THEIR OWN SHADOWS...
BUT WHEN SHE STARTS TO LEAVE...
WHA-WHAT DO YOU WANT, MATE?!
DON'T BE AFRAID! JUST STAY STILL AND I WON'T HURT YOU!
PLEASE! PUT THAT KNIFE AWAY!!
NO-- STAY BACK!
IT WON'T HURT A BIT--I PROMISE!
I CAN'T FIND THIS STREET ON THE MAP, ANYWHERE!
WALK THROUGH LONDON

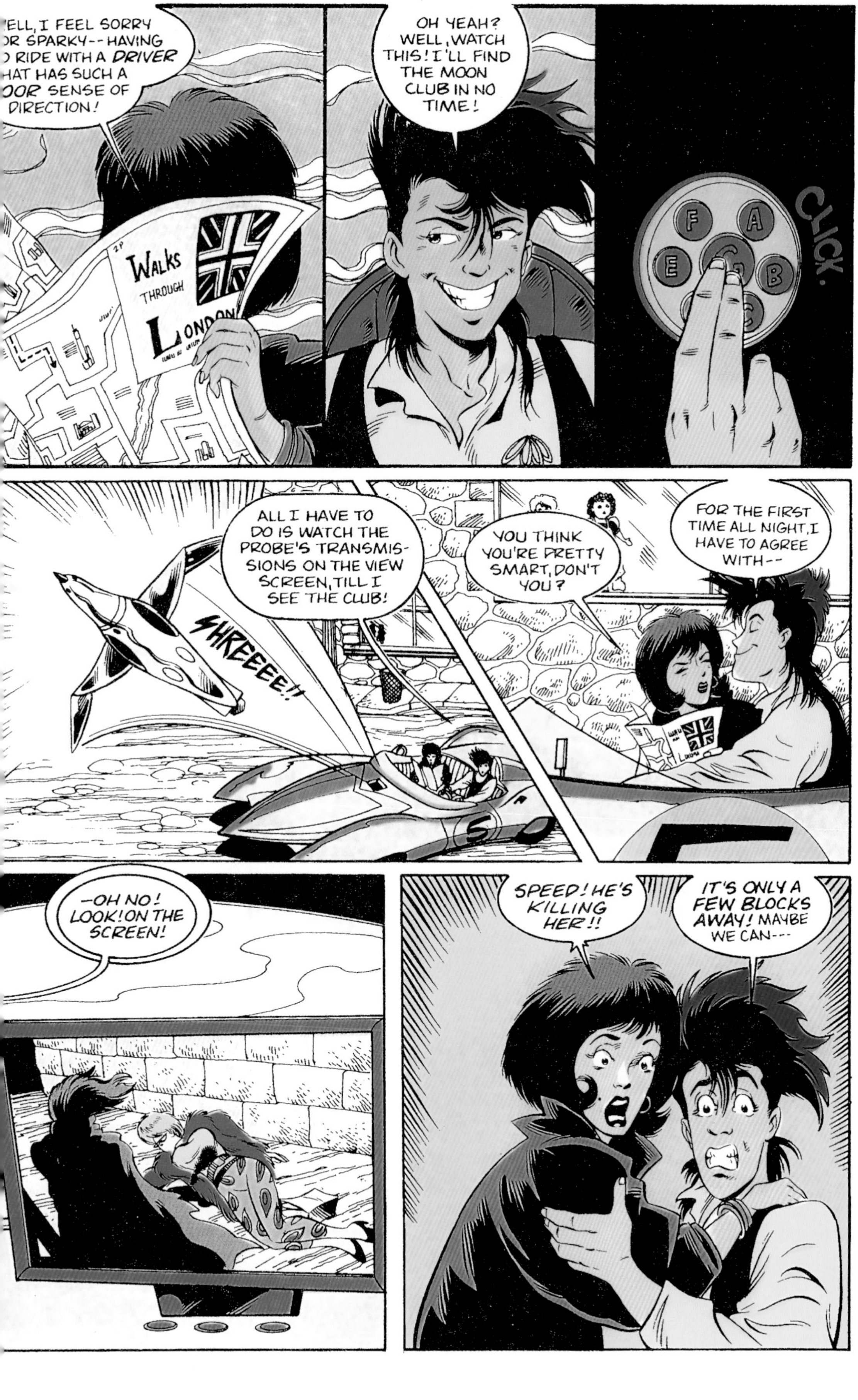
ELL, I FEEL SORRY
OR SPARKY--HAVING
O RIDE WITH A DRIVER
HAT HAS SUCH A
OOR SENSE OF
DIRECTION!
WALKS THROUGH LONDON
OH YEAH? WELL, WATCH THIS! I'LL FIND THE MOON CLUB IN NO TIME!
CLICK.
ALL I HAVE TO DO IS WATCH THE PROBE'S TRANSMISSIONS ON THE VIEW SCREEN, TILL I SEE THE CLUB!
SHREEEEE!!
YOU THINK YOU'RE PRETTY SMART, DON'T YOU?
FOR THE FIRST TIME ALL NIGHT, I HAVE TO AGREE WITH--
-OH NO! LOOK! ON THE SCREEN!
SPEED! HE'S KILLING HER!!
IT'S ONLY A FEW BLOCKS AWAY! MAYBE WE CAN---

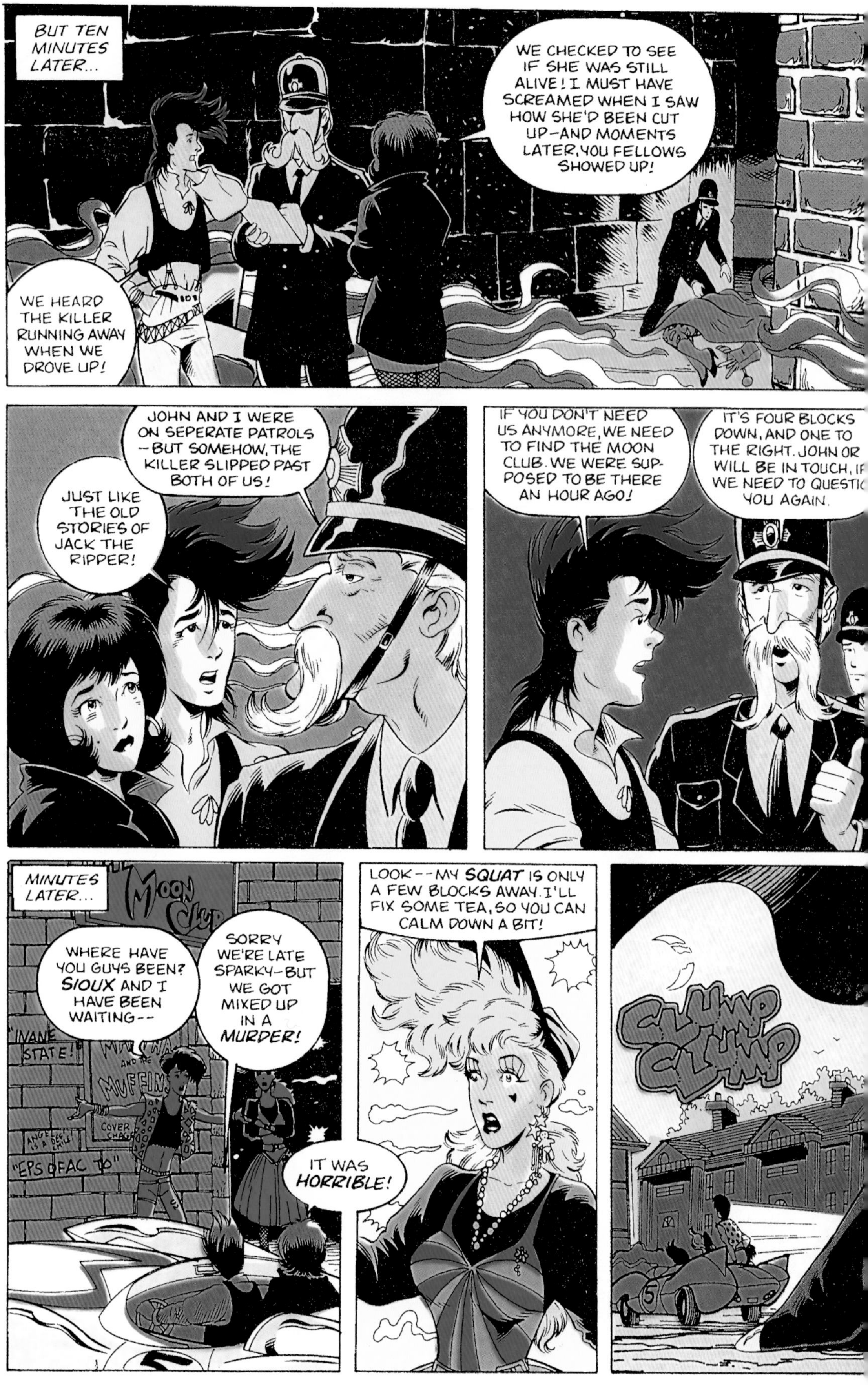
BUT TEN MINUTES LATER...
WE CHECKED TO SEE IF SHE WAS STILL ALIVE! I MUST HAVE SCREAMED WHEN I SAW HOW SHE'D BEEN CUT UP--AND MOMENTS LATER, YOU FELLOWS SHOWED UP!
WE HEARD THE KILLER RUNNING AWAY WHEN WE DROVE UP!
JOHN AND I WERE ON SEPERATE PATROLS --BUT SOMEHOW, THE KILLER SLIPPED PAST BOTH OF US!
JUST LIKE THE OLD STORIES OF JACK THE RIPPER!
IF YOU DON'T NEED US ANYMORE, WE NEED TO FIND THE MOON CLUB. WE WERE SUPPOSED TO BE THERE AN HOUR AGO!
IT'S FOUR BLOCKS DOWN, AND ONE TO THE RIGHT. JOHN OR WILL BE IN TOUCH, IF WE NEED TO QUESTIC YOU AGAIN.
MINUTES LATER...
MOON CLUB
WHERE HAVE YOU GUYS BEEN? SIOUX AND I HAVE BEEN WAITING--
SORRY WE'RE LATE SPARKY--BUT WE GOT MIXED UP IN A MURDER!
IT WAS HORRIBLE!
"INANE STATE!
MUFFINS
COVER CHARGE
"EPS OFAC TO"
LOOK--MY SQUAT IS ONLY A FEW BLOCKS AWAY. I'LL FIX SOME TEA, SO YOU CAN CALM DOWN A BIT!
CLUMP CLUMP

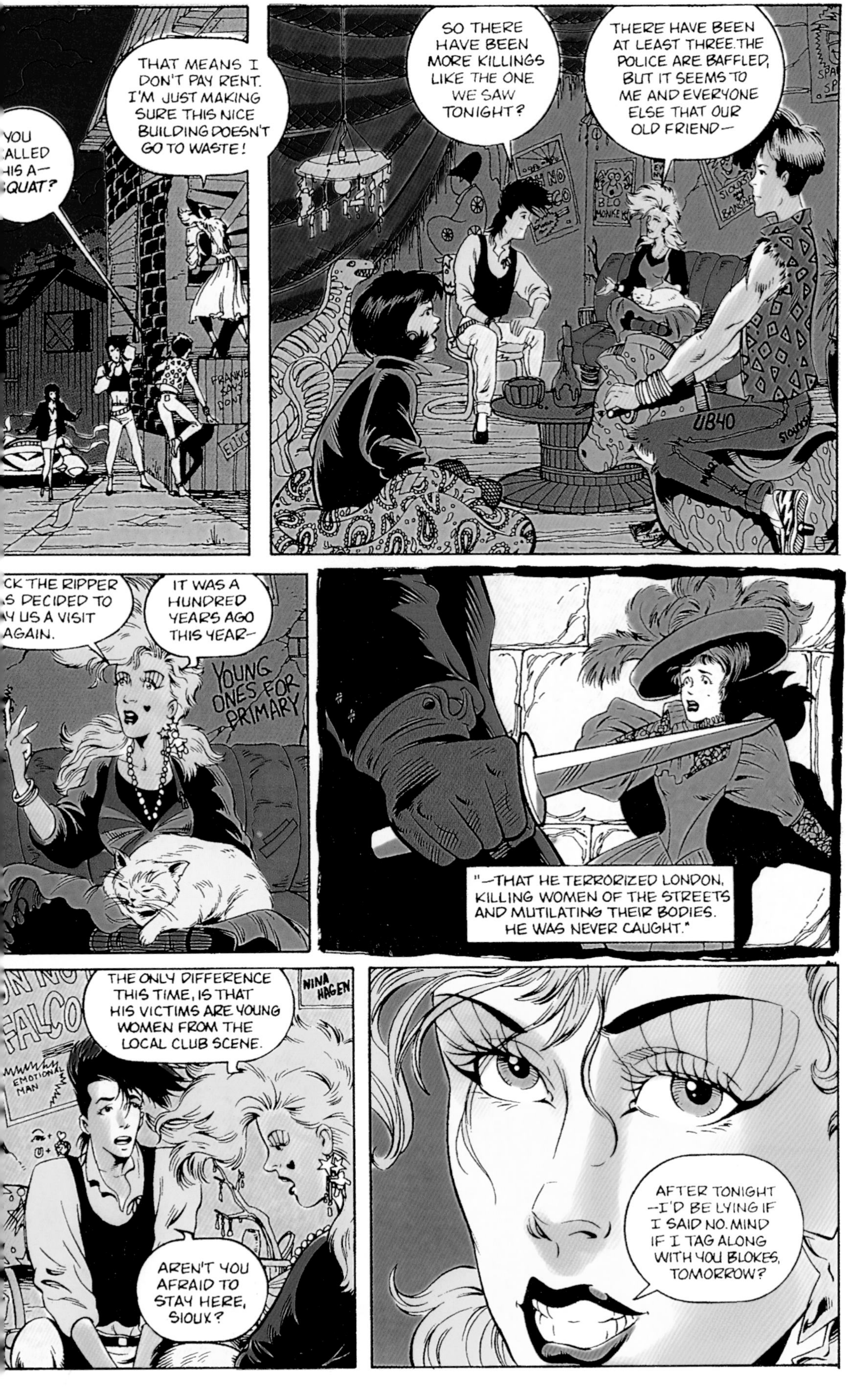
YOU
ALLED
HIS A–
QUAT?
THAT MEANS I DON'T PAY RENT. I'M JUST MAKING SURE THIS NICE BUILDING DOESN'T GO TO WASTE!
FRANKIE SAYS DON'T
SO THERE HAVE BEEN MORE KILLINGS LIKE THE ONE WE SAW TONIGHT?
THERE HAVE BEEN AT LEAST THREE. THE POLICE ARE BAFFLED, BUT IT SEEMS TO ME AND EVERYONE ELSE THAT OUR OLD FRIEND—
UB40
CK THE RIPPER
S DECIDED TO
Y US A VISIT
AGAIN.
IT WAS A HUNDRED YEARS AGO THIS YEAR—
YOUNG ONES FOR PRIMARY
"—THAT HE TERRORIZED LONDON, KILLING WOMEN OF THE STREETS AND MUTILATING THEIR BODIES. HE WAS NEVER CAUGHT."
THE ONLY DIFFERENCE THIS TIME, IS THAT HIS VICTIMS ARE YOUNG WOMEN FROM THE LOCAL CLUB SCENE.
NINA HAGEN
EMOTIONAL MAN
AREN'T YOU AFRAID TO STAY HERE, SIOUX?
AFTER TONIGHT —I'D BE LYING IF I SAID NO. MIND IF I TAG ALONG WITH YOU BLOKES, TOMORROW?

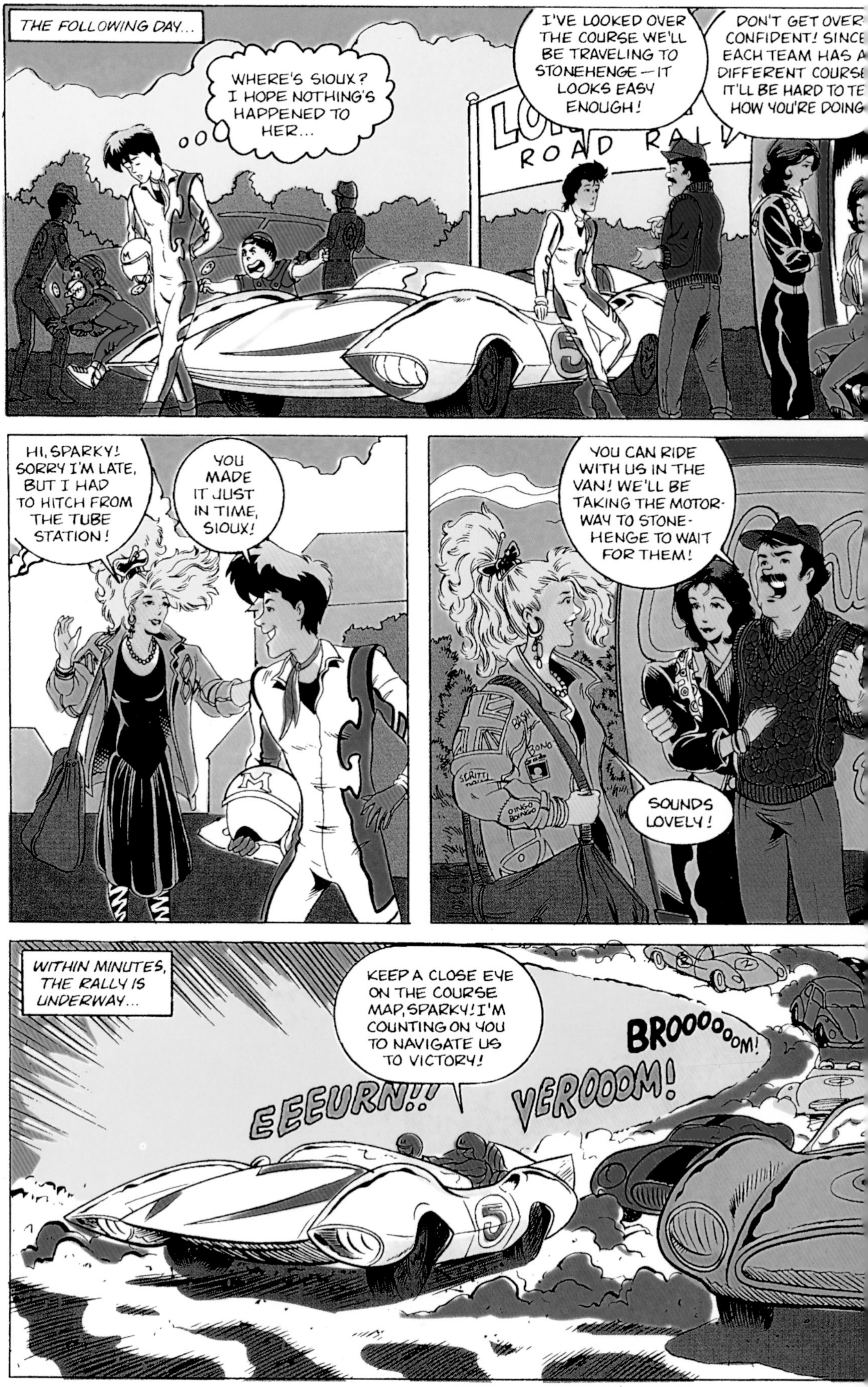
THE FOLLOWING DAY...
WHERE'S SIOUX? I HOPE NOTHING'S HAPPENED TO HER...
I'VE LOOKED OVER THE COURSE WE'LL BE TRAVELING TO STONEHENGE — IT LOOKS EASY ENOUGH!
DON'T GET OVER- CONFIDENT! SINC EACH TEAM HAS A DIFFERENT COURS IT'LL BE HARD TO TE HOW YOU'RE DOING
ROAD
HI, SPARKY! SORRY I'M LATE, BUT I HAD TO HITCH FROM THE TUBE STATION!
YOU MADE IT JUST IN TIME, SIOUX!
YOU CAN RIDE WITH US IN THE VAN! WE'LL BE TAKING THE MOTOR-WAY TO STONE-HENGE TO WAIT FOR THEM!
SOUNDS LOVELY!
WITHIN MINUTES, THE RALLY IS UNDERWAY...
KEEP A CLOSE EYE ON THE COURSE MAP, SPARKY! I'M COUNTING ON YOU TO NAVIGATE US TO VICTORY!
BROOOoooOM!
EEEURN!!
VEROOOM!

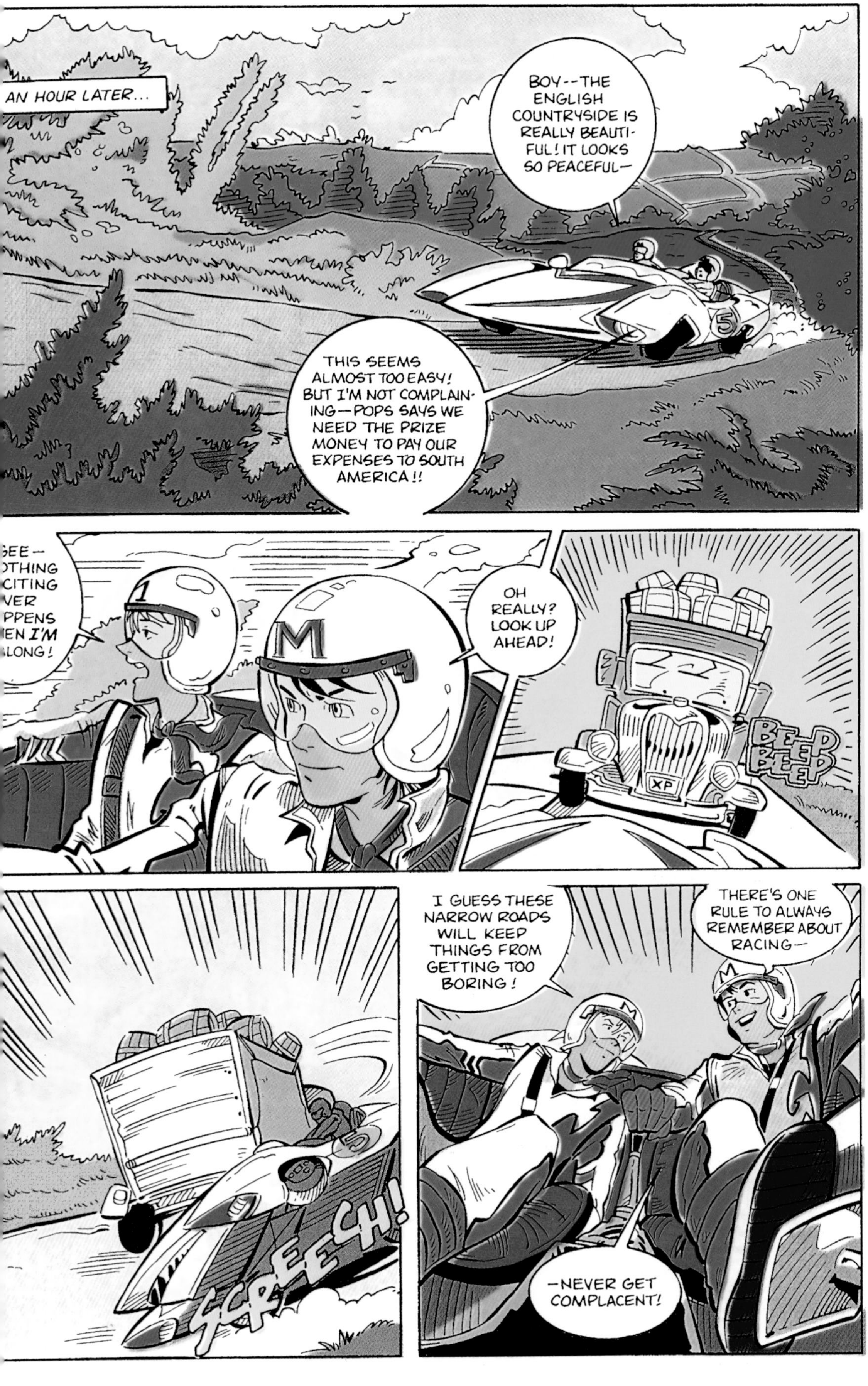
AN HOUR LATER...
BOY--THE ENGLISH COUNTRYSIDE IS REALLY BEAUTIFUL! IT LOOKS SO PEACEFUL—
THIS SEEMS ALMOST TOO EASY! BUT I'M NOT COMPLAINING—POPS SAYS WE NEED THE PRIZE MONEY TO PAY OUR EXPENSES TO SOUTH AMERICA!!
OH REALLY? LOOK UP AHEAD!
BEEP BEEP
XP
SCREECH!
I GUESS THESE NARROW ROADS WILL KEEP THINGS FROM GETTING TOO BORING!
THERE'S ONE RULE TO ALWAYS REMEMBER ABOUT RACING—
—NEVER GET COMPLACENT!

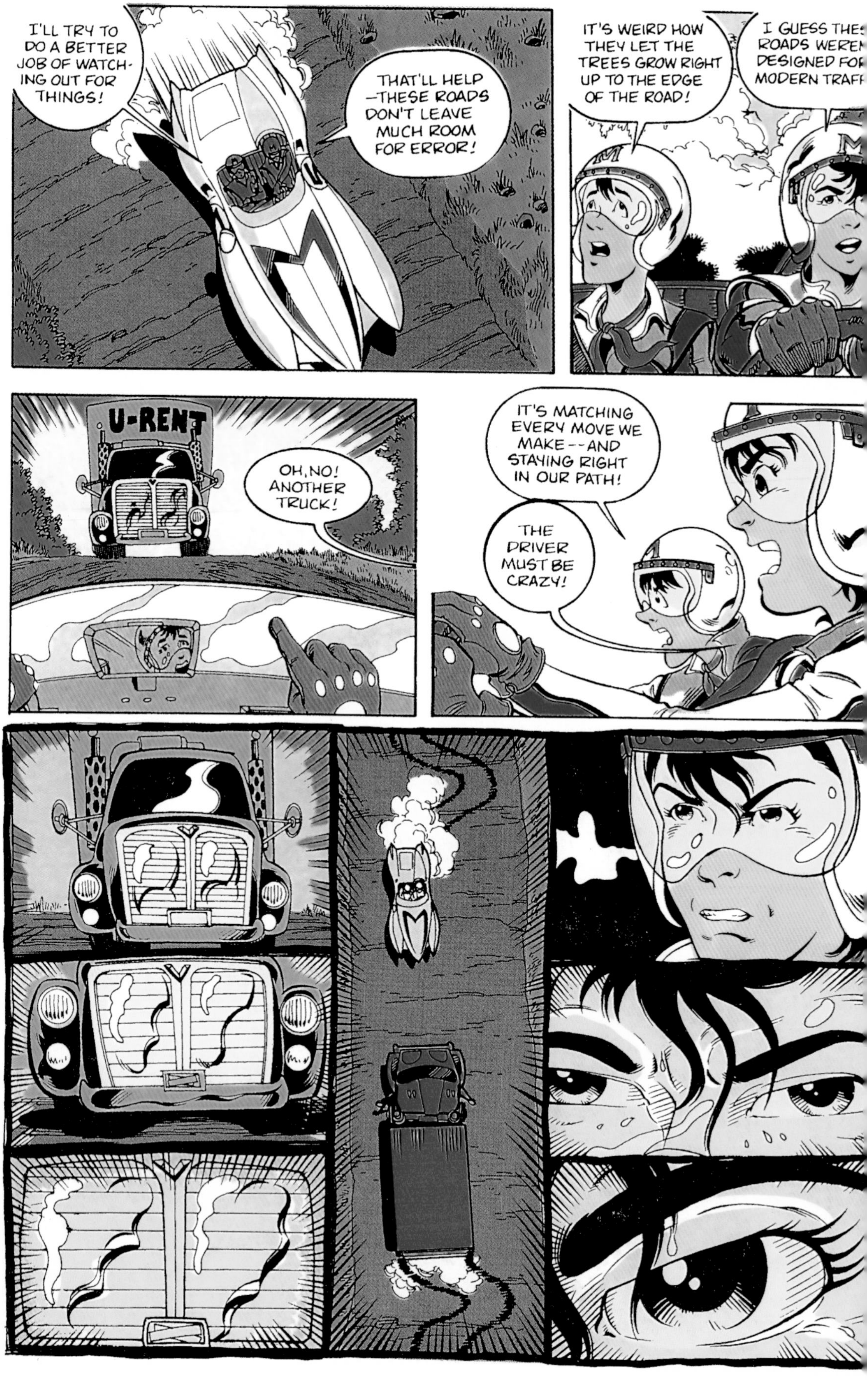

I'LL TRY TO DO A BETTER JOB OF WATCHING OUT FOR THINGS!
THAT'LL HELP —THESE ROADS DON'T LEAVE MUCH ROOM FOR ERROR!
IT'S WEIRD HOW THEY LET THE TREES GROW RIGHT UP TO THE EDGE OF THE ROAD!
I GUESS THES ROADS WEREN DESIGNED FOR MODERN TRAFF
U-RENT
OH, NO! ANOTHER TRUCK!
IT'S MATCHING EVERY MOVE WE MAKE--AND STAYING RIGHT IN OUR PATH!
THE DRIVER MUST BE CRAZY!

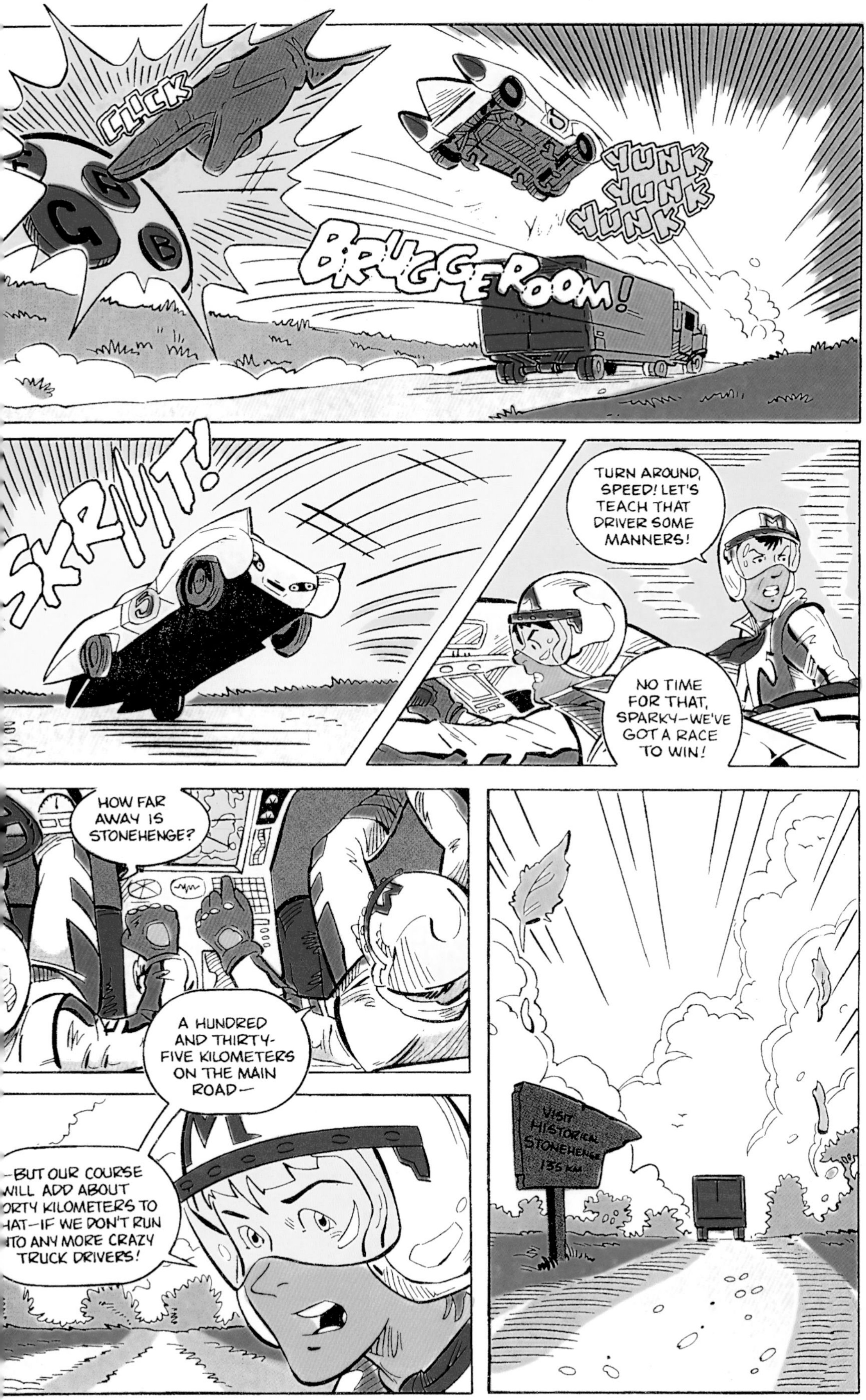
CLICK
YUNK YUNK YUNK
BRUGGEROOM!
SKRIIIT!
TURN AROUND, SPEED! LET'S TEACH THAT DRIVER SOME MANNERS!
NO TIME FOR THAT, SPARKY—WE'VE GOT A RACE TO WIN!
HOW FAR AWAY IS STONEHENGE?
A HUNDRED AND THIRTY-FIVE KILOMETERS ON THE MAIN ROAD—
—BUT OUR COURSE WILL ADD ABOUT ORTY KILOMETERS TO HAT—IF WE DON'T RUN NTO ANY MORE CRAZY TRUCK DRIVERS!
VISIT HISTORICAL STONEHENGE 135 KM

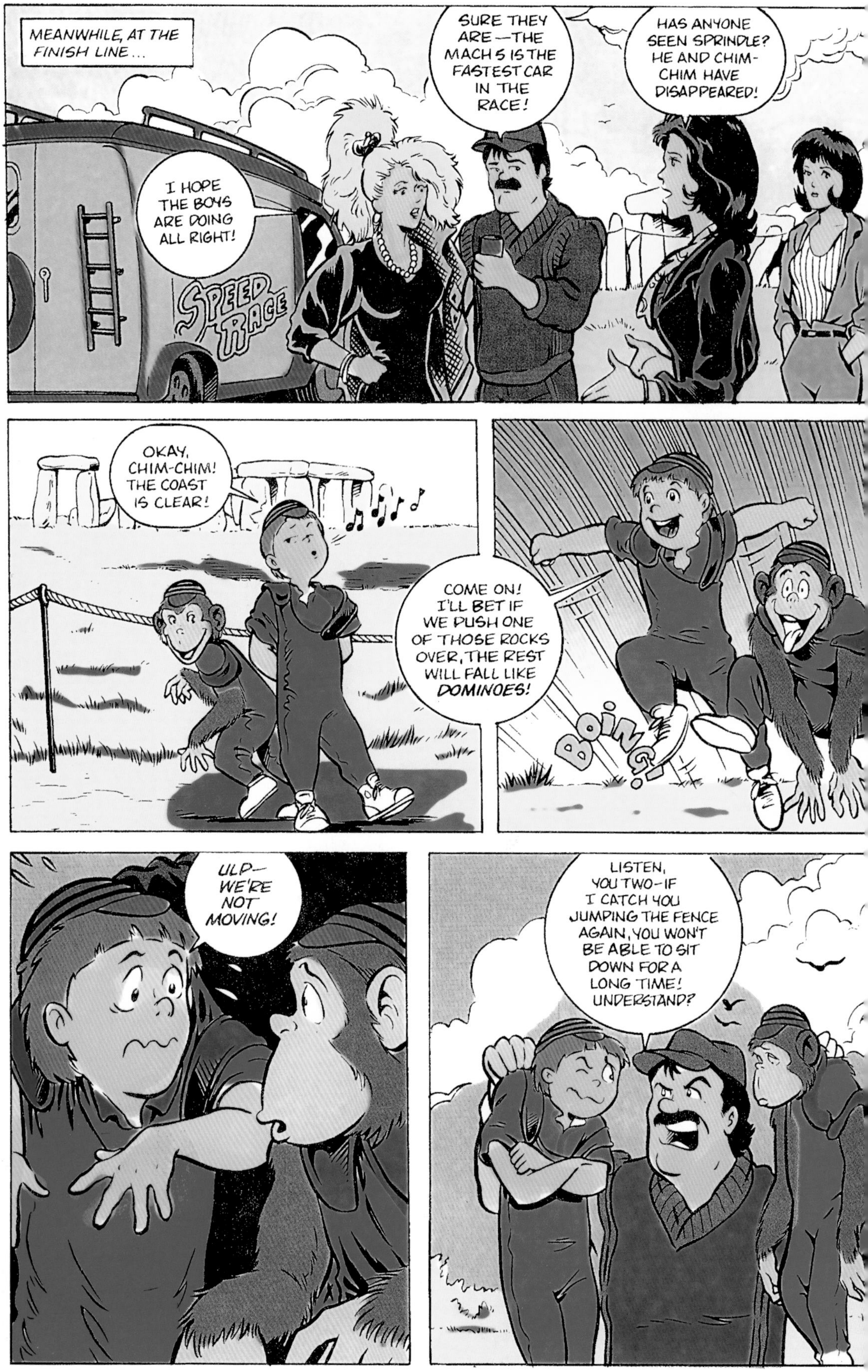

MEANWHILE, AT THE FINISH LINE...
I HOPE THE BOYS ARE DOING ALL RIGHT!
SURE THEY ARE—THE MACH 5 IS THE FASTEST CAR IN THE RACE!
HAS ANYONE SEEN SPRINDLE? HE AND CHIM-CHIM HAVE DISAPPEARED!
SPEED RACER
OKAY, CHIM-CHIM! THE COAST IS CLEAR!
COME ON! I'LL BET IF WE PUSH ONE OF THOSE ROCKS OVER, THE REST WILL FALL LIKE DOMINOES!
BOING!
ULP—WE'RE NOT MOVING!
LISTEN, YOU TWO—IF I CATCH YOU JUMPING THE FENCE AGAIN, YOU WON'T BE ABLE TO SIT DOWN FOR A LONG TIME! UNDERSTAND?

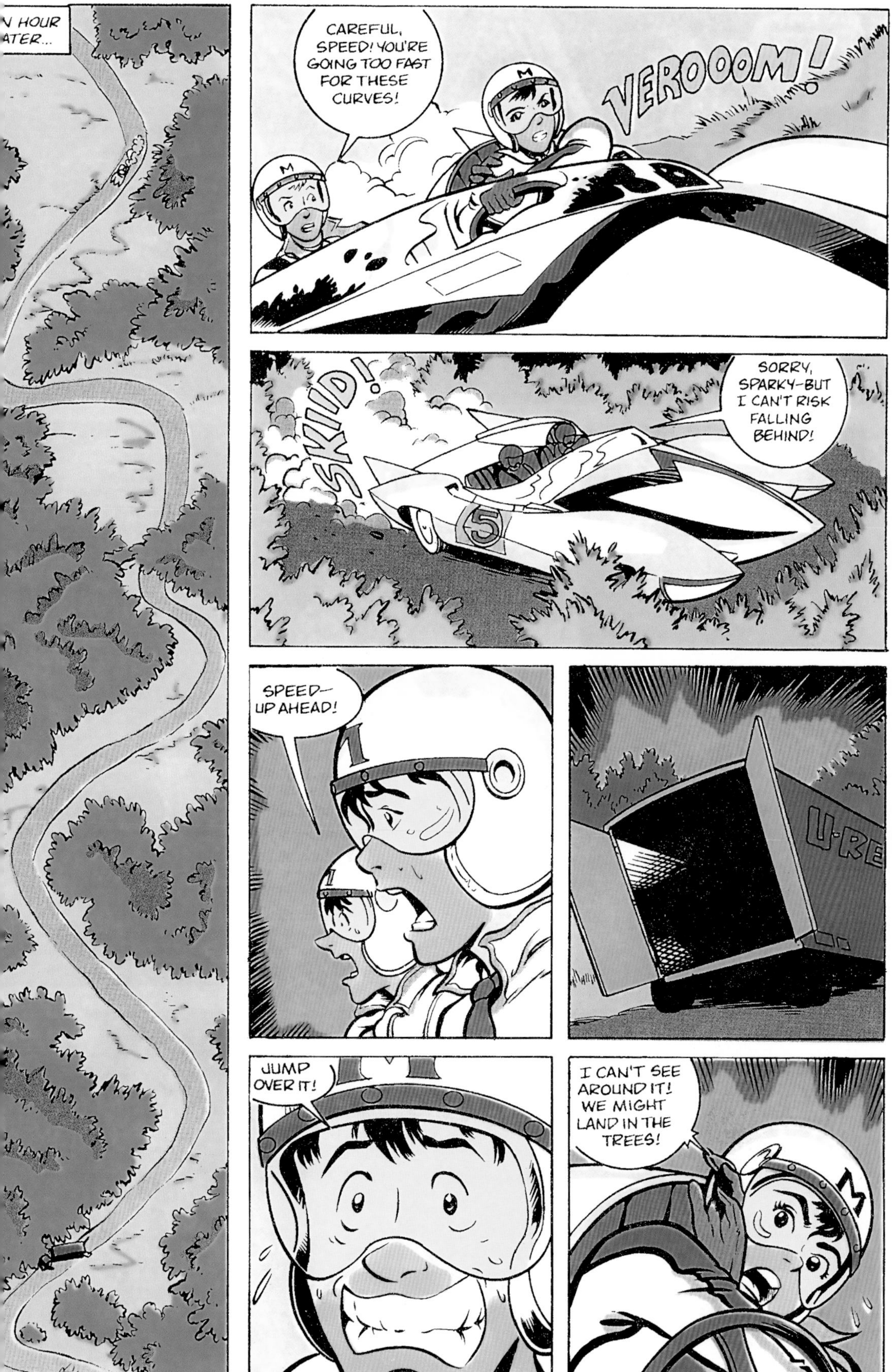
N HOUR
ATER...
CAREFUL, SPEED! YOU'RE GOING TOO FAST FOR THESE CURVES!
VEROOOM!
SKIID!
SORRY, SPARKY—BUT I CAN'T RISK FALLING BEHIND!
SPEED—UP AHEAD!
U-RE
JUMP OVER IT!
I CAN'T SEE AROUND IT! WE MIGHT LAND IN THE TREES!

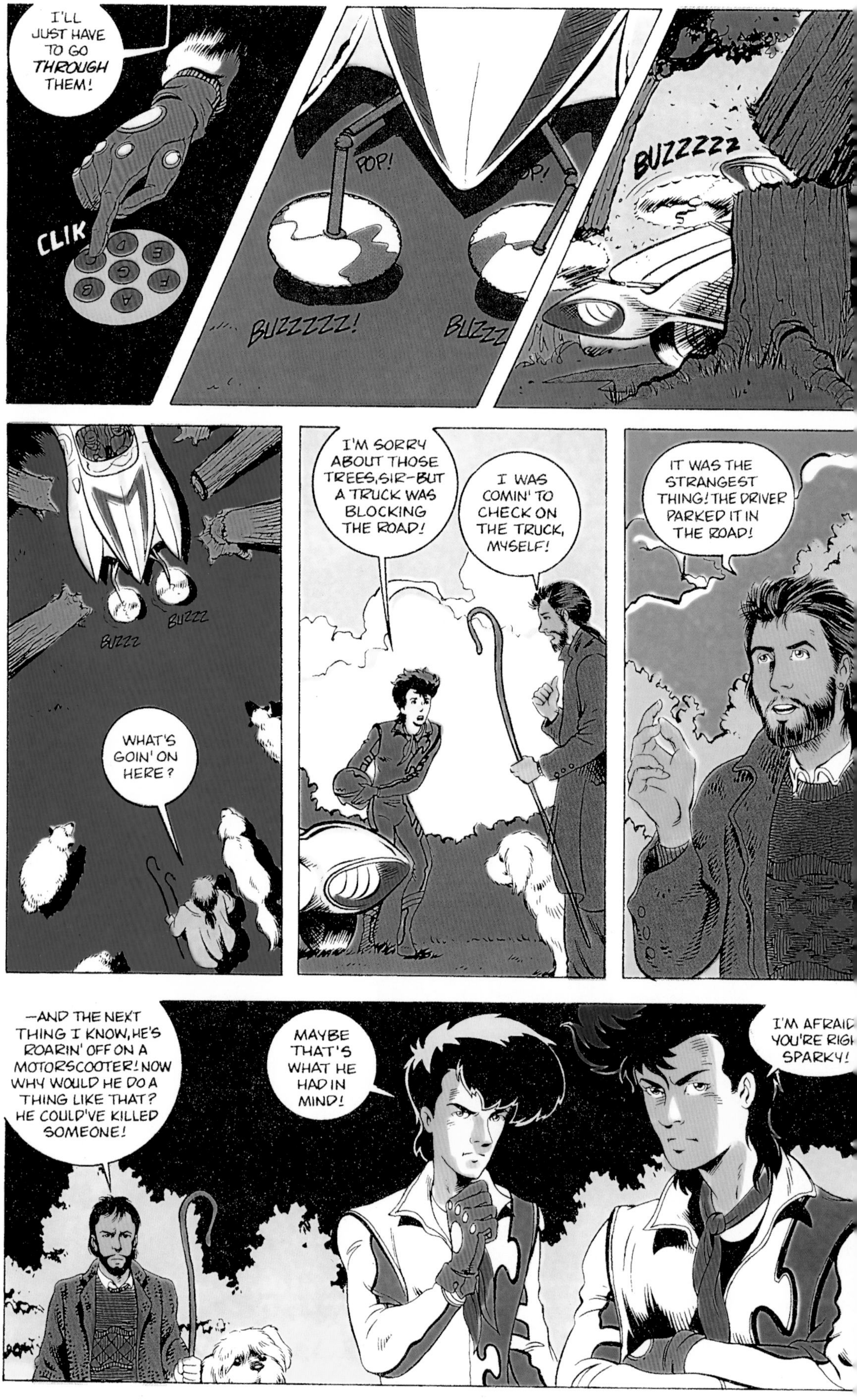
I'LL JUST HAVE TO GO THROUGH THEM!
CLIK
POP!
POP!
BUZZZZZ!
BUZZZ
BUZZZZZ
BUZZZ
BUZZZ
WHAT'S GOIN' ON HERE?
I'M SORRY ABOUT THOSE TREES, SIR–BUT A TRUCK WAS BLOCKING THE ROAD!
I WAS COMIN' TO CHECK ON THE TRUCK, MYSELF!
IT WAS THE STRANGEST THING! THE DRIVER PARKED IT IN THE ROAD!
—AND THE NEXT THING I KNOW, HE'S ROARIN' OFF ON A MOTORSCOOTER! NOW WHY WOULD HE DO A THING LIKE THAT? HE COULD'VE KILLED SOMEONE!
MAYBE THAT'S WHAT HE HAD IN MIND!
I'M AFRAID YOU'RE RIGH SPARKY!

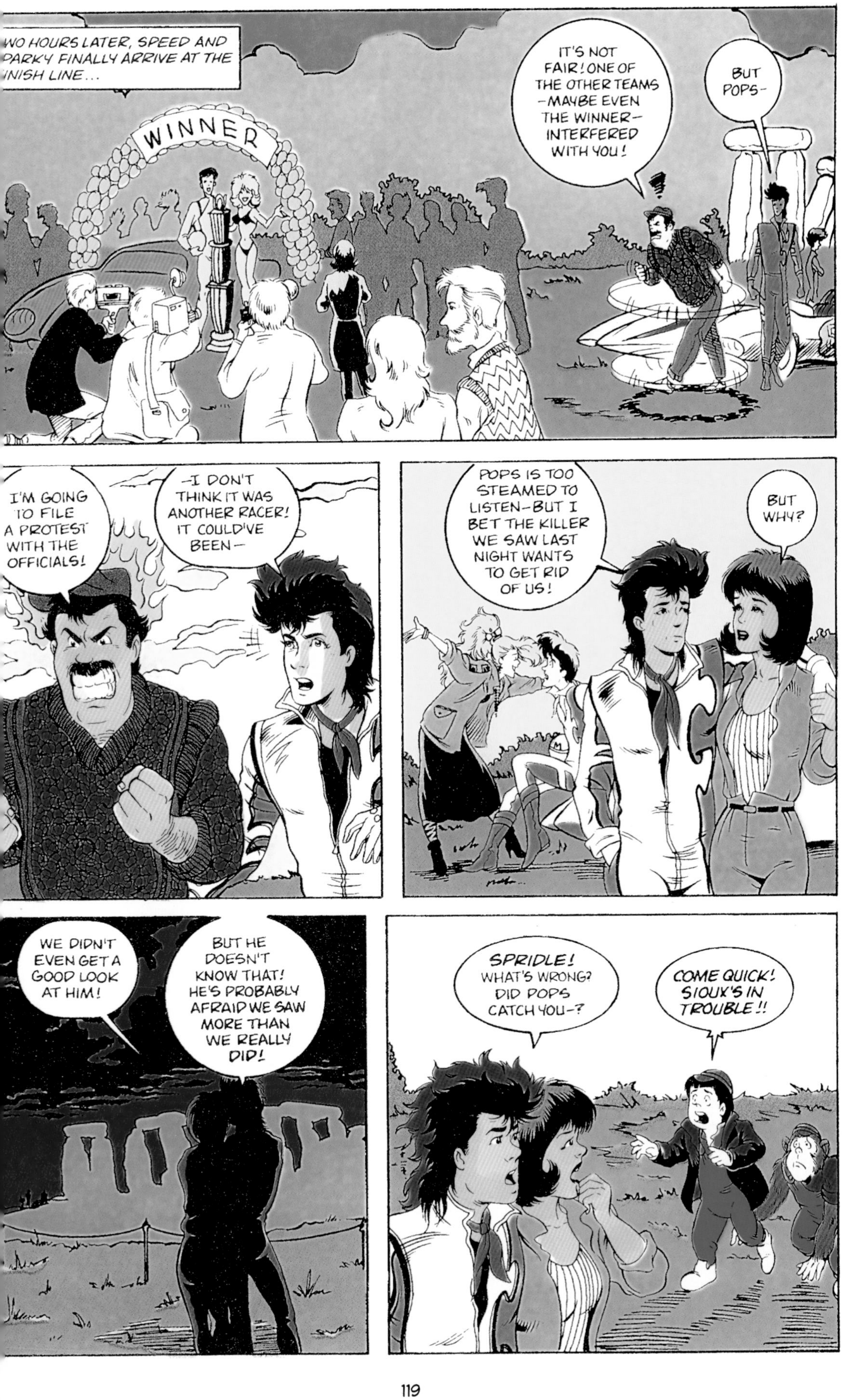
WO HOURS LATER, SPEED AND PARKY FINALLY ARRIVE AT THE INISH LINE...
WINNER
IT'S NOT FAIR! ONE OF THE OTHER TEAMS —MAYBE EVEN THE WINNER— INTERFERED WITH YOU!
BUT POPS—
I'M GOING TO FILE A PROTEST WITH THE OFFICIALS!
—I DON'T THINK IT WAS ANOTHER RACER! IT COULD'VE BEEN—
POPS IS TOO STEAMED TO LISTEN—BUT I BET THE KILLER WE SAW LAST NIGHT WANTS TO GET RID OF US!
BUT WHY?
WE DIDN'T EVEN GET A GOOD LOOK AT HIM!
BUT HE DOESN'T KNOW THAT! HE'S PROBABLY AFRAID WE SAW MORE THAN WE REALLY DID!
SPRIDLE! WHAT'S WRONG? DID POPS CATCH YOU—?
COME QUICK! SIOUX'S IN TROUBLE!!

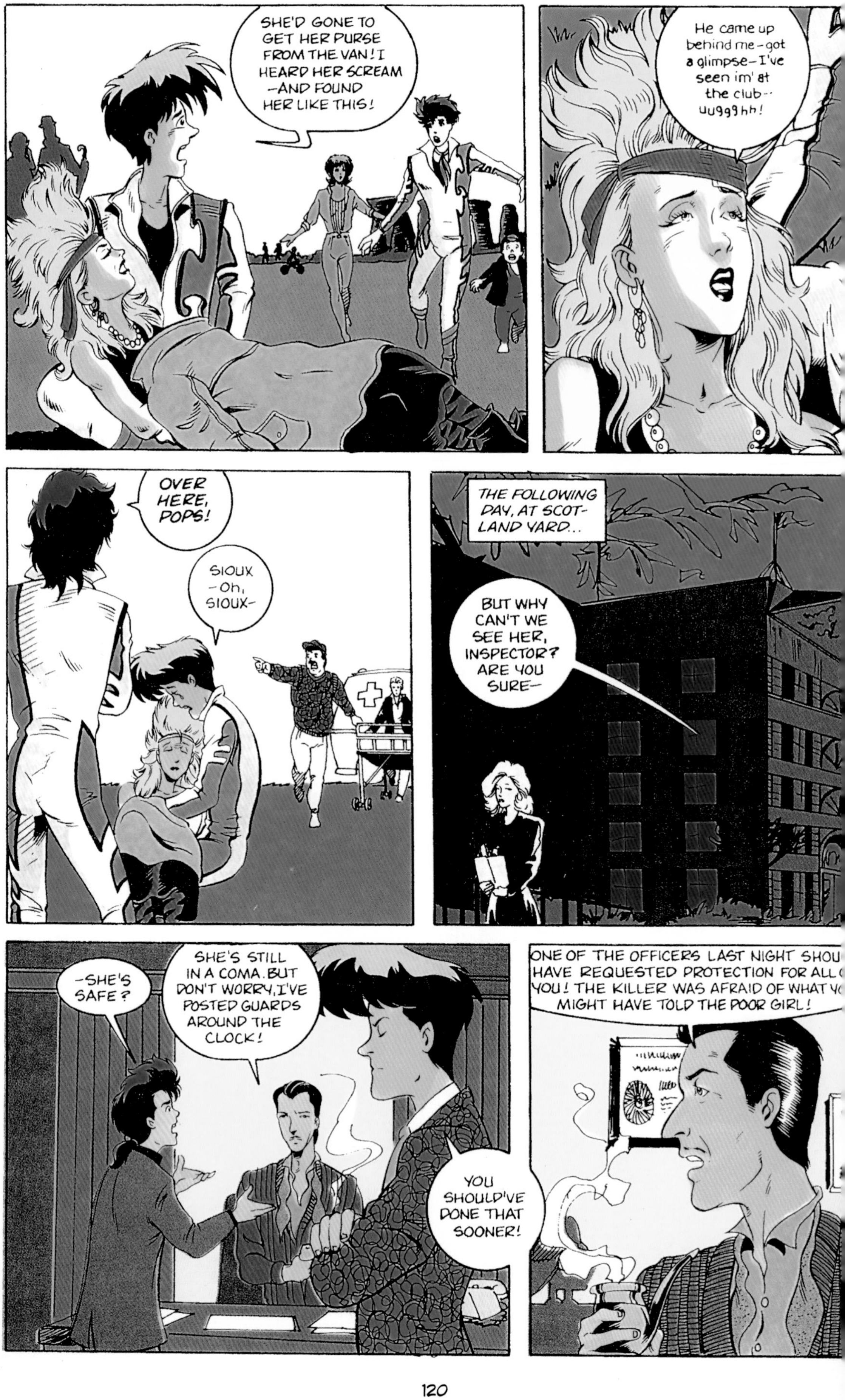
SHE'D GONE TO GET HER PURSE FROM THE VAN! I HEARD HER SCREAM —AND FOUND HER LIKE THIS!
He came up behind me—got a glimpse—I've seen im' at the club— uugggh!
OVER HERE, POPS!
SIOUX —Oh, SIOUX—
THE FOLLOWING DAY, AT SCOTLAND YARD...
BUT WHY CAN'T WE SEE HER, INSPECTOR? ARE YOU SURE—
—SHE'S SAFE?
SHE'S STILL IN A COMA. BUT DON'T WORRY, I'VE POSTED GUARDS AROUND THE CLOCK!
YOU SHOULD'VE DONE THAT SOONER!
ONE OF THE OFFICERS LAST NIGHT SHOU
HAVE REQUESTED PROTECTION FOR ALL
YOU! THE KILLER WAS AFRAID OF WHAT YO
MIGHT HAVE TOLD THE POOR GIRL!

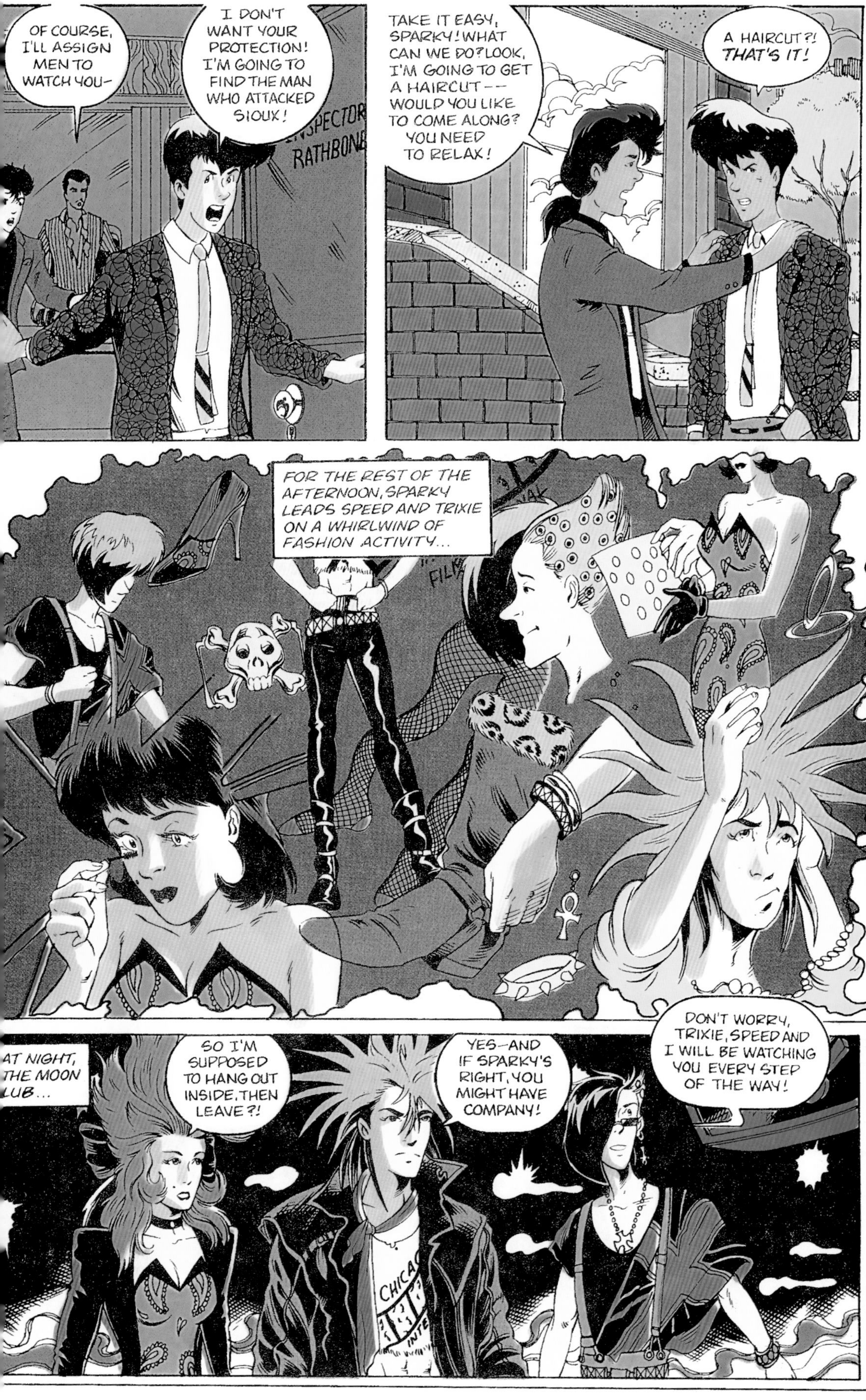
OF COURSE, I'LL ASSIGN MEN TO WATCH YOU-
I DON'T WANT YOUR PROTECTION! I'M GOING TO FIND THE MAN WHO ATTACKED SIOUX!
INSPECTOR RATHBONE
TAKE IT EASY, SPARKY! WHAT CAN WE DO? LOOK, I'M GOING TO GET A HAIRCUT -- WOULD YOU LIKE TO COME ALONG? YOU NEED TO RELAX!
A HAIRCUT?! THAT'S IT!
FOR THE REST OF THE AFTERNOON, SPARKY LEADS SPEED AND TRIXIE ON A WHIRLWIND OF FASHION ACTIVITY...
AT NIGHT, THE MOON LUB...
SO I'M SUPPOSED TO HANG OUT INSIDE, THEN LEAVE?!
YES--AND IF SPARKY'S RIGHT, YOU MIGHT HAVE COMPANY!
DON'T WORRY, TRIXIE, SPEED AND I WILL BE WATCHING YOU EVERY STEP OF THE WAY!

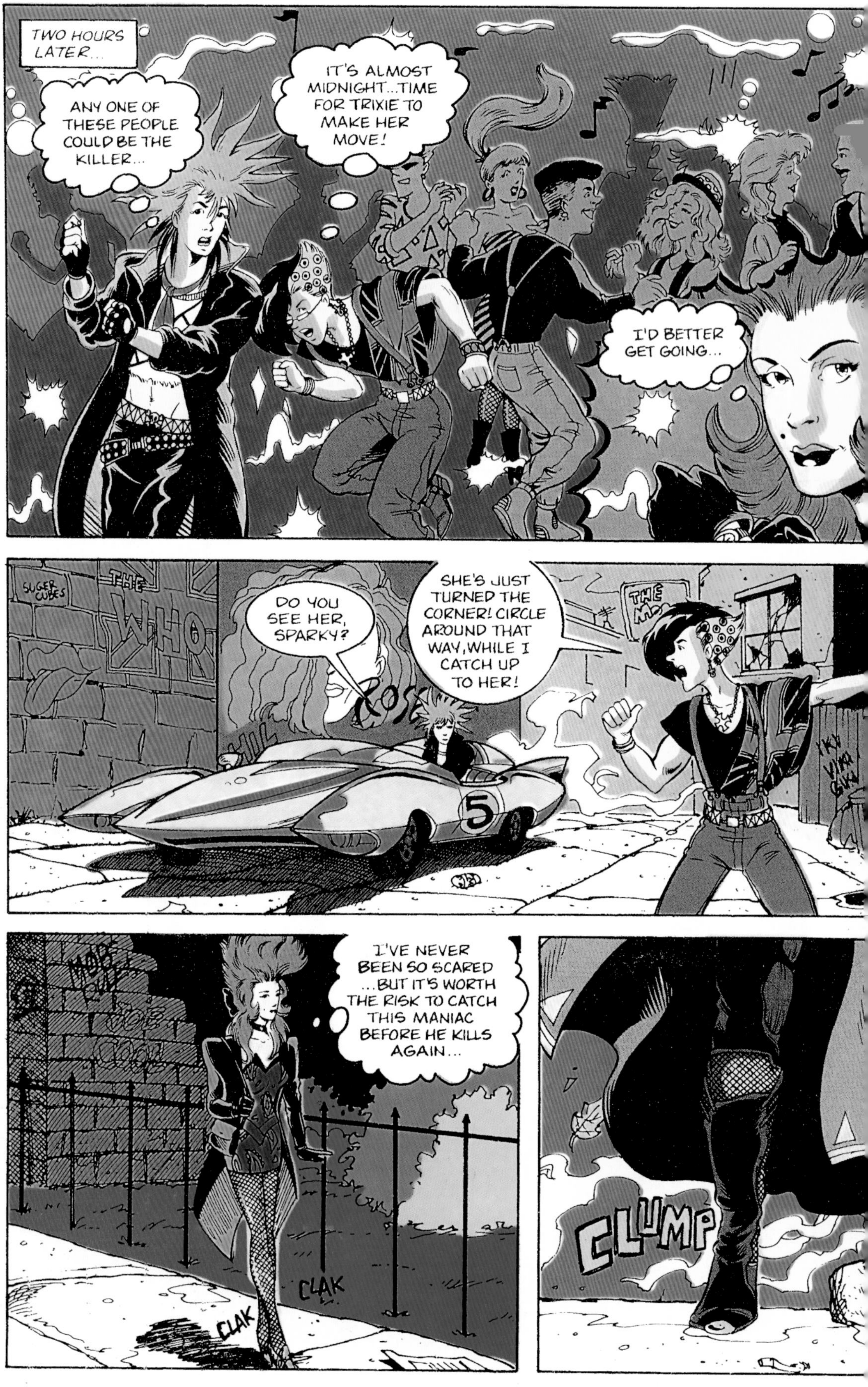
TWO HOURS LATER...
ANY ONE OF THESE PEOPLE COULD BE THE KILLER...
IT'S ALMOST MIDNIGHT...TIME FOR TRIXIE TO MAKE HER MOVE!
I'D BETTER GET GOING...
SUGER CUBES
THE WHO
DO YOU SEE HER, SPARKY?
SHE'S JUST TURNED THE CORNER! CIRCLE AROUND THAT WAY, WHILE I CATCH UP TO HER!
I'VE NEVER BEEN SO SCARED ...BUT IT'S WORTH THE RISK TO CATCH THIS MANIAC BEFORE HE KILLS AGAIN...
CLAK
CLAK
CLUMP

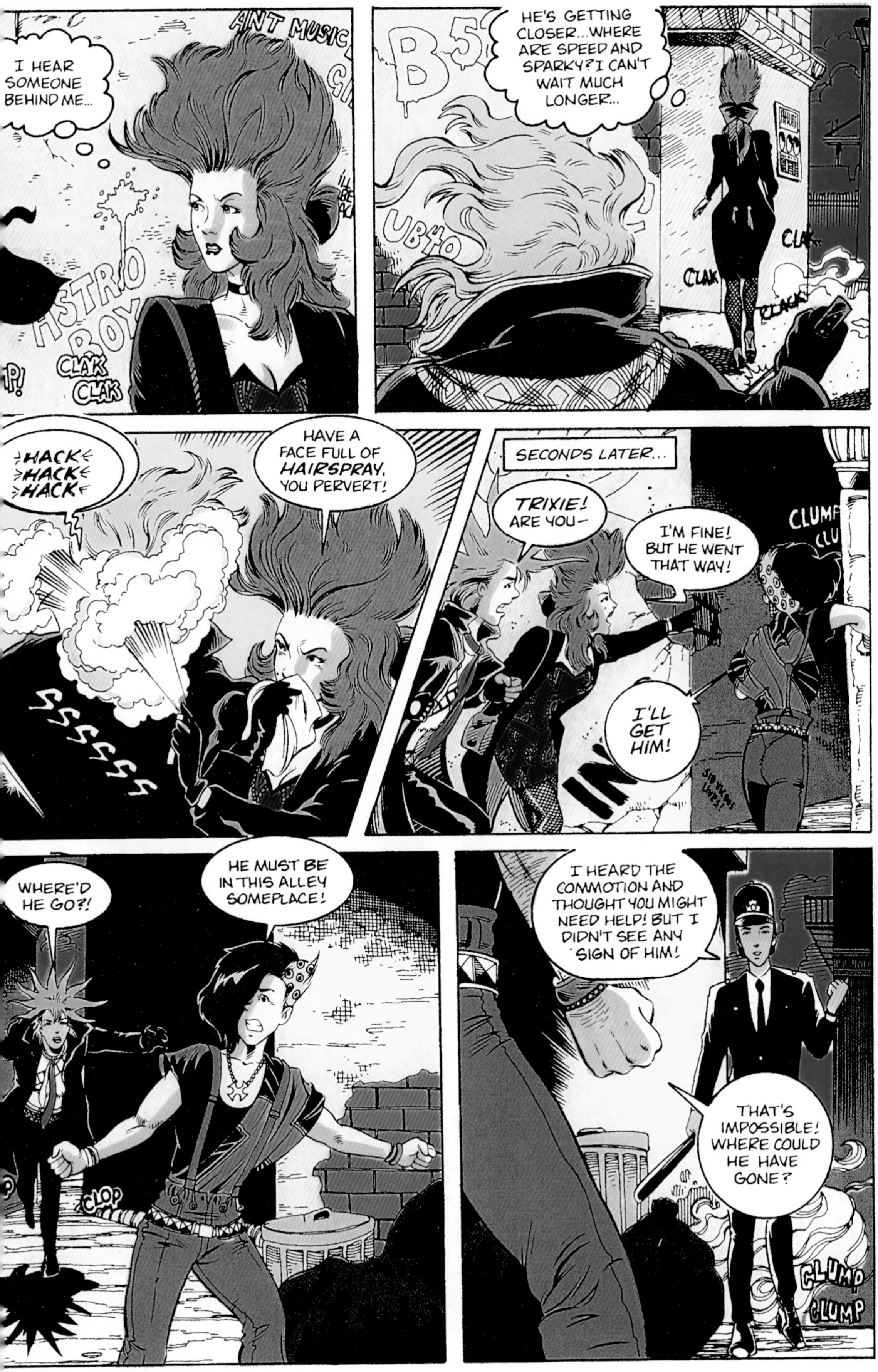
I HEAR SOMEONE BEHIND ME...
ANT MUSIC
ASTRO BOY
CLAK CLAK
HE'S GETTING CLOSER... WHERE ARE SPEED AND SPARKY? I CAN'T WAIT MUCH LONGER...
UB40
CLAK
CLAK
CLACK
HACK HACK HACK
HAVE A FACE FULL OF HAIRSPRAY, YOU PERVERT!
SSSSSS
SECONDS LATER...
TRIXIE! ARE YOU—
I'M FINE! BUT HE WENT THAT WAY!
I'LL GET HIM!
WHERE'D HE GO?!
HE MUST BE IN THIS ALLEY SOMEPLACE!
CLOP
I HEARD THE COMMOTION AND THOUGHT YOU MIGHT NEED HELP! BUT I DIDN'T SEE ANY SIGN OF HIM!
THAT'S IMPOSSIBLE! WHERE COULD HE HAVE GONE?
CLUMP
CLUMP

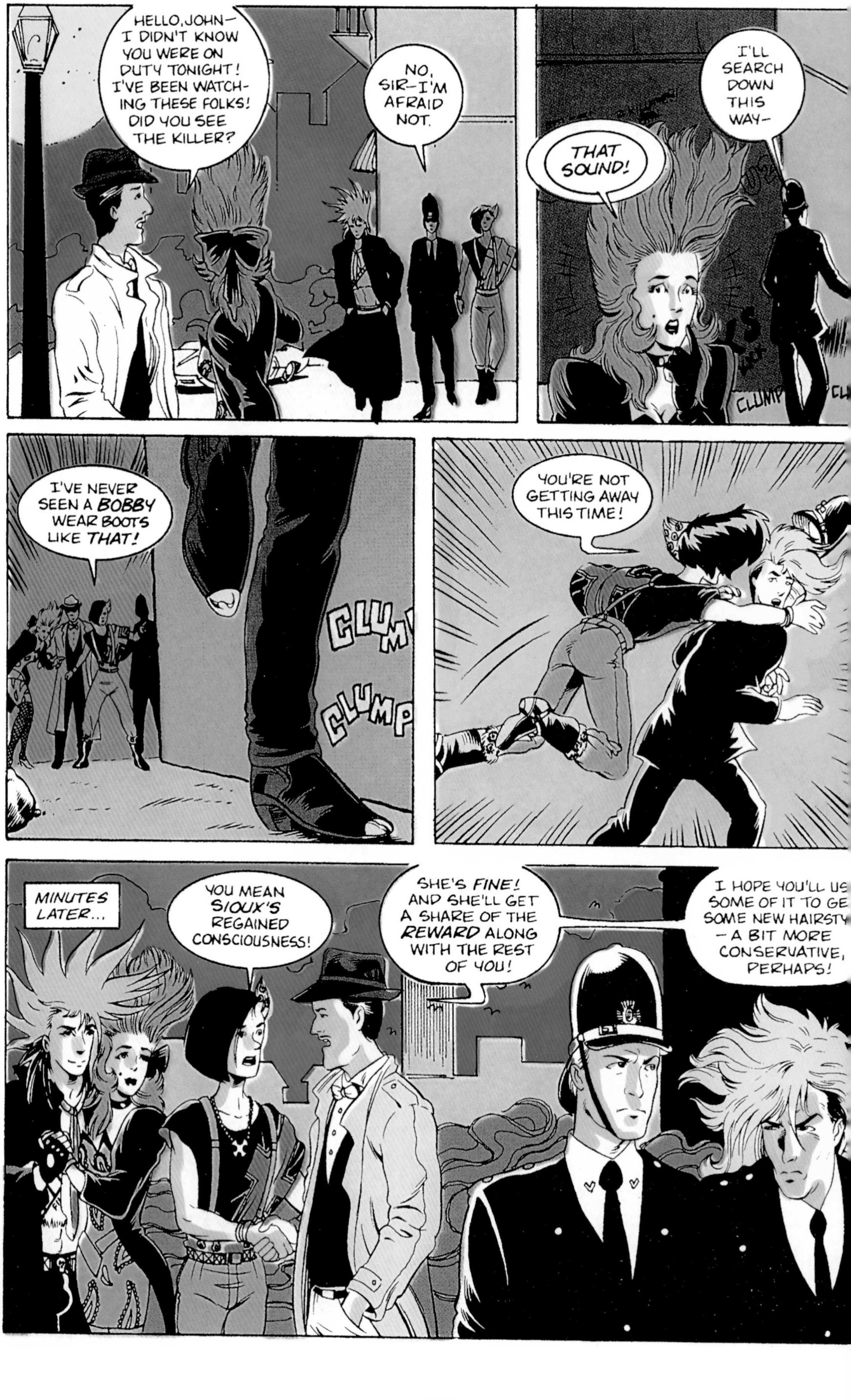
HELLO, JOHN— I DIDN'T KNOW YOU WERE ON DUTY TONIGHT! I'VE BEEN WATCHING THESE FOLKS! DID YOU SEE THE KILLER?
NO, SIR—I'M AFRAID NOT.
I'LL SEARCH DOWN THIS WAY—
THAT SOUND!
CLUMP
I'VE NEVER SEEN A BOBBY WEAR BOOTS LIKE THAT!
CLUMP
YOU'RE NOT GETTING AWAY THIS TIME!
MINUTES LATER...
YOU MEAN SIOUX'S REGAINED CONSCIOUSNESS!
SHE'S FINE! AND SHE'LL GET A SHARE OF THE REWARD ALONG WITH THE REST OF YOU!
I HOPE YOU'LL US SOME OF IT TO GE SOME NEW HAIRSTY —A BIT MORE CONSERVATIVE, PERHAPS!

Speed Racer #19

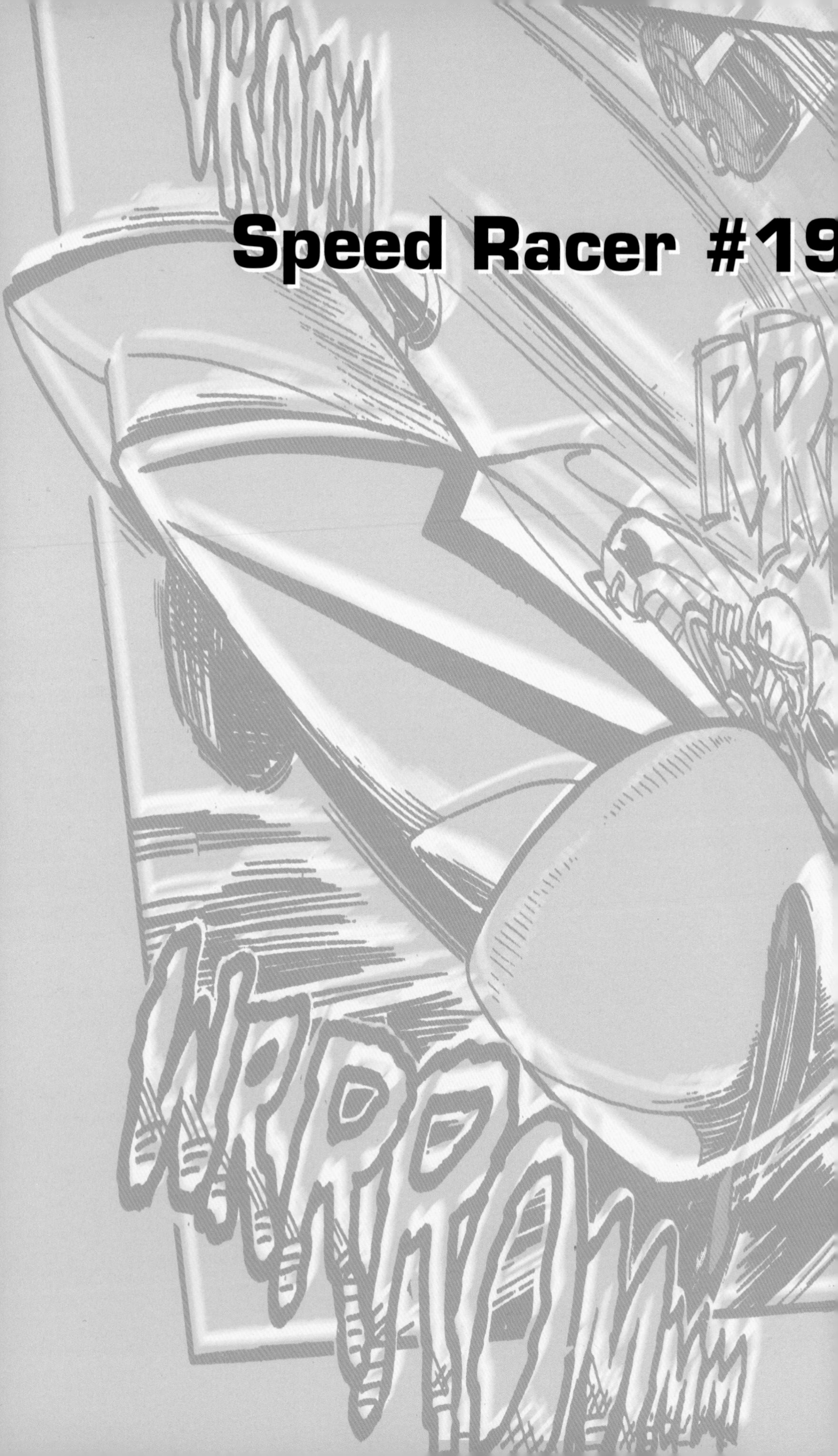

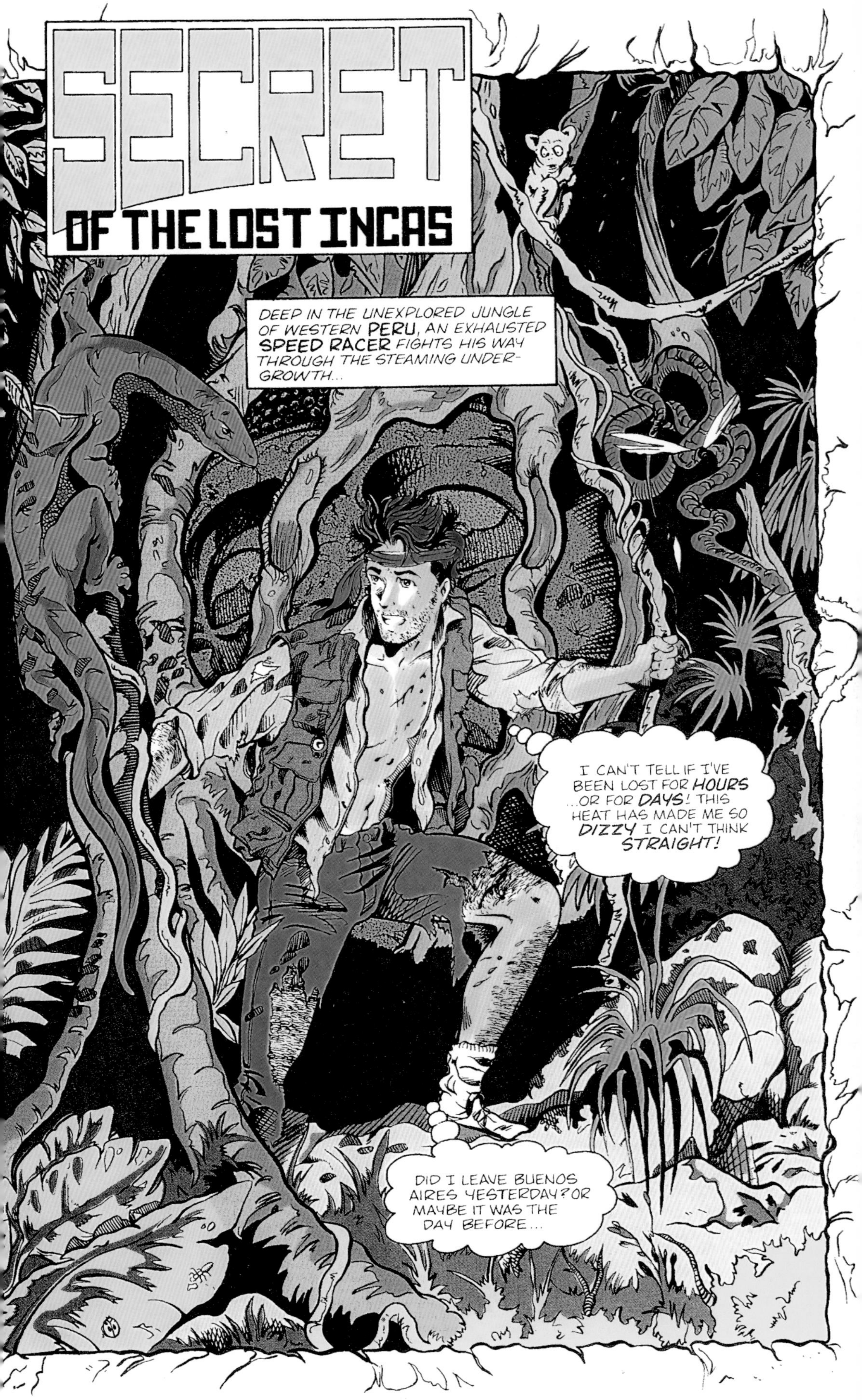
SECRET OF THE LOST INCAS
DEEP IN THE UNEXPLORED JUNGLE OF WESTERN PERU, AN EXHAUSTED SPEED RACER FIGHTS HIS WAY THROUGH THE STEAMING UNDER-GROWTH...
I CAN'T TELL IF I'VE BEEN LOST FOR HOURS ...OR FOR DAYS! THIS HEAT HAS MADE ME SO DIZZY I CAN'T THINK STRAIGHT!
DID I LEAVE BUENOS AIRES YESTERDAY? OR MAYBE IT WAS THE DAY BEFORE...

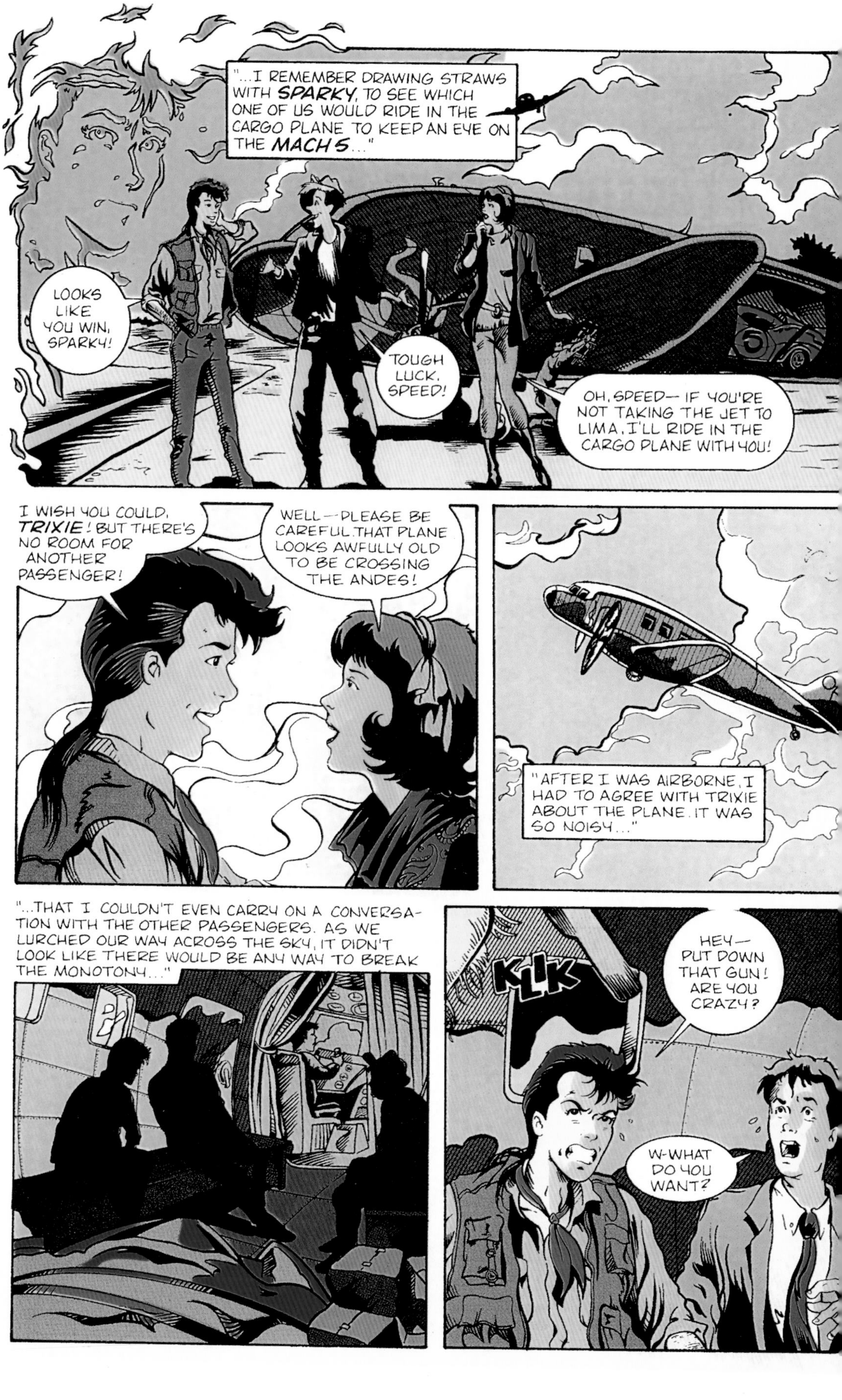
"...I REMEMBER DRAWING STRAWS WITH SPARKY, TO SEE WHICH ONE OF US WOULD RIDE IN THE CARGO PLANE TO KEEP AN EYE ON THE MACH 5..."
LOOKS LIKE YOU WIN, SPARKY!
TOUGH LUCK, SPEED!
OH, SPEED— IF YOU'RE NOT TAKING THE JET TO LIMA, I'LL RIDE IN THE CARGO PLANE WITH YOU!
I WISH YOU COULD, TRIXIE! BUT THERE'S NO ROOM FOR ANOTHER PASSENGER!
WELL—PLEASE BE CAREFUL. THAT PLANE LOOKS AWFULLY OLD TO BE CROSSING THE ANDES!
"AFTER I WAS AIRBORNE, I HAD TO AGREE WITH TRIXIE ABOUT THE PLANE. IT WAS SO NOISY..."
"...THAT I COULDN'T EVEN CARRY ON A CONVERSATION WITH THE OTHER PASSENGERS. AS WE LURCHED OUR WAY ACROSS THE SKY, IT DIDN'T LOOK LIKE THERE WOULD BE ANY WAY TO BREAK THE MONOTONY..."
KLIK
HEY— PUT DOWN THAT GUN! ARE YOU CRAZY?
W-WHAT DO YOU WANT?

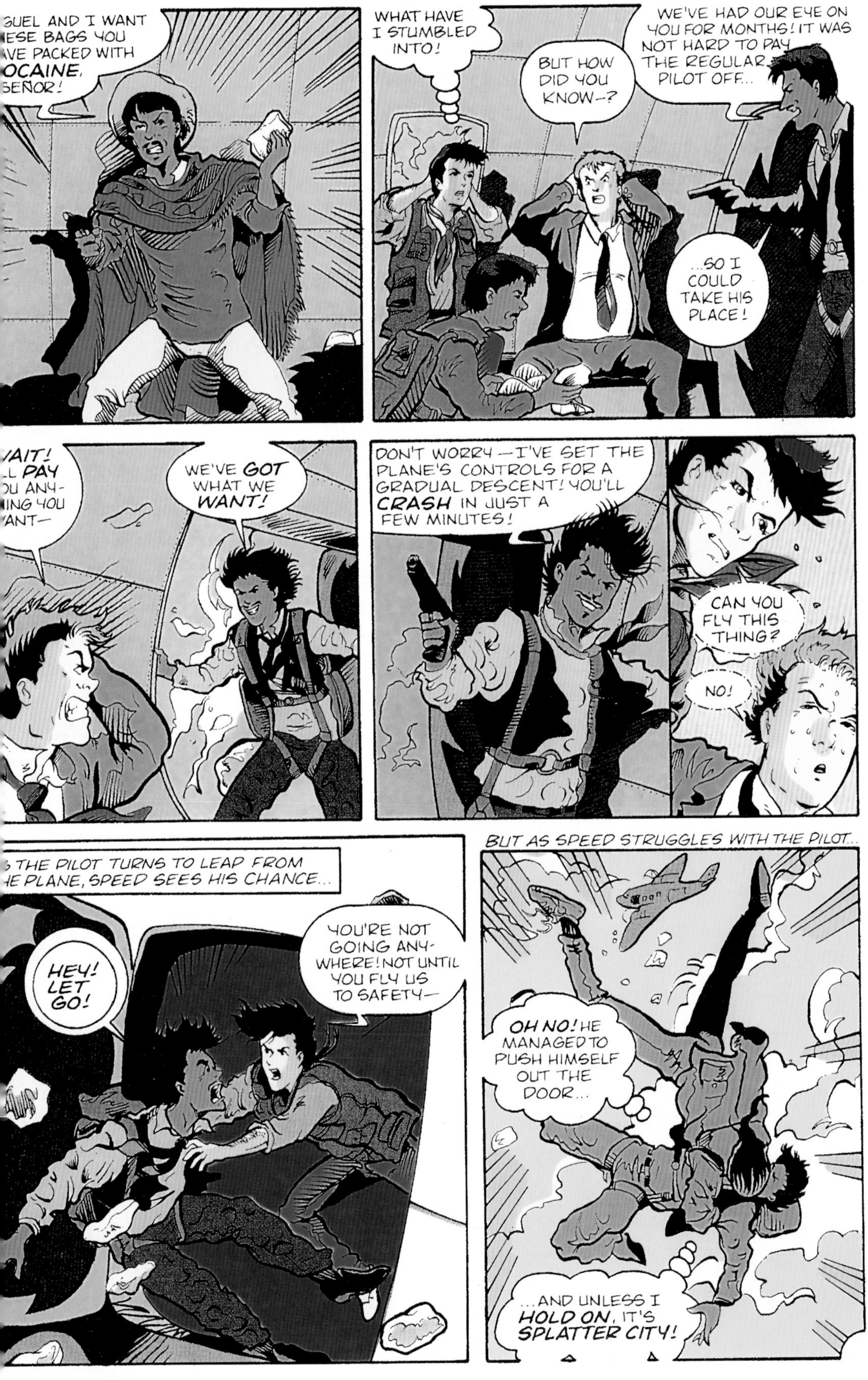

GUEL AND I WANT
IESE BAGS YOU
IVE PACKED WITH
OCAINE,
SEÑOR!
WHAT HAVE I STUMBLED INTO!
BUT HOW DID YOU KNOW--?
WE'VE HAD OUR EYE ON YOU FOR MONTHS! IT WAS NOT HARD TO PAY THE REGULAR PILOT OFF...
...SO I COULD TAKE HIS PLACE!
VAIT!
L PAY
OU ANY-
ING YOU
VANT—
WE'VE GOT WHAT WE WANT!
DON'T WORRY—I'VE SET THE PLANE'S CONTROLS FOR A GRADUAL DESCENT! YOU'LL CRASH IN JUST A FEW MINUTES!
CAN YOU FLY THIS THING?
NO!
S THE PILOT TURNS TO LEAP FROM
HE PLANE, SPEED SEES HIS CHANCE...
HEY! LET GO!
YOU'RE NOT GOING ANYWHERE! NOT UNTIL YOU FLY US TO SAFETY—
BUT AS SPEED STRUGGLES WITH THE PILOT...
OH NO! HE MANAGED TO PUSH HIMSELF OUT THE DOOR...
...AND UNLESS I HOLD ON, IT'S SPLATTER CITY!

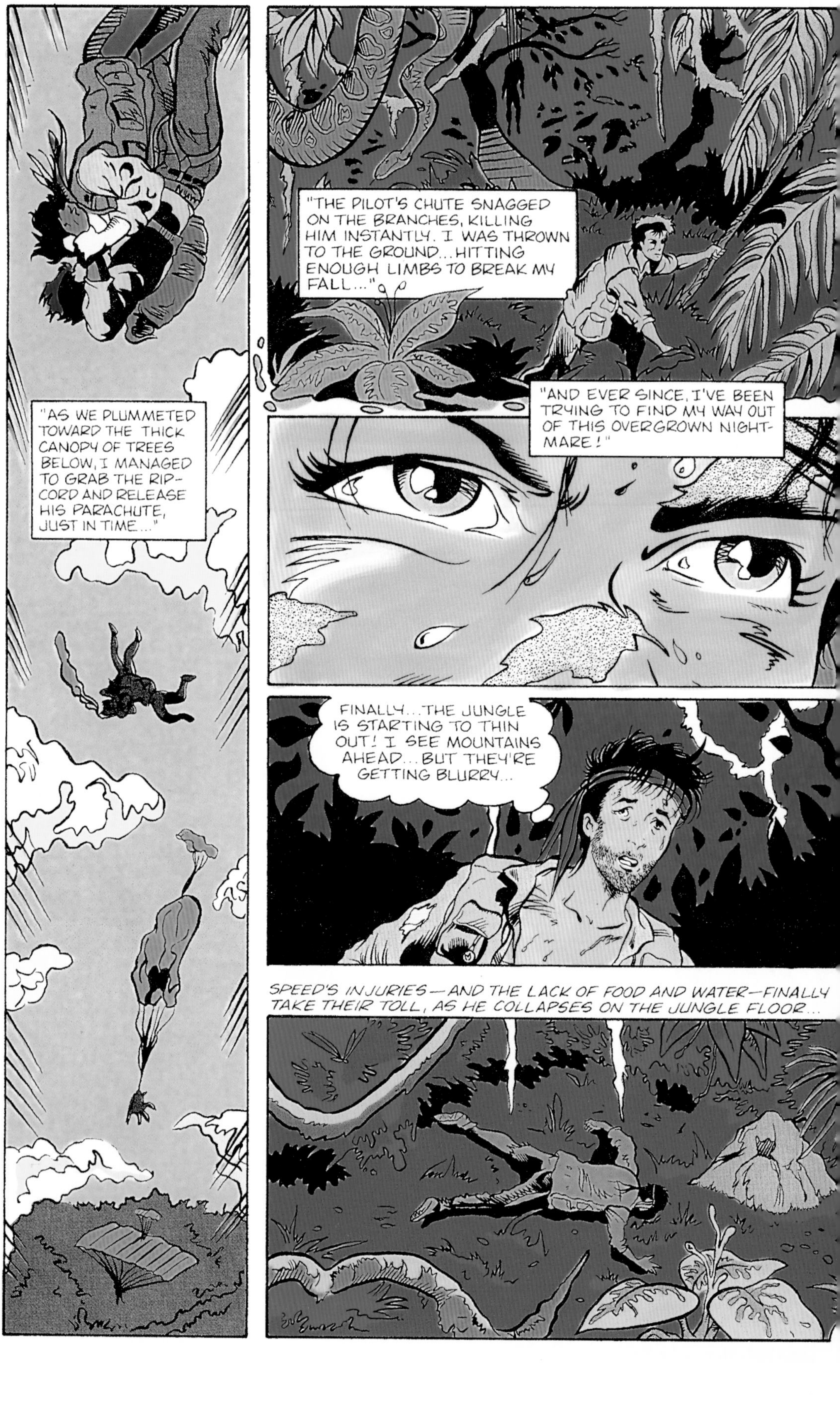
"AS WE PLUMMETED TOWARD THE THICK CANOPY OF TREES BELOW, I MANAGED TO GRAB THE RIP-CORD AND RELEASE HIS PARACHUTE, JUST IN TIME..."
"THE PILOT'S CHUTE SNAGGED ON THE BRANCHES, KILLING HIM INSTANTLY. I WAS THROWN TO THE GROUND... HITTING ENOUGH LIMBS TO BREAK MY FALL..."
"AND EVER SINCE, I'VE BEEN TRYING TO FIND MY WAY OUT OF THIS OVERGROWN NIGHT-MARE!"
FINALLY... THE JUNGLE IS STARTING TO THIN OUT! I SEE MOUNTAINS AHEAD... BUT THEY'RE GETTING BLURRY...
SPEED'S INJURIES—AND THE LACK OF FOOD AND WATER—FINALLY TAKE THEIR TOLL, AS HE COLLAPSES ON THE JUNGLE FLOOR...

THE FOLLOWING DAY...

WHAT— WHERE AM I?

THE LAST THING I REMEMBER, I WAS LOST IN THE JUNGLE!

PLEASE BE QUIET! DON'T MAKE TOO MUCH NOISE, OR THEY'LL HEAR THAT YOU'VE REGAINED CONSCIOUSNESS!

WHO ARE YOU—AND HOW DID I GET HERE?

YOU WERE FOUND AT THE EDGE OF THE JUNGLE·AND BROUGHT HERE TO *VILCABRA*. MY NAME IS *REENA*, AND I AM A DAUGHTER OF THE SUN.

NOW, LIE DOWN—YOU NEED TO REST AT LEAST ONE MORE DAY!

BUT I'VE GOT TO GET TO LIMA, IN TIME FOR THE RACE!

RACE? DON'T SPEAK OF SUCH THINGS—AND DON'T OPEN THAT DOOR! PLEASE!

SORRY, REENA. BUT I CAN'T STAY FOR YOUR *COSTUME PARTY*!

I NEED TO—

—I CAN'T BELIEVE MY EYES!

I-IT'S INCREDIBLE!

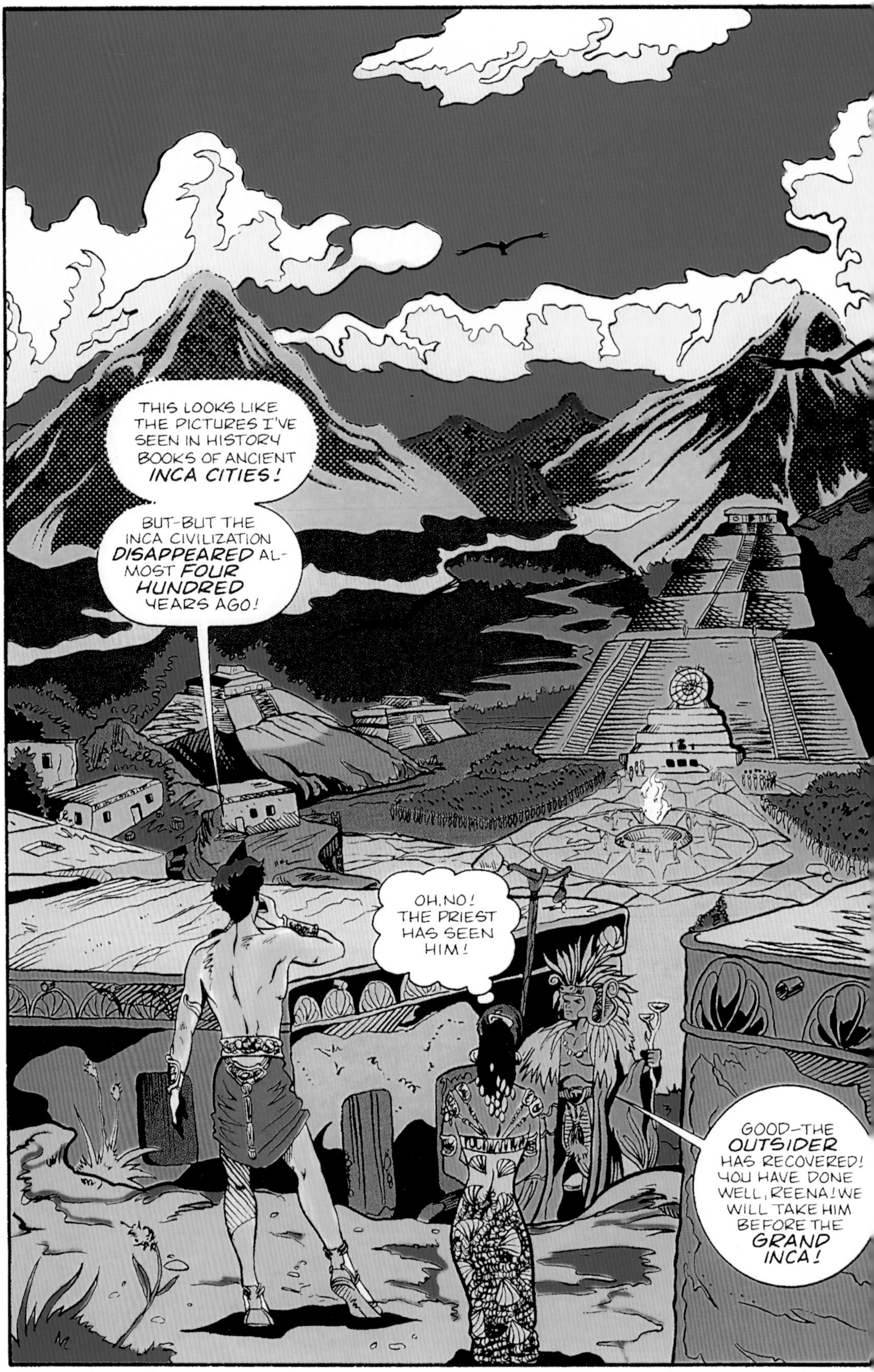
THIS LOOKS LIKE THE PICTURES I'VE SEEN IN HISTORY BOOKS OF ANCIENT INCA CITIES!
BUT-BUT THE INCA CIVILIZATION DISAPPEARED ALMOST FOUR HUNDRED YEARS AGO!
OH, NO! THE PRIEST HAS SEEN HIM!
GOOD-THE OUTSIDER HAS RECOVERED! YOU HAVE DONE WELL, REENA! WE WILL TAKE HIM BEFORE THE GRAND INCA!

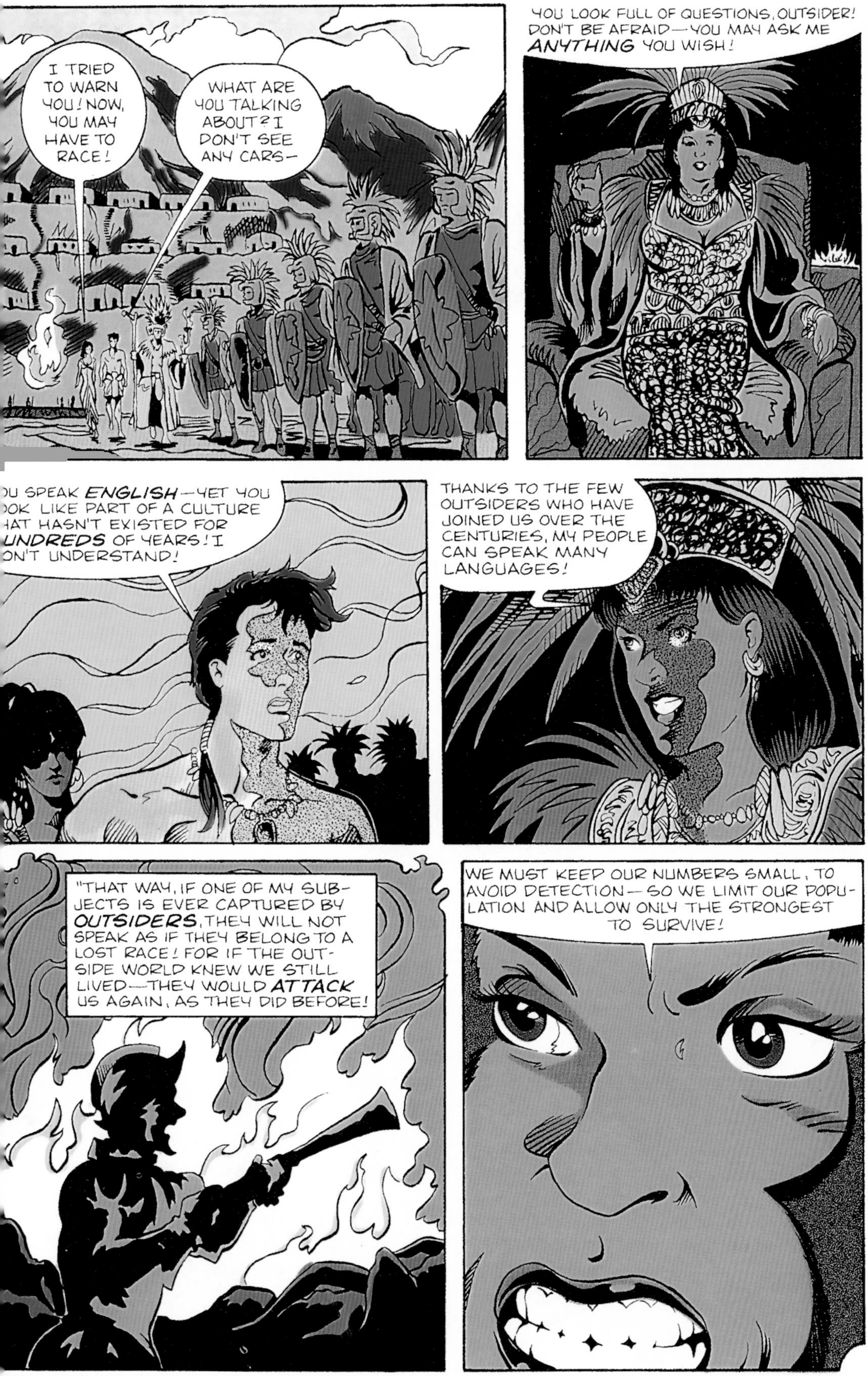
I TRIED TO WARN YOU! NOW, YOU MAY HAVE TO RACE!
WHAT ARE YOU TALKING ABOUT? I DON'T SEE ANY CARS—
YOU LOOK FULL OF QUESTIONS, OUTSIDER! DON'T BE AFRAID—YOU MAY ASK ME ANYTHING YOU WISH!
OU SPEAK ENGLISH—YET YOU OOK LIKE PART OF A CULTURE HAT HASN'T EXISTED FOR UNDREDS OF YEARS! I ON'T UNDERSTAND!
THANKS TO THE FEW OUTSIDERS WHO HAVE JOINED US OVER THE CENTURIES, MY PEOPLE CAN SPEAK MANY LANGUAGES!
"THAT WAY, IF ONE OF MY SUBJECTS IS EVER CAPTURED BY OUTSIDERS, THEY WILL NOT SPEAK AS IF THEY BELONG TO A LOST RACE! FOR IF THE OUTSIDE WORLD KNEW WE STILL LIVED—THEY WOULD ATTACK US AGAIN, AS THEY DID BEFORE!
WE MUST KEEP OUR NUMBERS SMALL, TO AVOID DETECTION—SO WE LIMIT OUR POPULATION AND ALLOW ONLY THE STRONGEST TO SURVIVE!

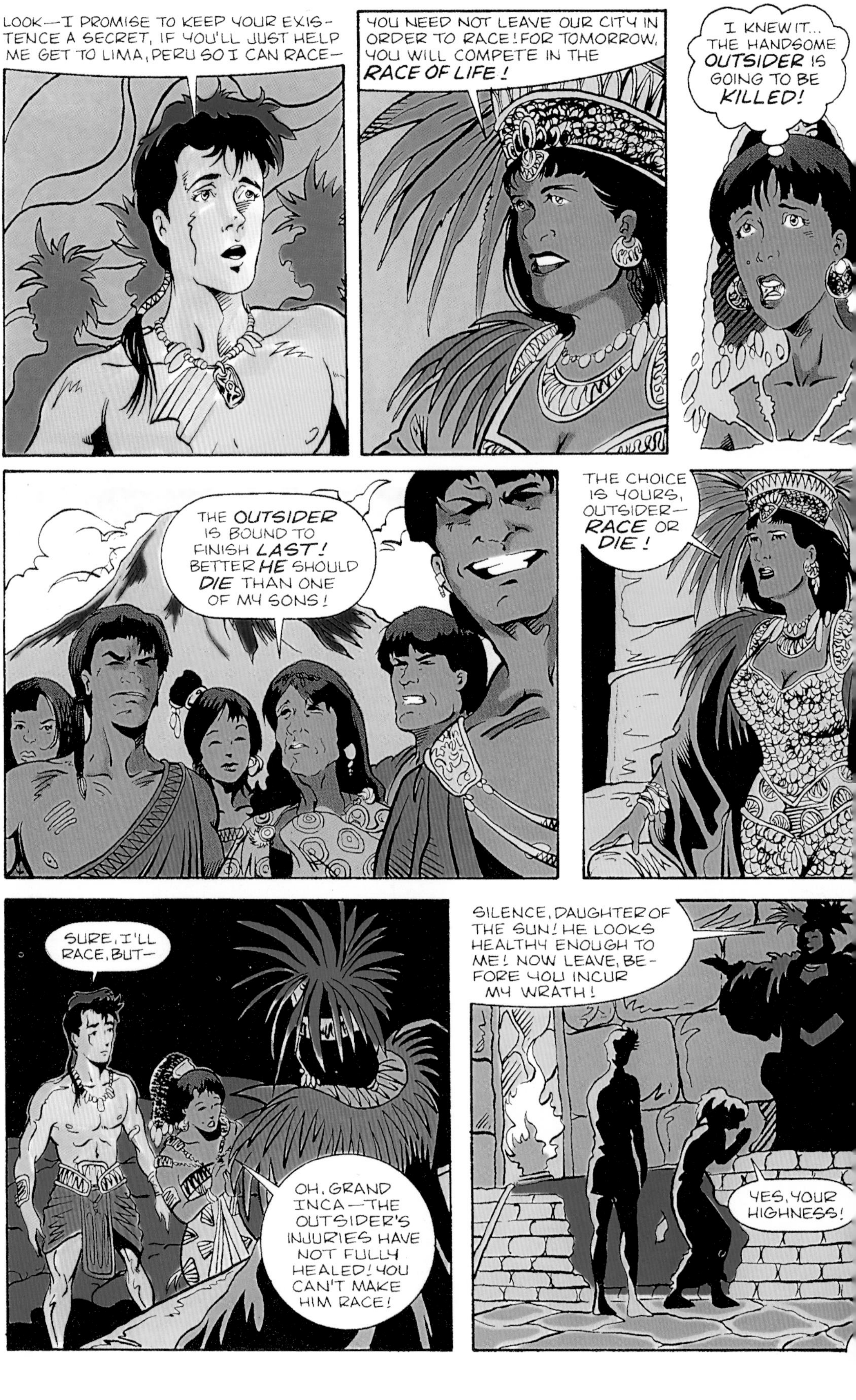
LOOK—I PROMISE TO KEEP YOUR EXIS-TENCE A SECRET, IF YOU'LL JUST HELP ME GET TO LIMA, PERU SO I CAN RACE—
YOU NEED NOT LEAVE OUR CITY IN ORDER TO RACE! FOR TOMORROW, YOU WILL COMPETE IN THE RACE OF LIFE!
I KNEW IT... THE HANDSOME OUTSIDER IS GOING TO BE KILLED!
THE OUTSIDER IS BOUND TO FINISH LAST! BETTER HE SHOULD DIE THAN ONE OF MY SONS!
THE CHOICE IS YOURS, OUTSIDER— RACE OR DIE!
SURE, I'LL RACE, BUT—
OH, GRAND INCA—THE OUTSIDER'S INJURIES HAVE NOT FULLY HEALED! YOU CAN'T MAKE HIM RACE!
SILENCE, DAUGHTER OF THE SUN! HE LOOKS HEALTHY ENOUGH TO ME! NOW LEAVE, BE-FORE YOU INCUR MY WRATH!
YES, YOUR HIGHNESS!

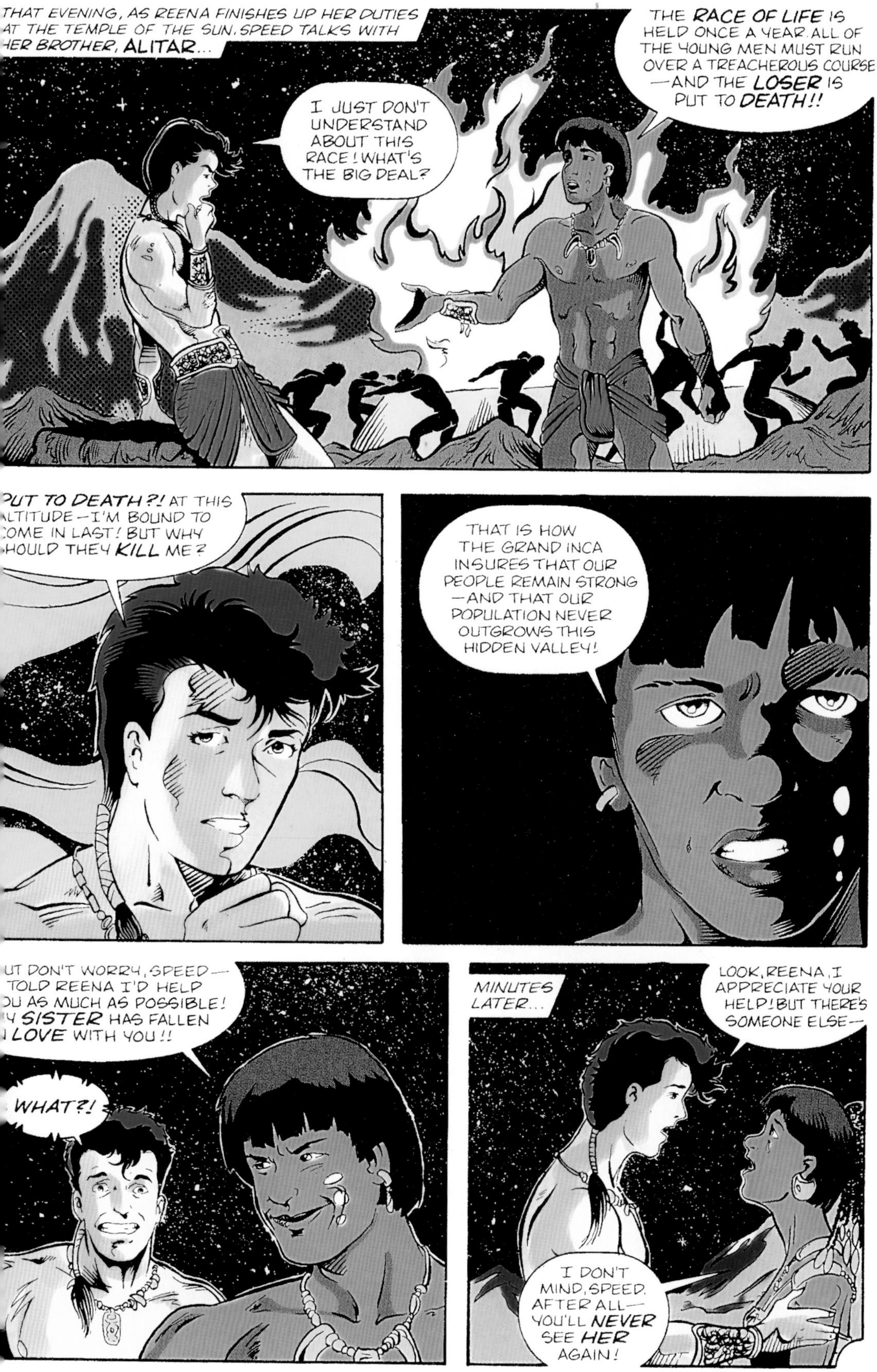
THAT EVENING, AS REENA FINISHES UP HER DUTIES AT THE TEMPLE OF THE SUN, SPEED TALKS WITH HER BROTHER, ALITAR...
I JUST DON'T UNDERSTAND ABOUT THIS RACE! WHAT'S THE BIG DEAL?
THE RACE OF LIFE IS HELD ONCE A YEAR. ALL OF THE YOUNG MEN MUST RUN OVER A TREACHEROUS COURSE —AND THE LOSER IS PUT TO DEATH!!
PUT TO DEATH?! AT THIS ALTITUDE—I'M BOUND TO COME IN LAST! BUT WHY SHOULD THEY KILL ME?
THAT IS HOW THE GRAND INCA INSURES THAT OUR PEOPLE REMAIN STRONG —AND THAT OUR POPULATION NEVER OUTGROWS THIS HIDDEN VALLEY!
BUT DON'T WORRY, SPEED— I TOLD REENA I'D HELP YOU AS MUCH AS POSSIBLE! MY SISTER HAS FALLEN IN LOVE WITH YOU!!
WHAT?!
MINUTES LATER...
LOOK, REENA, I APPRECIATE YOUR HELP! BUT THERE'S SOMEONE ELSE—
I DON'T MIND, SPEED. AFTER ALL— YOU'LL NEVER SEE HER AGAIN!

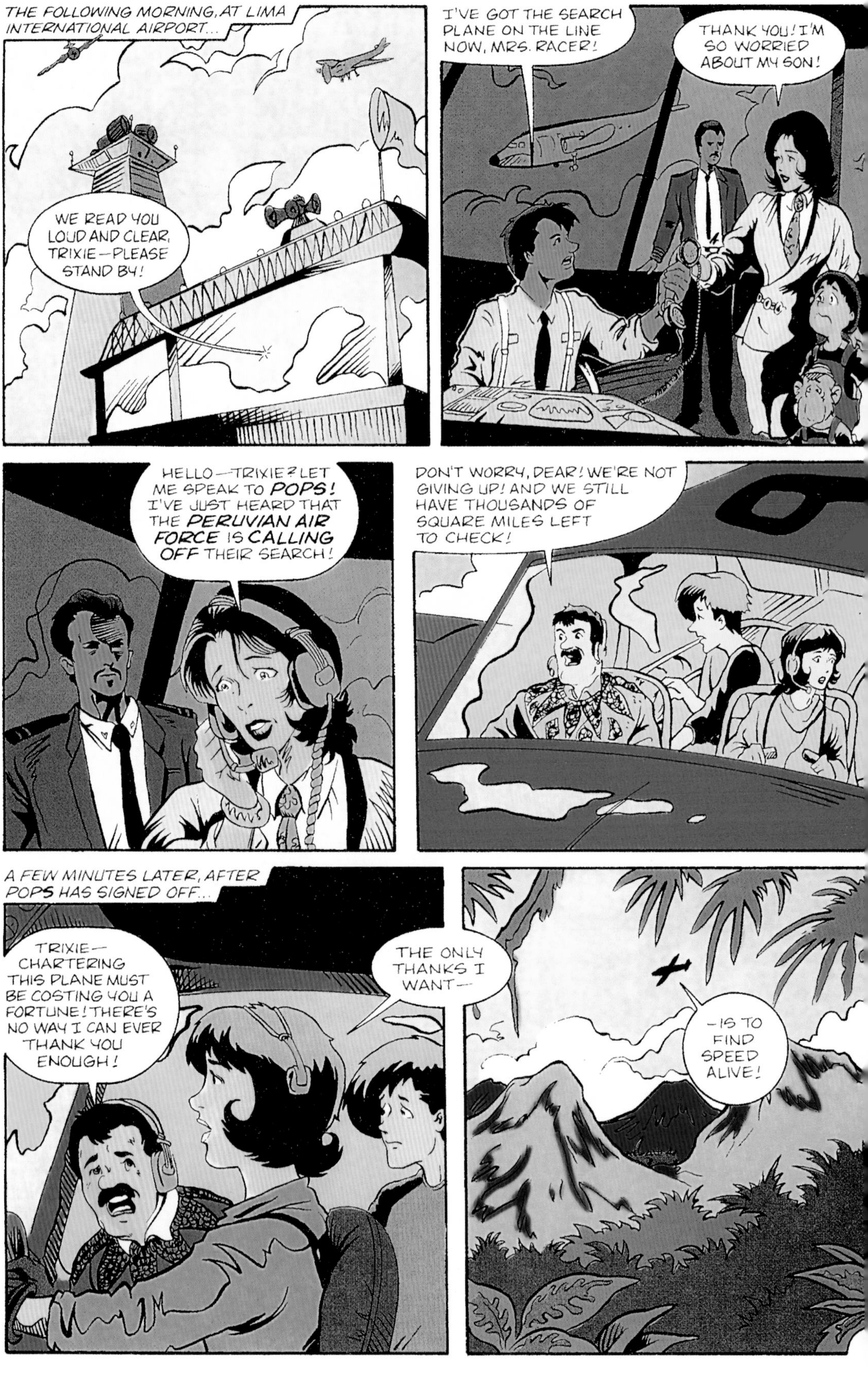
THE FOLLOWING MORNING, AT LIMA INTERNATIONAL AIRPORT...
WE READ YOU LOUD AND CLEAR, TRIXIE—PLEASE STAND BY!
I'VE GOT THE SEARCH PLANE ON THE LINE NOW, MRS. RACER!
THANK YOU! I'M SO WORRIED ABOUT MY SON!
HELLO—TRIXIE? LET ME SPEAK TO POPS! I'VE JUST HEARD THAT THE PERUVIAN AIR FORCE IS CALLING OFF THEIR SEARCH!
DON'T WORRY, DEAR! WE'RE NOT GIVING UP! AND WE STILL HAVE THOUSANDS OF SQUARE MILES LEFT TO CHECK!
A FEW MINUTES LATER, AFTER POPS HAS SIGNED OFF...
TRIXIE—CHARTERING THIS PLANE MUST BE COSTING YOU A FORTUNE! THERE'S NO WAY I CAN EVER THANK YOU ENOUGH!
THE ONLY THANKS I WANT—
—IS TO FIND SPEED ALIVE!

MEANWHILE, THE YOUNG MEN OF **VILCABRA** PREPARE FOR THEIR DEADLY RACE...

SPEED—I WOULD LIKE YOU TO WEAR THIS FOR **GOOD LUCK!** IT'S MY FAVORITE SCARF!

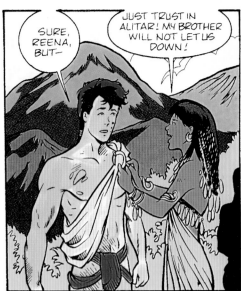

SURE, REENA, BUT—

JUST TRUST IN ALITAR! MY BROTHER WILL NOT LET US DOWN!

HEAR ME, YOUNG RUNNERS AND **HEED** MY WORDS! THE COURSE OF THE RACE THIS YEAR RUNS THROUGH THE WESTERN HILLS—

—AND ALONG THE RIVER. REMEMBER, THAT ANY DEVIATION FROM THE COURSE WILL RESULT IN DISQUALIFICATION—AND **DEATH!**

MAY THE **SUN GOD** BE WITH YOU ALL!

YOU—OUTSIDER!

huh?!

WHO ARE YOU?

I AM **TORGU!** REENA WAS **MINE**, UNTIL YOU CAME TO VILCABRA—

—AND SHE WILL BE MINE AGAIN ONCE YOU ARE **DEAD!**

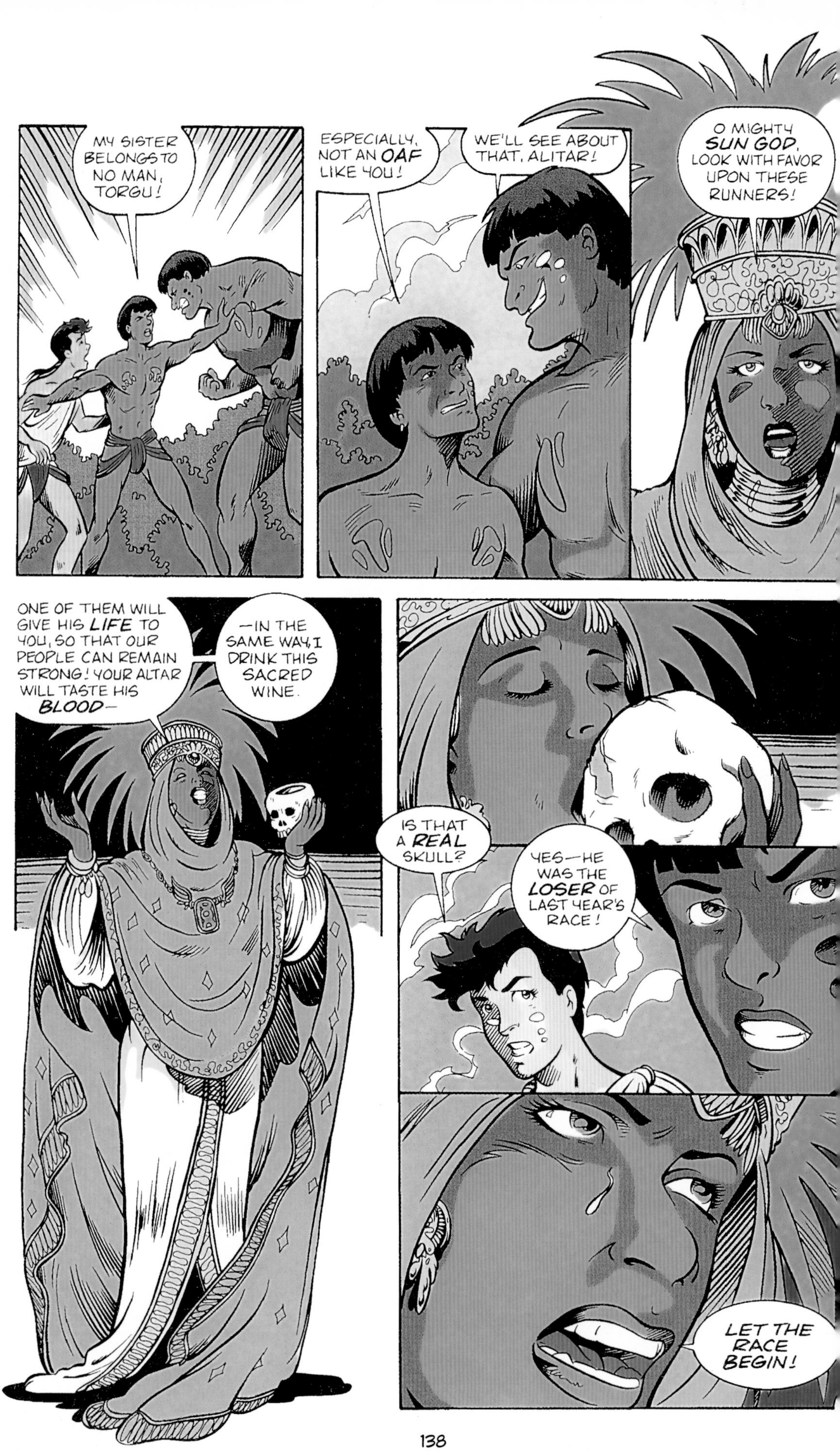
MY SISTER BELONGS TO NO MAN, TORGU!
ESPECIALLY, NOT AN OAF LIKE YOU!
WE'LL SEE ABOUT THAT, ALITAR!
O MIGHTY SUN GOD, LOOK WITH FAVOR UPON THESE RUNNERS!
ONE OF THEM WILL GIVE HIS LIFE TO YOU, SO THAT OUR PEOPLE CAN REMAIN STRONG! YOUR ALTAR WILL TASTE HIS BLOOD—
—IN THE SAME WAY, I DRINK THIS SACRED WINE.
IS THAT A REAL SKULL?
YES—HE WAS THE LOSER OF LAST YEAR'S RACE!
LET THE RACE BEGIN!

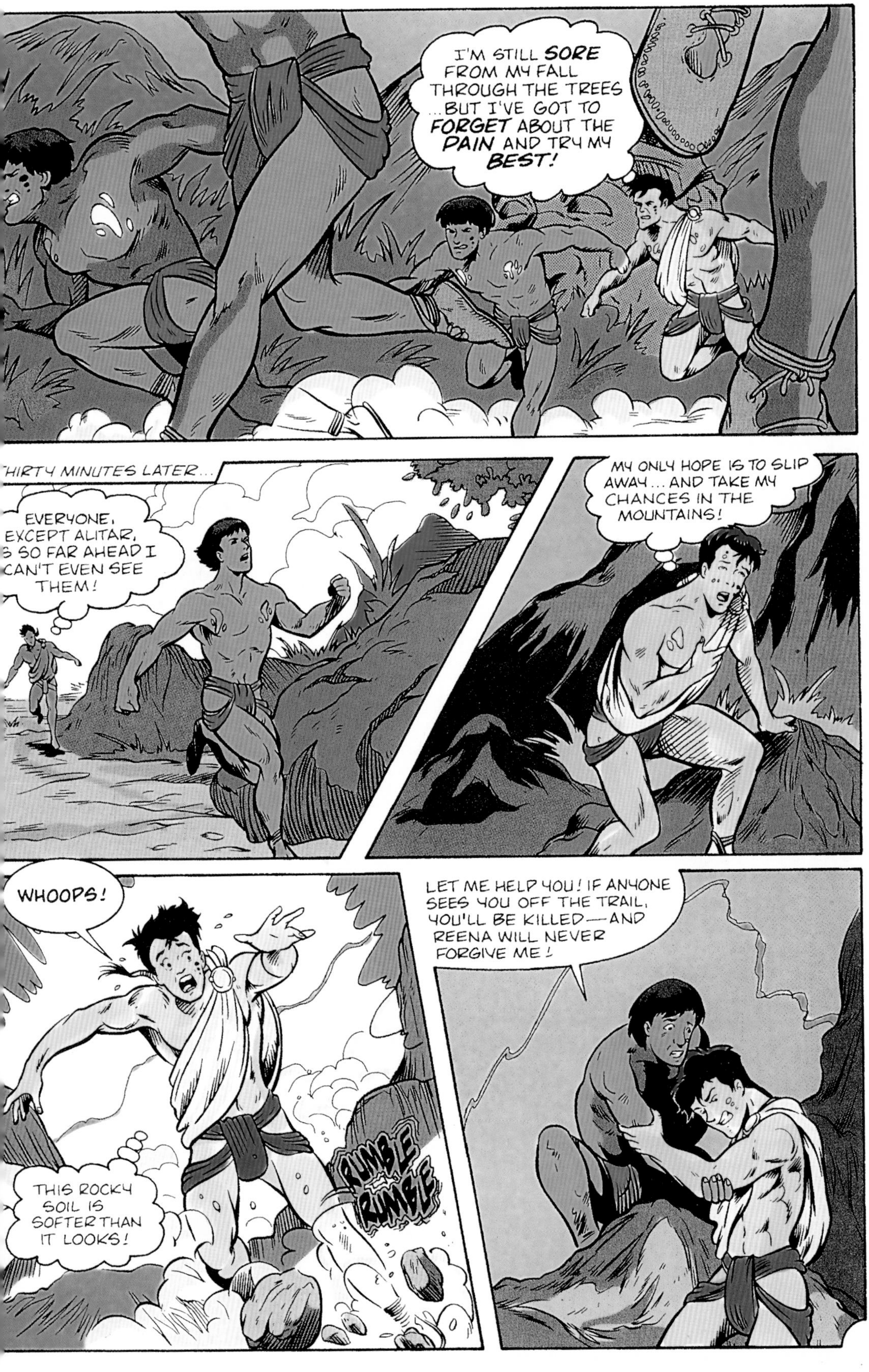
I'M STILL SORE FROM MY FALL THROUGH THE TREES ...BUT I'VE GOT TO FORGET ABOUT THE PAIN AND TRY MY BEST!
THIRTY MINUTES LATER...
EVERYONE, EXCEPT ALITAR, IS SO FAR AHEAD I CAN'T EVEN SEE THEM!
MY ONLY HOPE IS TO SLIP AWAY... AND TAKE MY CHANCES IN THE MOUNTAINS!
WHOOPS!
RUMBLE RUMBLE
THIS ROCKY SOIL IS SOFTER THAN IT LOOKS!
LET ME HELP YOU! IF ANYONE SEES YOU OFF THE TRAIL, YOU'LL BE KILLED—AND REENA WILL NEVER FORGIVE ME!

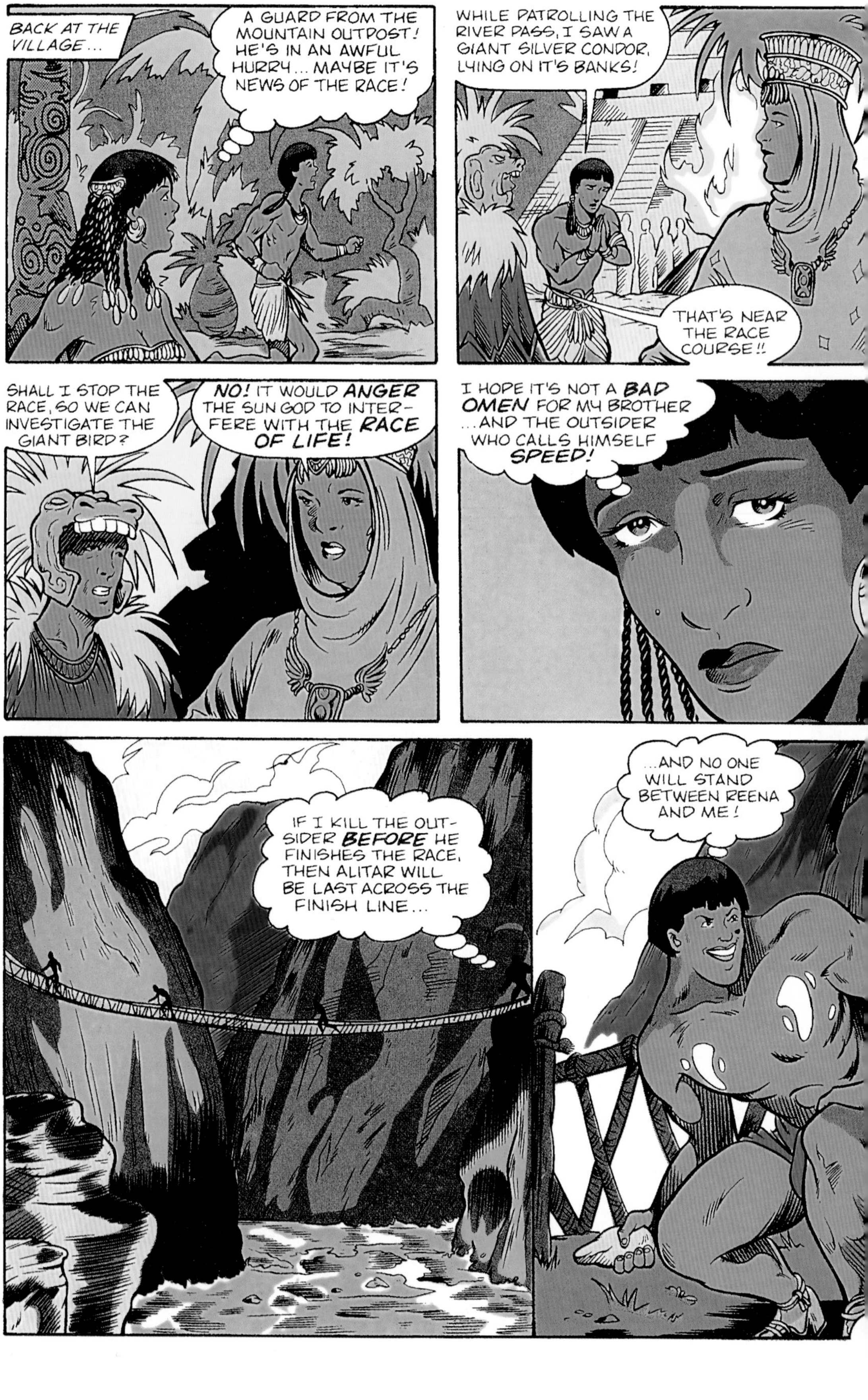
BACK AT THE VILLAGE...
A GUARD FROM THE MOUNTAIN OUTPOST! HE'S IN AN AWFUL HURRY... MAYBE IT'S NEWS OF THE RACE!
WHILE PATROLLING THE RIVER PASS, I SAW A GIANT SILVER CONDOR, LYING ON IT'S BANKS!
THAT'S NEAR THE RACE COURSE!!
SHALL I STOP THE RACE, SO WE CAN INVESTIGATE THE GIANT BIRD?
NO! IT WOULD ANGER THE SUN GOD TO INTERFERE WITH THE RACE OF LIFE!
I HOPE IT'S NOT A BAD OMEN FOR MY BROTHER ...AND THE OUTSIDER WHO CALLS HIMSELF SPEED!
IF I KILL THE OUTSIDER BEFORE HE FINISHES THE RACE, THEN ALITAR WILL BE LAST ACROSS THE FINISH LINE...
...AND NO ONE WILL STAND BETWEEN REENA AND ME!

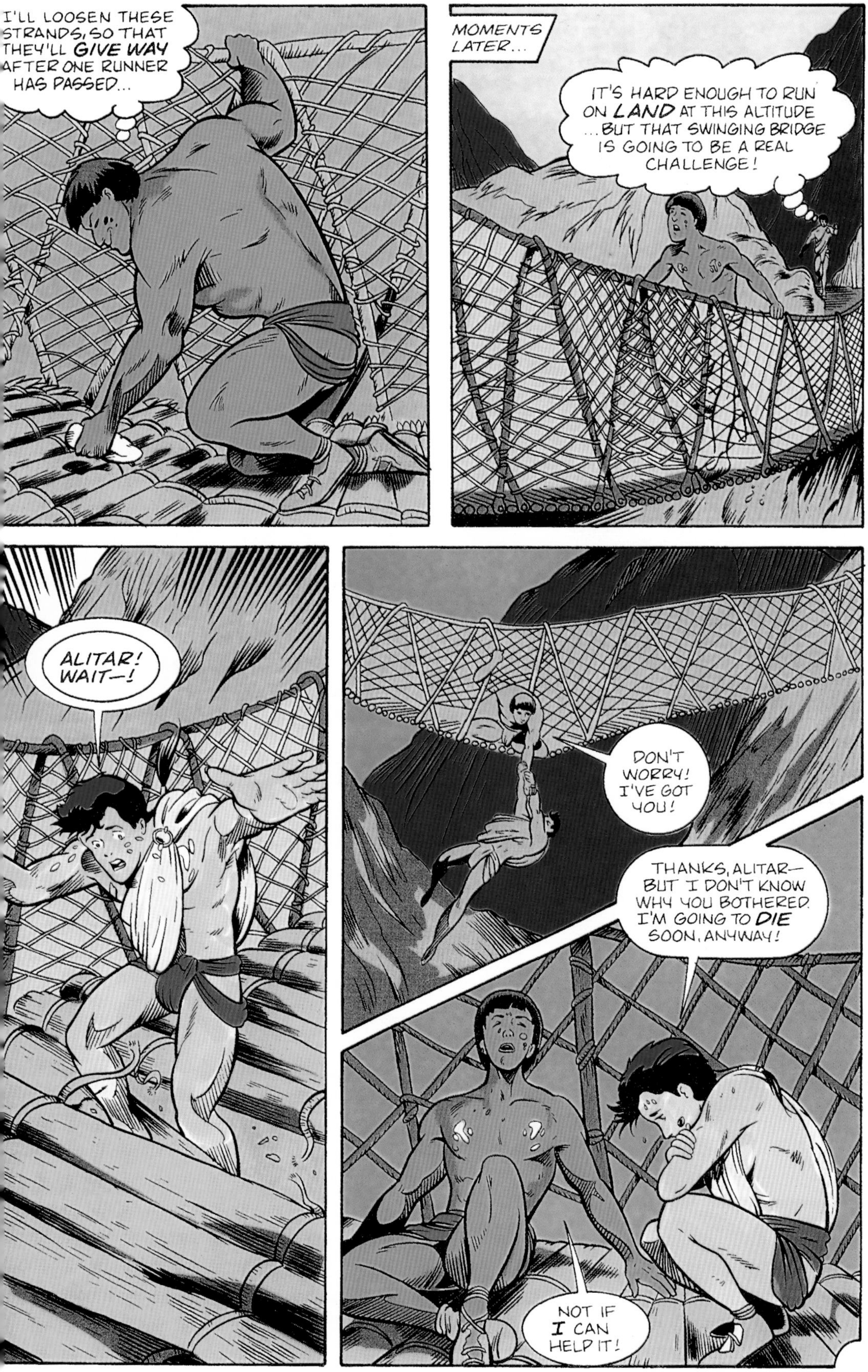
I'LL LOOSEN THESE STRANDS, SO THAT THEY'LL GIVE WAY AFTER ONE RUNNER HAS PASSED...
MOMENTS LATER...
IT'S HARD ENOUGH TO RUN ON LAND AT THIS ALTITUDE ...BUT THAT SWINGING BRIDGE IS GOING TO BE A REAL CHALLENGE!
ALITAR! WAIT--!
DON'T WORRY! I'VE GOT YOU!
THANKS, ALITAR-- BUT I DON'T KNOW WHY YOU BOTHERED. I'M GOING TO DIE SOON, ANYWAY!
NOT IF I CAN HELP IT!

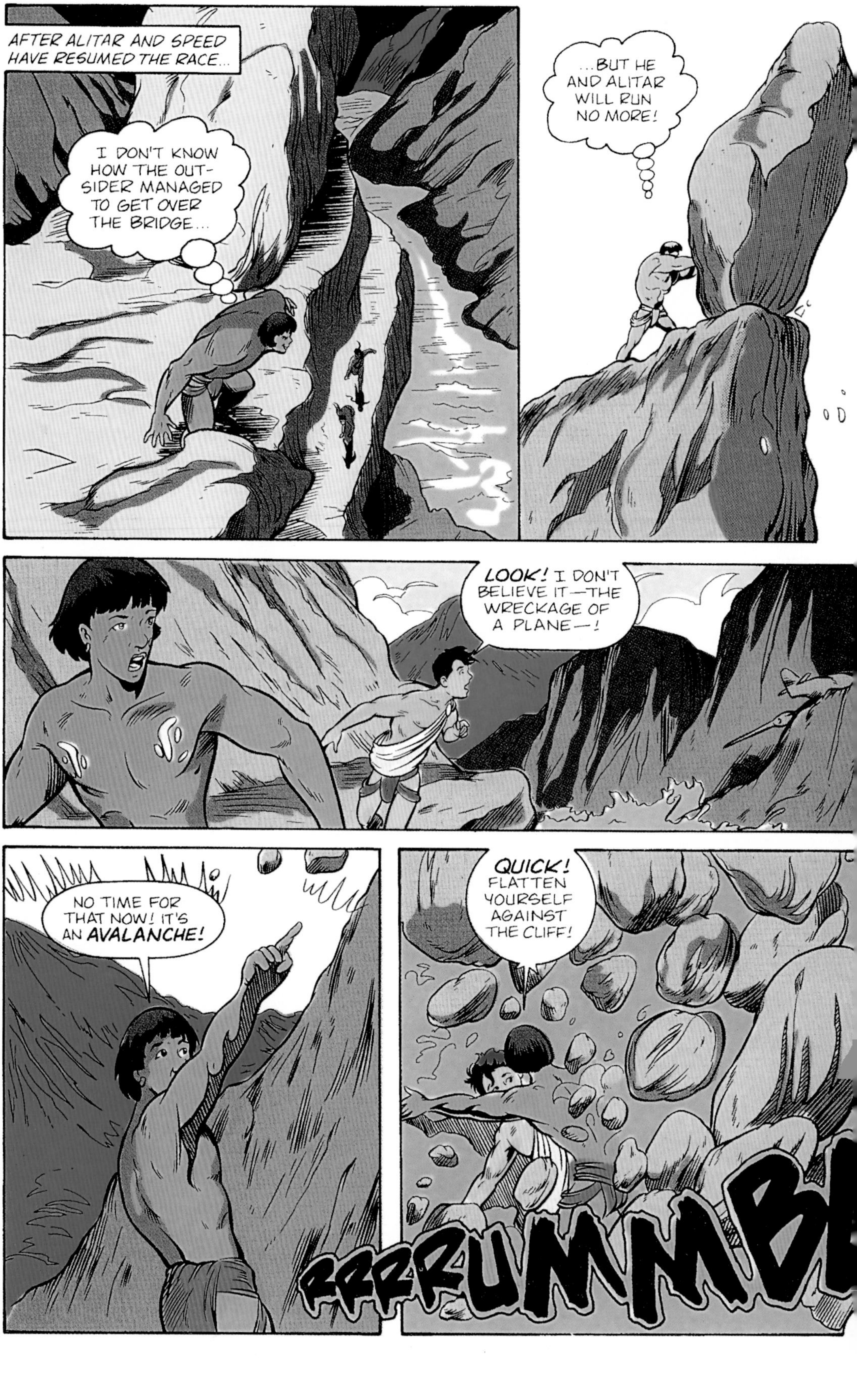
AFTER ALITAR AND SPEED HAVE RESUMED THE RACE...
I DON'T KNOW HOW THE OUT-SIDER MANAGED TO GET OVER THE BRIDGE...
...BUT HE AND ALITAR WILL RUN NO MORE!
LOOK! I DON'T BELIEVE IT—THE WRECKAGE OF A PLANE—!
NO TIME FOR THAT NOW! IT'S AN AVALANCHE!
QUICK! FLATTEN YOURSELF AGAINST THE CLIFF!
RRRRUMMB

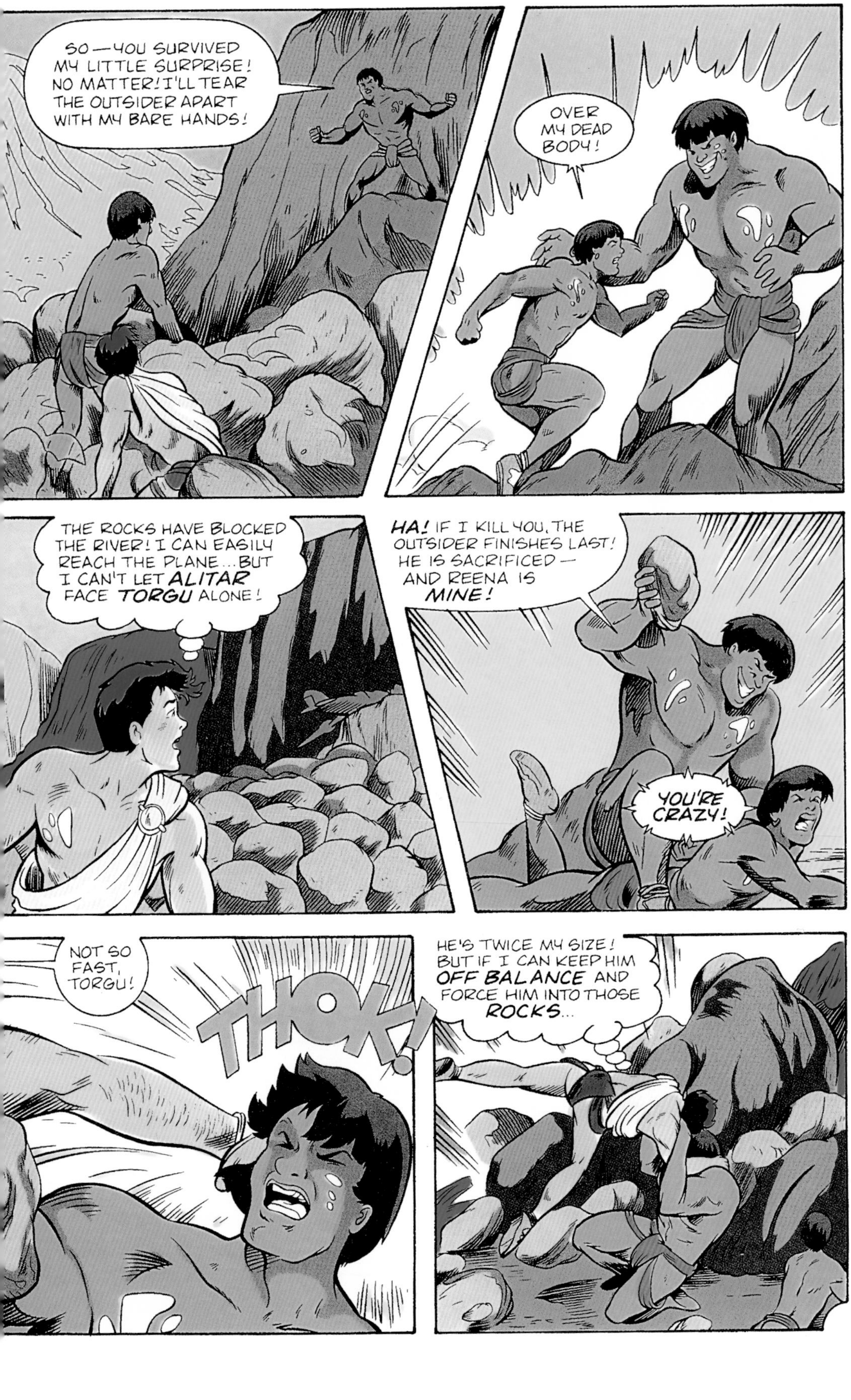
SO—YOU SURVIVED MY LITTLE SURPRISE! NO MATTER! I'LL TEAR THE OUTSIDER APART WITH MY BARE HANDS!
OVER MY DEAD BODY!
THE ROCKS HAVE BLOCKED THE RIVER! I CAN EASILY REACH THE PLANE... BUT I CAN'T LET ALITAR FACE TORGU ALONE!
HA! IF I KILL YOU, THE OUTSIDER FINISHES LAST! HE IS SACRIFICED—AND REENA IS MINE!
YOU'RE CRAZY!
NOT SO FAST, TORGU!
THOK!
HE'S TWICE MY SIZE! BUT IF I CAN KEEP HIM OFF BALANCE AND FORCE HIM INTO THOSE ROCKS...

AAAAAWW— MY FOOT!

HE TWISTED IT UNDER THAT ROCK! THAT OUGHT TO HOLD HIM...

...LONG ENOUGH FOR ME TO MAKE MY ESCAPE!

HEY! WHERE ARE YOU GOING?

I'M GOING TO TAKE MY CHANCES, USING THE SUP-PLIES LEFT IN THE PLANE! TELL REENA I'M SORRY!

I OWE YOU MY LIFE — SO I'LL LEAVE YOU IN *PEACE,* MY FRIEND.

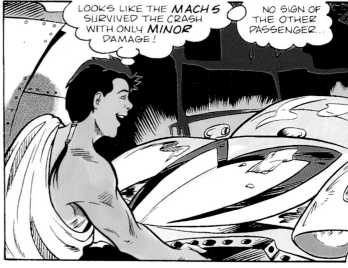

I NEVER DARED TO HOPE... BUT THERE *IT* IS!

LOOKS LIKE THE *MACH 5* SURVIVED THE CRASH WITH ONLY *MINOR* DAMAGE!

NO SIGN OF THE OTHER PASSENGER...

...AND I'D BETTER GET GOING BEFORE ANY MORE INCAS SHOW UP!

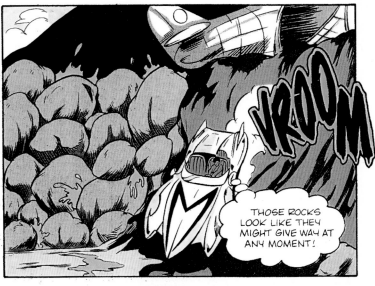

THOSE ROCKS LOOK LIKE THEY MIGHT GIVE WAY AT ANY MOMENT!

VROOM

UH-OH! HERE IT COMES!

VROOOM

RUMBLE

THIS RIVER BED LOOKS LIKE MY *ONLY* WAY THROUGH THESE TREACHEROUS MOUNTAINS!

THREE HOURS LATER...

SPLASH

NO CHOICE BUT TO PULL ONTO THE RIVER BANK...I'M ALMOST *OUT* OF *GAS!*

THE DAY'S STRENUOUS ACTIVITIES IN THIN MOUNTAIN AIR FINALLY TAKE THEIR TOLL...

I FEEL TOTALLY EXHAUSTED ...CAN'T STAY AWAKE ANY LONGER...

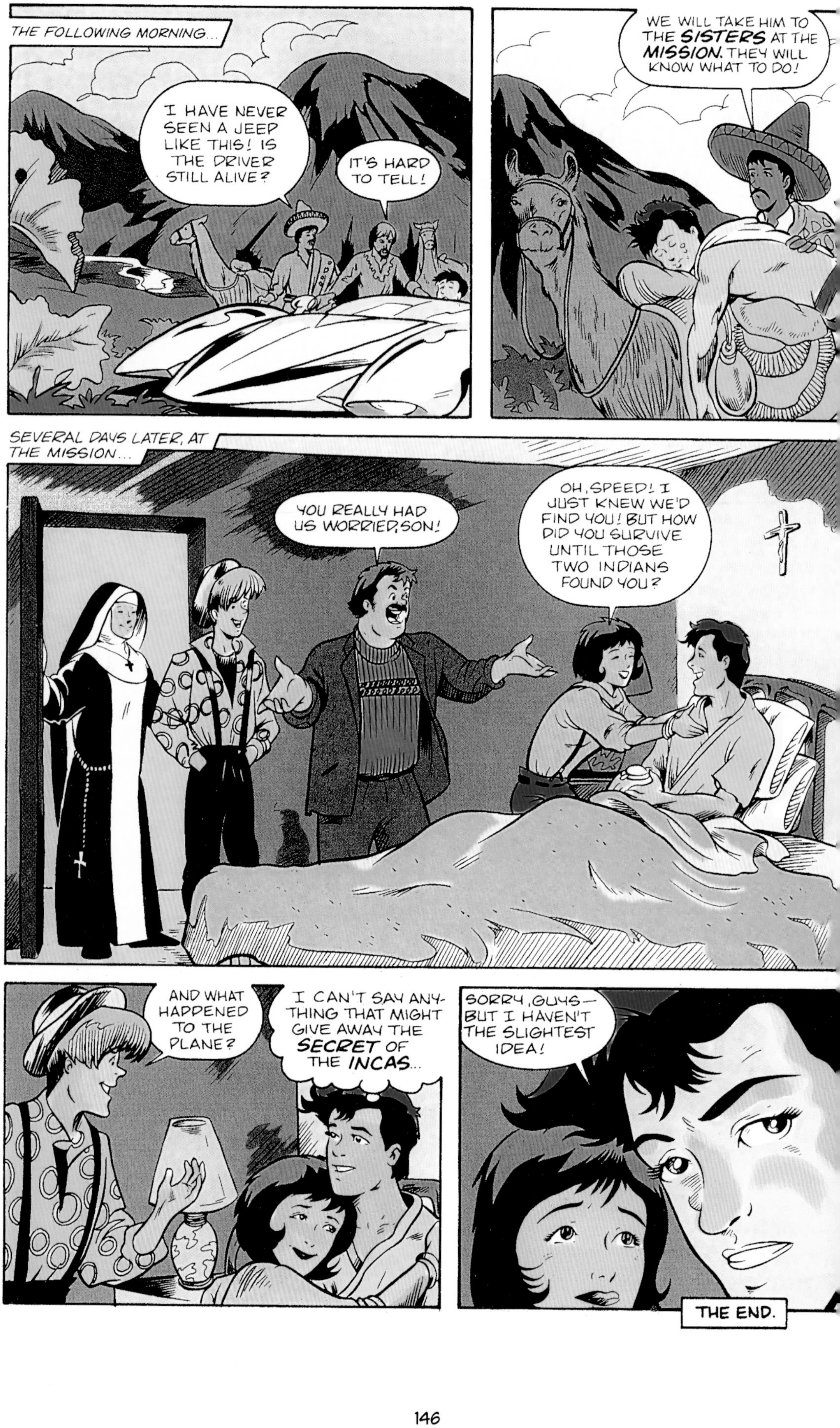
THE FOLLOWING MORNING...
I HAVE NEVER SEEN A JEEP LIKE THIS! IS THE DRIVER STILL ALIVE?
IT'S HARD TO TELL!
WE WILL TAKE HIM TO THE SISTERS AT THE MISSION. THEY WILL KNOW WHAT TO DO!
SEVERAL DAYS LATER, AT THE MISSION...
YOU REALLY HAD US WORRIED, SON!
OH, SPEED! I JUST KNEW WE'D FIND YOU! BUT HOW DID YOU SURVIVE UNTIL THOSE TWO INDIANS FOUND YOU?
AND WHAT HAPPENED TO THE PLANE?
I CAN'T SAY ANY-THING THAT MIGHT GIVE AWAY THE SECRET OF THE INCAS...
SORRY, GUYS— BUT I HAVEN'T THE SLIGHTEST IDEA!
THE END.

Art of Speed Racer

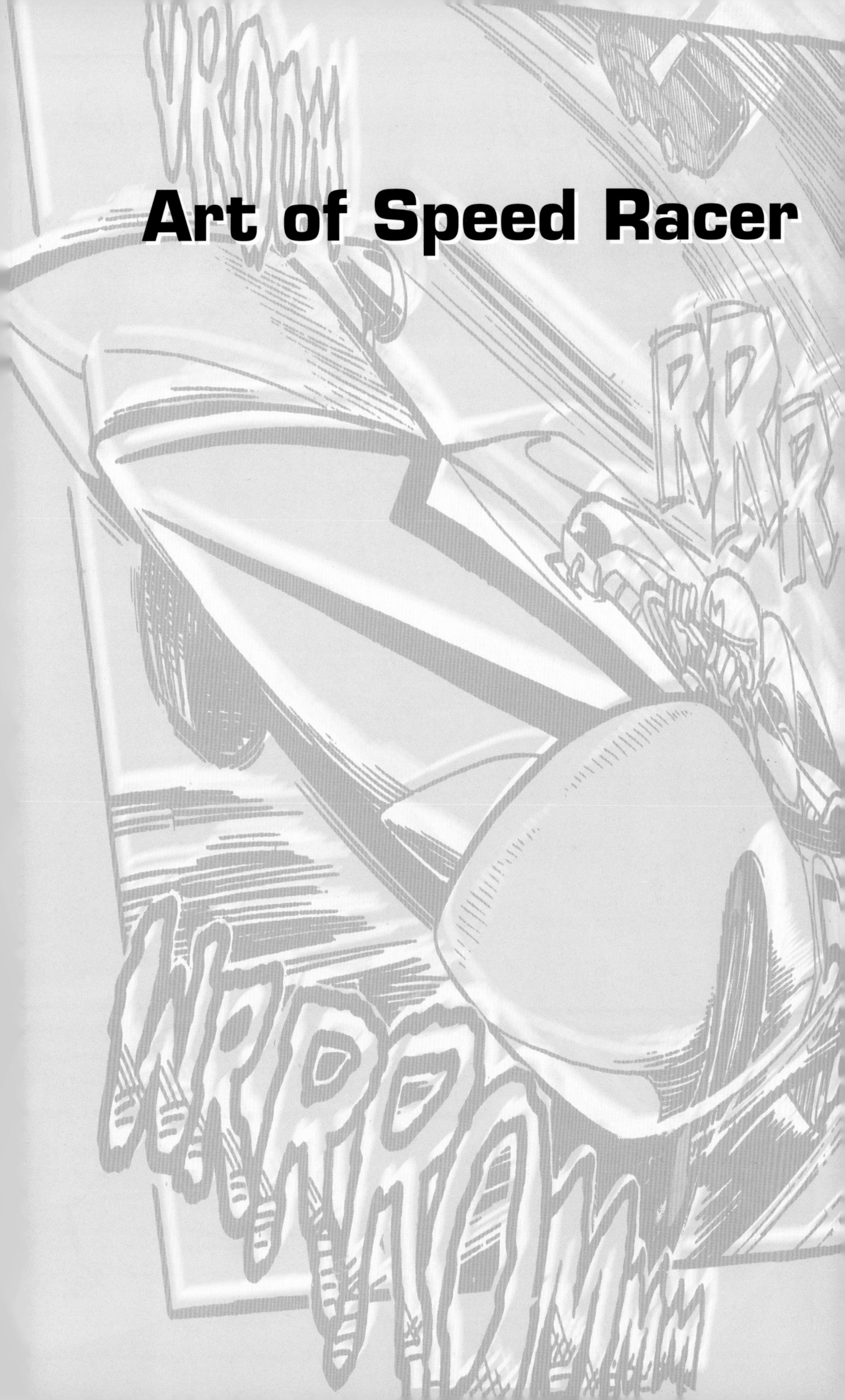

Art by ***Ken Holewczynski***

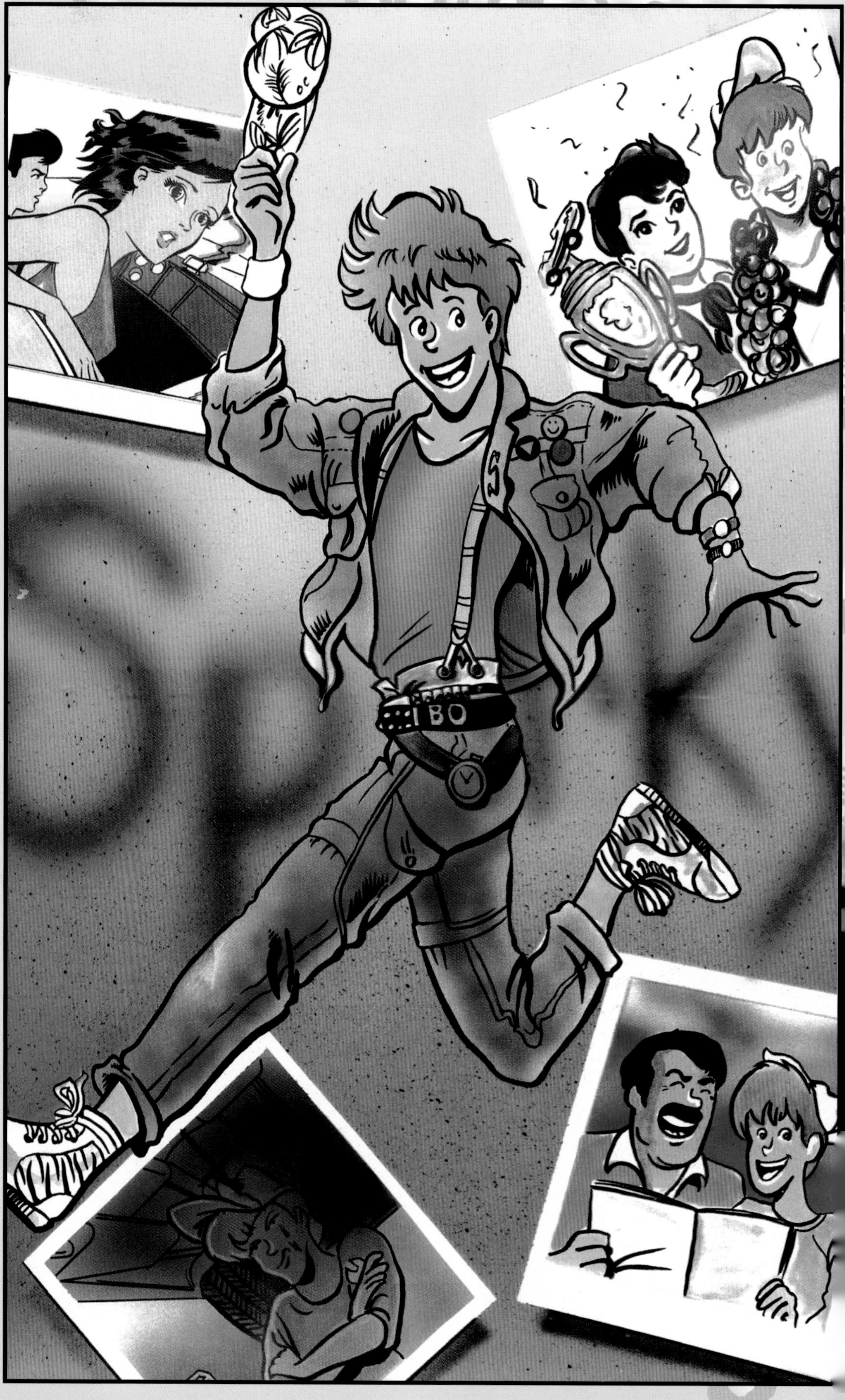
BO

Art by **Ken Holewczynski**

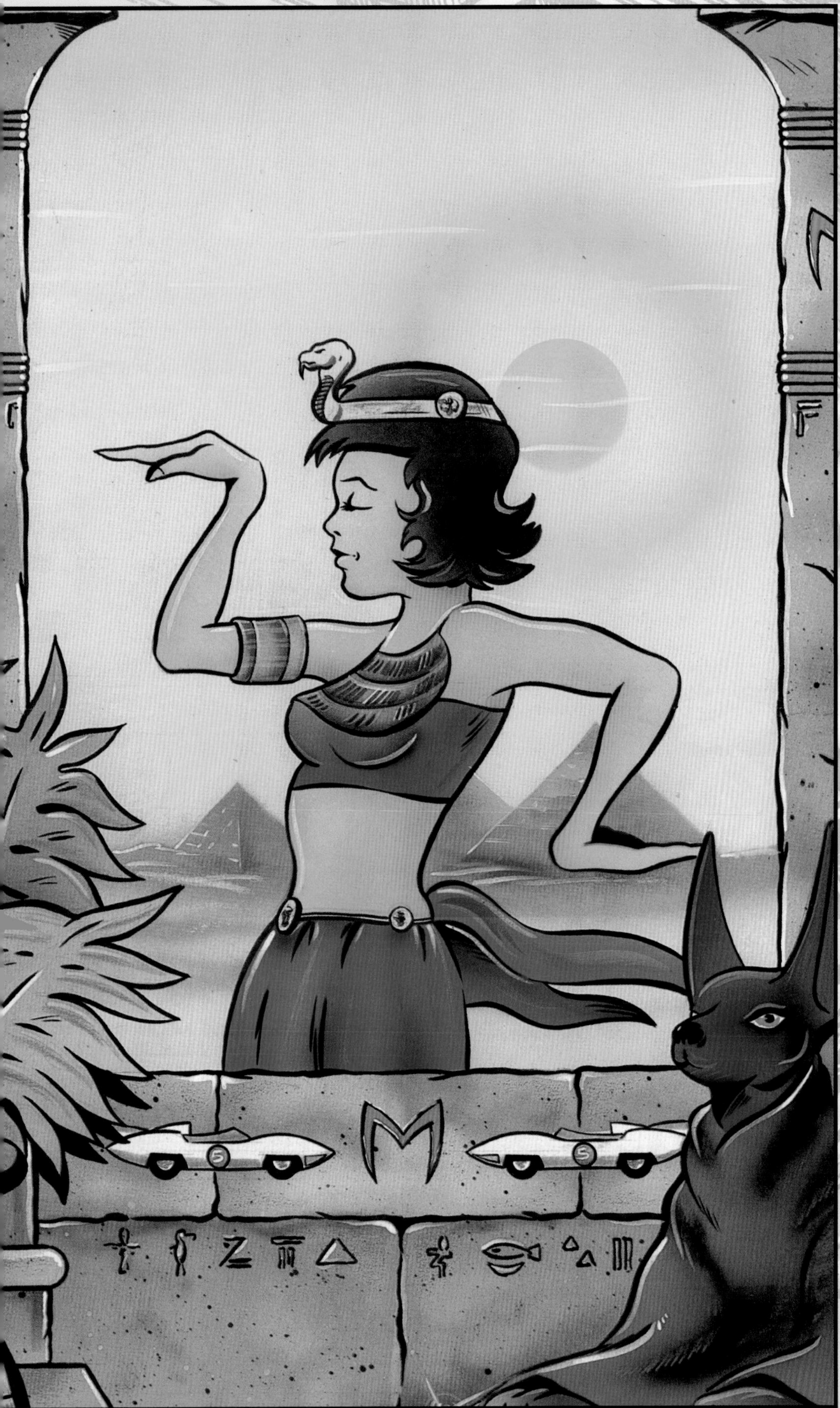
M

Art by **Mitch O'Connell**

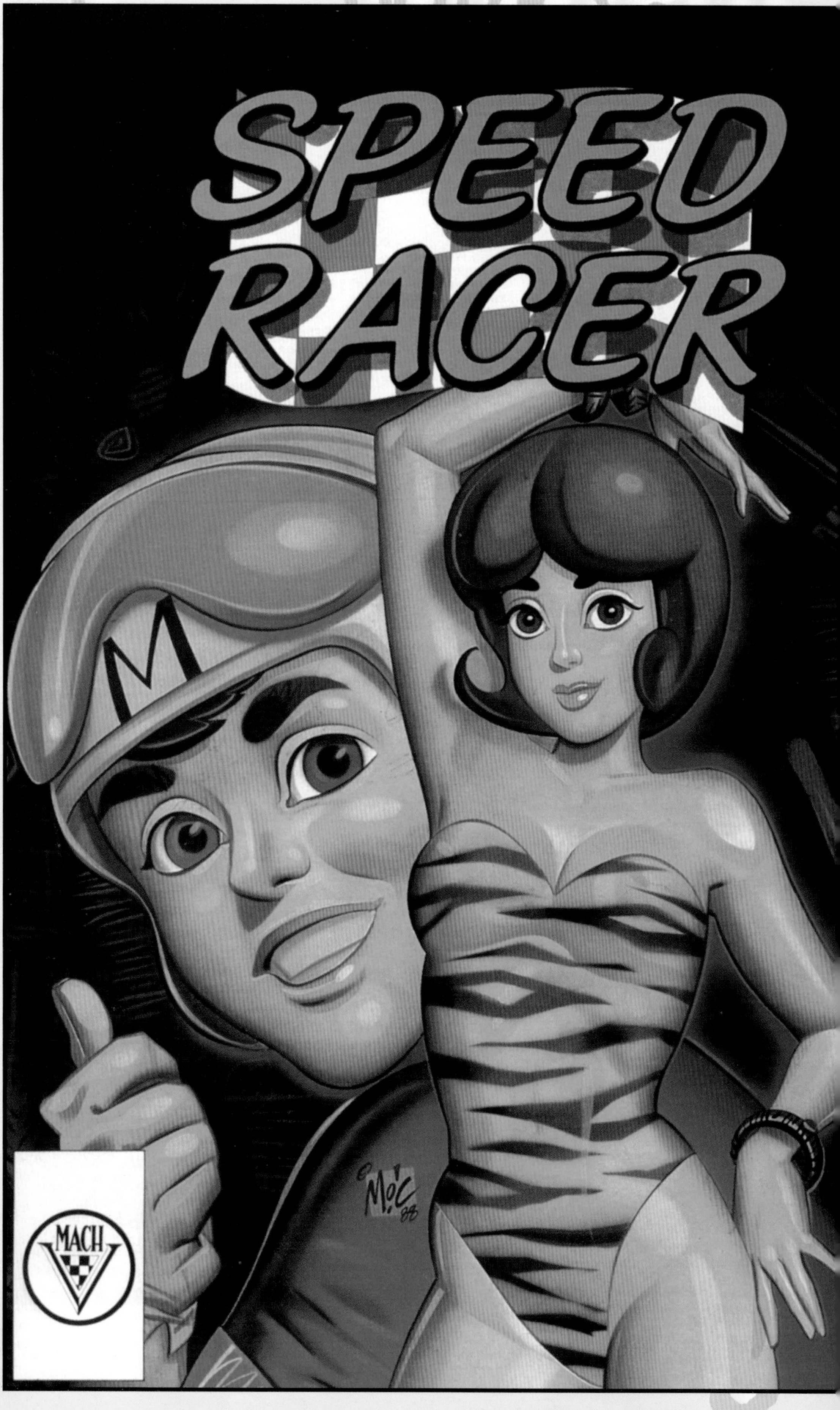
SPEED RACER
M
M.O'C 88
MACH V

Art by **Joe Phillips**

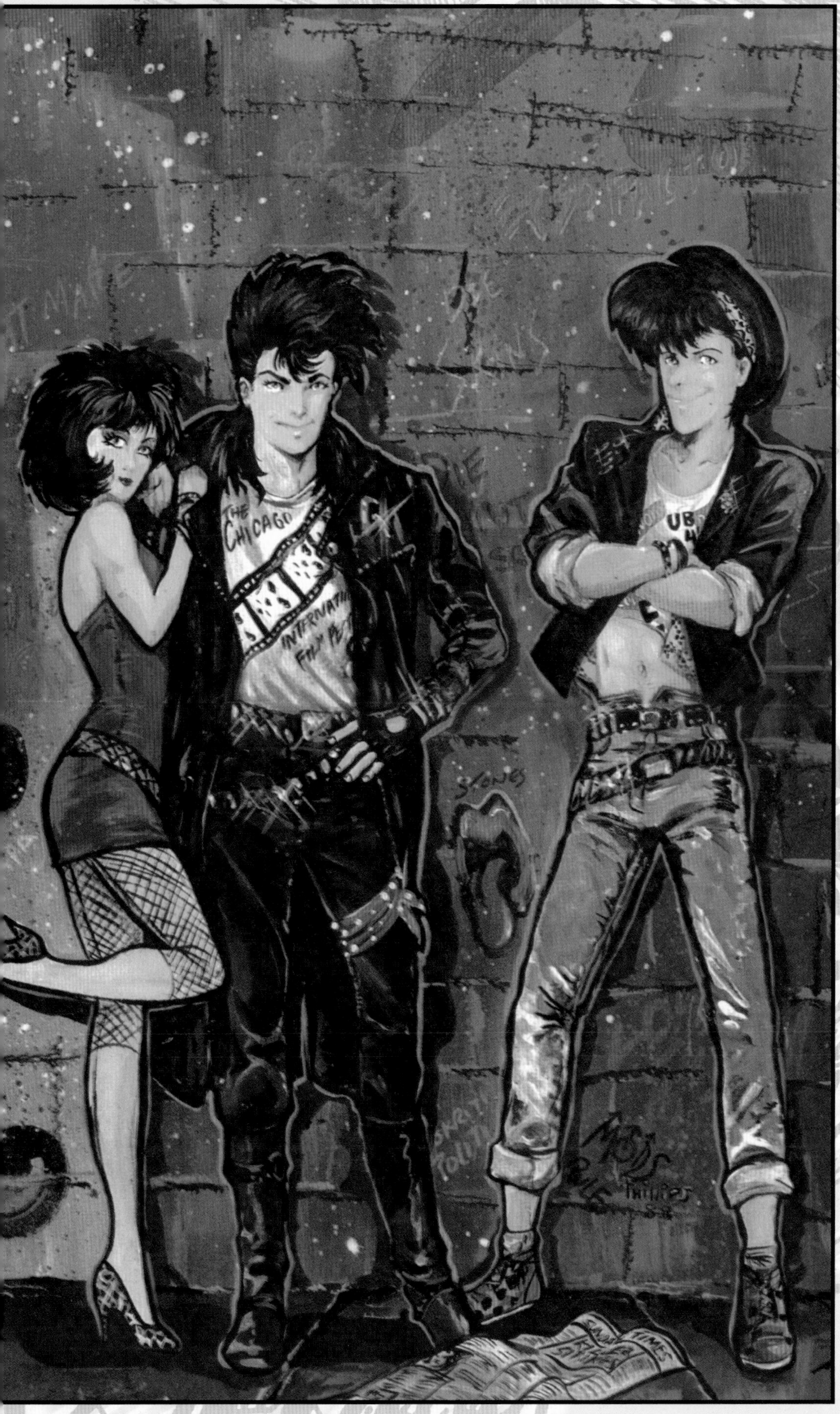
THE CHICAGO
STONES

CATCH UP ON SPEED!

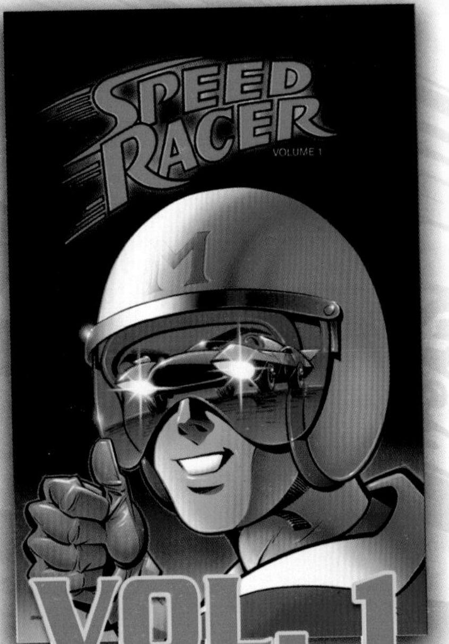
SPEED RACER
VOLUME 1

VOL. 1
COLLECTS ISSUES 1-5
ISBN: 978-1-60010-174-8

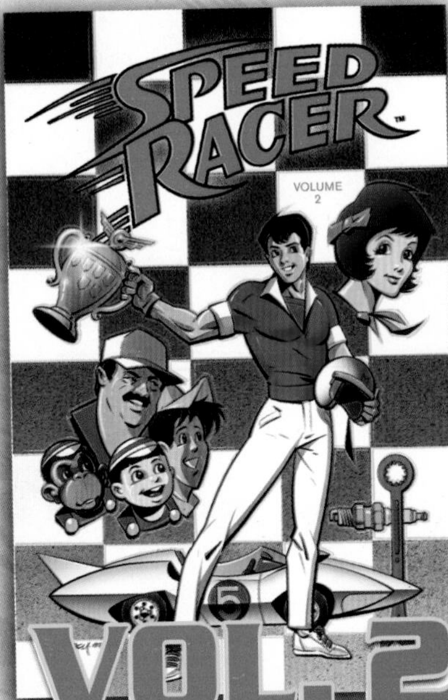
SPEED RACER™
VOLUME 2

VOL. 2
COLLECTS ISSUES 6-13
ISBN: 978-1-60010-175-5

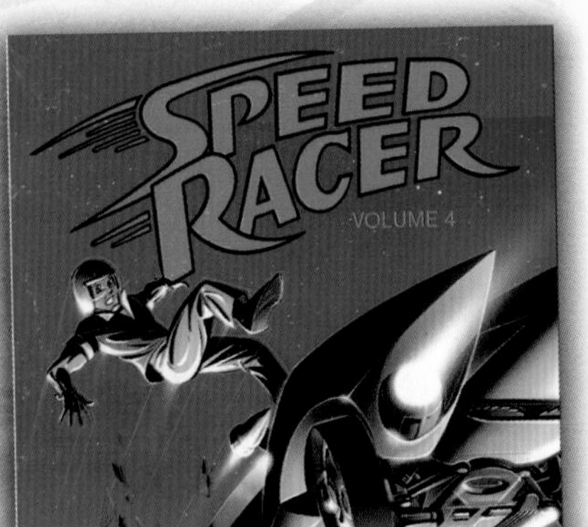
SPEED RACER
VOLUME 4

V
COLL ... 26

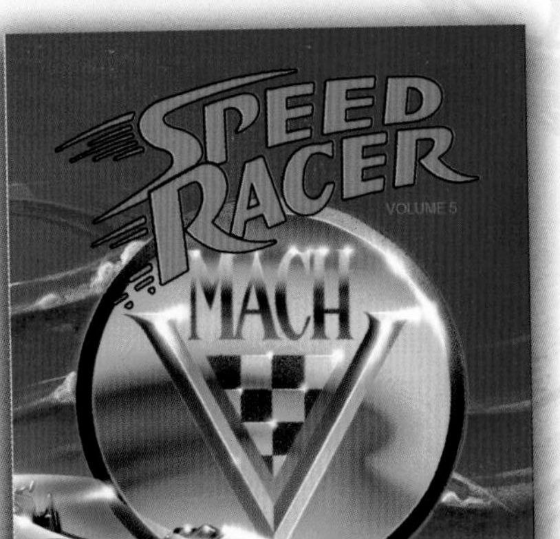
SPEED RACER
VOLUME 5
MACH V

VOL. 5
COLLECTS ISSUES 27-32
ISBN: 978-1-60010-178-6

The classic Now Comics *Speed Racer* series from 20 years ago gets the deluxe reprint treatment from IDW, including reproductions of Ken Steacy's amazing painted covers, too.

www.idwpublishing.com • www.speedracer.com